ON THE BIBLE

ON THE BIBLE

Eighteen Studies by

Martin Buber

Edited by NAHUM N. GLATZER
Introduction by HAROLD BLOOM

SCHOCKEN BOOKS · NEW YORK

First published by Schocken Books 1982
10 9 8 7 6 5 4 3 2 1   82 83 84 85
Copyright © 1968 by Schocken Books Inc.
Introduction copyright © 1982 by Harold Bloom

Library of Congress Cataloging in Publication Data
Buber, Martin, 1878–1965.
On the Bible.
Includes bibliographical references and index.
1. Bible. O.T.—Addresses, essays, lectures.
I. Glatzer, Nahum Norbert, 1903–   . II. Title.
BS1192.B8   1982   2211′.6   81-16555
AACR2

Manufactured in the United States of America
ISBN 0–8052–3796–8 (hardback)
ISBN 0–8052–0691–4 (paperback)

CONTENTS

[v]

[vi]   Contents

PUBLISHER'S NOTE

THE INTENT of the present selection is to acquaint the reader—both student and interested layman—with the major concerns of Buber's biblical research and of his attempt to interpret biblical concepts to modern man. Included are significant chapters from *Moses, The Prophetic Faith,* and *Israel and Palestine,* and studies, articles, and lectures that appeared in periodicals and collections of essays. Three essays appear here for the first time in English translation. For the sake of easier reading, English spelling, italicization, and transliteration of Hebrew terms, which vary in the original works from which the selections are reprinted, follow one consistent usage. The notes have been checked and, in the case of Buber's own writings cited, English book titles and page numbers have been substituted for the original Hebrew references. References to J. [Yehezkel] Kaufmann's *Toledot ha-Emunah ha-Yisreelit* (cited as *History of the Religion of Israel*) have been left in their original form; the English reader will find the translation and abridgment by Moshe Greenberg (*The Religion of Israel,* 1960) of welcome assistance. A fairly complete corpus of Buber's studies on the Bible appeared as volume II of his Collected Works (*Werke*) in 1964; additional material is contained in *Darko shel Mikra* (The Way of Scripture), 1964.

INTRODUCTION
Harold Bloom

T HE HEBREW BIBLE, in whatever version we read it, is an immensely difficult sequence or series of books. This difficulty cannot be too much emphasized. It has been masked by familiarity and by two thousand years of normative interpretation, ranging from the subtlest analyses of possible meaning to the astonishing literalism we confront nightly when viewing evangelists on television. Stories and poems that are so worn by repetition as to be beyond surprise, and yet remain so esoteric, are texts necessarily in Freud's category of "the uncanny." We read them and feel at once estranged and yet at home.

Modern Biblical scholarship, though now two hundred years old, is inadequate as literary criticism. Much of what this scholarship insists upon calling literary criticism would be dismissed as trivial or rudimentary by the advanced criticism of secular literature. Martin Buber's writings on the Bible were not intended as scholarship or as specifically literary criticism but as a religious testimony. In my judgment, at their best they are precisely instances of an authentic *literary* criticism and, as such, are likely to survive Buber's writings on Hasidism or his more direct presentations of his own spiritual stance.

Buber on Hasidism and on the concept of Judaism has suffered the formidable criticism of Gershom Scholem, the leading scholar of myth and mysticism in Jewish tradition. Acknowledging Buber as precursor in the exploration of esoteric Judaism, Scholem nevertheless puts into question the descriptive accuracy of his older contemporary:

> In the reports of the Torah, which he considers unhistorical, he seeks the "core" of an original event, namely that "encounter" in the highest sense, and he finds the latter by the application of a purely pneumatic exegesis, the subjectivity of which bewilders the reader.

"Pneumatic exegesis" is Scholem's sly irony at Buber's expense, since the phrase can mean "gnostic interpretation," and so much of Buber's work is a moral polemic directed against Gnosticism. But the essence of Hasidism, as Scholem has shown against Buber, is in the Gnosticism of the Lurianic Kabbalah. Scholem's contention is that both he and Buber are religious anarchists, but Buber is a subjectivist masking as a Hasidic sage, while Scholem is an objective historian of Kabbalism. This is a little misleading, since Scholem's Kabbalah is in some sense as much his own creation as Buber's Hasidism is Buber's kind of strong misreading. But there is a vital difference, which establishes Scholem as the stronger of these two demonic interpreters. Scholem's "history" is essentially analytic and descriptive, however colored it may be by his own prophetic force of spiritual anarchy. Buber is rarely analytic and almost never descriptive.

Yet Buber on the Bible survives Scholem's critiques, precisely because he is the more literary of the two expositors. Buber, as Scholem once remarked, was an eloquent rhetorician, and his spiritual commentaries on the Bible tend to be remarkable instances of rhetorical criticism. Here is one example, in the vivid discussion of "The Burning Bush" from Buber's *Moses*:

> As reply to his question about the name, Moses is told: *Ehyeh asher ehyeh*. This is usually understood to mean "I am that I am" in the sense that YHVH describes Himself as the Being One or even the Everlast-

ing One. . . . Should we, however, really assume that in
the view of the narrator the God who came to inform His
people of their liberation wishes, at that hour of all
hours, merely to secure His distance, and not to grant
and warrant proximity as well?

From this powerful rhetorical question follows Buber's
reading of the *ehyeh asher ehyeh* as, in effect, "I shall be
present where and when I shall be present," the covenant
promise of perpetual presence. Buber in some sense shrewdly answers his own rhetorical prophecy, as stated in the 1926
lecture that the editor, Nahum Glatzer, selected as the
inaugural essay of *On the Bible*. Confronting the Bible, the
person of today must read it:

> . . . as though it were something entirely unfamil-
> iar, as though it had not been set before him ready-made,
> as though he has not been confronted all his life with
> sham concepts and sham statements that cited the Bible
> as their authority. He must face the Book with a new
> attitude, as something new. He must yield to it, withhold
> nothing of his being, and let whatever will occur between
> himself and it.

Buber seems to be describing the process of falling in
love, but his paradigm indeed is *'ahabah* or Yahweh's
Election-Love for Israel. That paradigm accounts for Buber's love of the Bible and for his intense confrontational
reading of *ehyeh asher ehyeh* as the uncanny or sublime
presence of Divine Love. Scholem, with his customary
exemplary harshness, criticized Buber's use of Rosenzweig's
terminology of creation, revelation, and redemption as the
basic categories of Judaism, observing that Buber's "revelation" is purely mystical, kabbalistic even, as Buber denied
any reliance upon mysticism. Certainly Buber's *rhetorical*
defense of his enterprise betrays the aura of a kabbalistic or
gnostic critique of Darwin, Freud, and Marx:

> We have already answerd the question of whether
> the man of today can believe by saying that, while he is

denied the certainty of faith, he has the power to hold
himself open to faith. But is not the strangeness of
biblical concepts a stumblingblock to his readiness to do
so? Has he not lost the reality of creation in his concept
of evolution, that of revelation in the theory of the
unconscious, and that of redemption in the setting up of
social or national goals?

In his rejection of "scientific" views, Buber still insists
that he does not resort to "the mystic interpretation, according to which the acts of creation are not acts, but emanations." Scholem's polemical point nevertheless holds, since
Buber also asserts a freedom from all historical considera-
tions that might circumscribe concepts of creation, revelation, and redemption. His rhetoric grants Buber only a
pragmatic freedom from the entrapments of temporality, a
freedom unearned dialectically. Skilled at detecting the
ironies of apprehension and of expression in Biblical texts,
Buber seems blind to the ironies implicit in his own dis-
course. His "I—Thou" doctrine, as Scholem demonstrates
so often, is essentially rhetorical rather than spiritual or
philosophical. It is a grand turning operation dependent
upon the traditional trope of apostrophe, the confrontation
between life and life, subject and subject, that always
conditions Western lyric poetry, and that attained its apotheosis in a radical lyricist like Shelley.

After this problematic introductory essay on "The Man
of Today and the Jewish Bible," the next seven pieces in this
volume address themselves to texts in Genesis and Exodus by
the greatest of Biblical authors, known to scholarly conven-
tion as the Jahvist, or J for shorthand. Buber had little
interest in what is called the "documentary hypothesis" of
Biblical scholarship, yet it is about as well established as
internal evidence can establish anything textual. In his book,
The Prophetic Faith, Buber says that the J document is "very
much more comprehensive than had been supposed," but
scholars like E.A. Speiser hardly show J as being less than

comprehensive. Buber's real point about J ought to have been that this author was badly misrepresented by normative commentary. Unfortunately, Buber sought to demonstrate that J was more prophet than priest and was even prophetic of Buber's dialogical vision. But J was more storyteller than prophet, and more interested in the relation of God's blessing to human struggle than in the blessing as an index to revelation and redemption. The Jahvist is the most problematic of writers, and though his work is the foundation of Western religion, he is hardly a religious writer as such. Something in Buber knew this and helped spark Buber's fury at Freud, whose *Moses and Monotheism*, problematic as it was, is so ferociously denounced in the opening footnote of Buber's book, *Moses*.

What allies Freud to the Jahvist in particular, and to Biblical writers in general, is the double problematic of authority and transference, a problematic more Hebraic than Greek. I mean by this a very specific and limited sense of both authority and transference, having to do with the representation of what Freud called "reality-testing," and of what the Biblical writers regarded as the transcendent reality of Yahweh. In Freud and the Bible, representation is antimimetic, in the uncanny mode that attains an apotheosis whenever Messianic speculations attempt to embody themselves in appropriate images. Scholem once associated a majestic saying from the *Zohar*: "The Messiah will not come until the tears of Esau will be exhausted," with the even more mysterious apothegm of the Hasidic Rabbi Israel of Rizhin: "The Messianic world will be a world without images in which the image and its object can no longer be related." In a postscript to his critique of Buber on Hasidism, Scholem recalled an exchange with Buber in which the expounder of Hasidism confessed his inability to understand that apothegm. Scholem's implication is, again, that Buber lacked imaginative sympathy for the apocalyptic impulse, an implication that suggests a correspondent weakness in Buber's Biblical criticism. But this weakness prevails in all Biblical criticism, which must confront the most difficult of all literary texts.

Our difficulties in reading J or the Jahvist stem primarily from his almost unique authority, an authority so long established that it cannot be undermined by mere disbelief, or by any supposed advances in modes of interpretation, or in historical knowledge. J's invention, so far as we can tell, was Yahweh, not the Yahweh of normative tradition, but the Yahweh who inspired the awe that made the tradition both necessary and inevitable. What texts concerning Yahweh were available to J we cannot know, though it seems likely that his sources were not confined to an oral tradition. We must read what we have, and the strongest and earliest chronicler of Yahweh available to us is J. What characterized Yahweh as J gives him to us?

To ask that question, from a literary perspective, is to ask also just *how* J presents Yahweh to us. What is J's tone or stance, and what modes of representation does he favor? Much scholarship, falling victim to J's irony, calls him a simple and naive writer, which is neither helpful nor true. Like Tolstoy or the early Wordsworth, both his close descendants, J is a massively self-confident writer, fierce and primal in his approach to human personality and totally daring in his apprehension of divine realities. Unlike Tolstoy and Wordsworth, J is almost invariably ironic when human personality and divine reality collide. But the irony of one age or culture is rarely the irony of another, and J's irony is neither classical nor romantic, Greek nor European. If irony is saying one thing while meaning another or provoking an expectation that will not be fulfilled, then J is no ironist. However, there is a more sublime irony, the irony say of Kafka's fragmentary story, "The Hunter Gracchus," which ends with a fussy seaport mayor nervously asking Gracchus (an undead phantasm floating about on his death ship) whether he means to go on docking in the mayor's domain and being answered that the hunter thinks not, since his ship is rudderless and is driven by a wind from the region of death. In Kafka, and more massively in J, irony comes from clashes or encounters between totally incommensurate orders of reality. J's most peculiar gift is his preternatural ease in so writing about Yahweh, in so making Yahweh act and speak, that no uncertainty or reservation is experienced when the reader moves from Yahweh to Jacob or to Moses. Yet this authority is quite knowingly ironic, in that no one is clearer than J as to where Yahweh ends and man begins.

One way of estimating J's extraordinary success in representing God is to contrast it with the vicissitudes of later representations of Yahweh in the normative tradition, both Jewish and Christian. The prophet Isaiah makes us a little uneasy by giving us a Yahweh seated upon a throne surrounded by an assembly of seraphs. Isaiah is a sublime poet, but his images of a high throne, six-winged angels, smoke, and a train of glory mix earthly emblems of power with aspects of the grotesque. Prophecy takes its point of origin from J's account of Moses (Buber would say from Abraham), but J's preternatural greatness as a writer transcended the necessity for the later prophetic imagery of kingly pomp. J does not need to see himself as standing in the presence of God in the heavenly council, there to receive the God-word. Jeremiah says: "The God-word was (came) to me," but that would be a weak perspective, to J. J precedes and has spiritual authority over kings and prophets alike. The prophet Micaiah ben Imlah (1 Kings 22:17) actually reports a dialogue in the heavenly court just as the poet of Job does, thus setting the bad precedent that causes Milton such esthetic grief in Book III of *Paradise Lost*. J's God does not preside over a royal council in the heavens, and indeed such a role or image is not conceivable for the uncanny Yahweh J chronicles.

To confine oneself only to J's share in Genesis, these are some of the representations of God that he gives us. Yahweh molds a man out of clods in the soil and plants a garden so as to make a home for this creature. Even in his creation, God is not unironic, since he first makes animals *as an aid for*

man's loneliness and fashions woman only as an after-
thought. Yahweh likes to walk around his garden toward
sundown, as even he prefers to keep cool, but this charming
touch is qualified by his bad temper after Adam and Eve
have devoured prohibited fruit. Still, this is a very intimate
God, who never shrinks from face-to-face conversation with
his creatures. Presumably the presence of this God is not just
a voice, though J is too canny to describe him. But then J,
and nearly all biblical writers after him, are not interested in
how persons or objects look anyway. Thorleif Boman acutely
notes that in biblical theophanies "sight and hearing pass
imperceptibly into one another," since the Hebraic images of
God were never visual but rather were motor, dynamic, and
auditive. So, in J's story of the tower of Babel, God descends
to look at the tower, though presumably he had a good
enough view of its presumption from above. But J's God is
highly dynamic; he *likes* to go down, walk about amidst
places, persons, and things, and see for himself from ground
level. Indeed, without such periodic descents, Yahweh evi-
dently does not allow himself to make covenants, since these
are very much on-the-ground affairs.

The intercessions at Mamre and on the road to Sodom
illustrate Yahweh's penchant for abrupt visits, but only our
consciousness feels the abruptness; J and Abraham do not
feel it. Rather than continue a citation of instances, I move to
what I would name as the esthetic principle involved, which
governs our responses: originality. J's strength, and difficulty, is that he remains more original than any other writer in
the entire tradition that he fostered. Such a statement makes
little literary sense unless I can define my use of the critical
term, "originality," within the context of biblical tradition.
That context is a history of interpretation, but by "interpretation" I mean also the use and readings of J that take place
as early as E, P, and D, the other narrative strands in the
Pentateuch.

Perhaps it was absolutely arbitrary that nearly all of the
biblical writers took J as their point of origin. But once they
did, the teleology of Jewish tradition became absolutely

inescapable. A kind of brute factuality or contingency in-
heres forever in every historical tradition, be it philosophy or
religion, literature or psychoanalysis, though such factuality
usually blinds later representatives of a tradition from seeing
that it is indeed factuality that imprisons them. J may have
been a kind of idiosyncratic accident, as Shakespeare perhaps
was, but once writers as overwhelming as J or Shakespeare or
Freud set a tradition, that tradition is doomed to shy away
from them even as it exalts them. J and the Priestly Author or
authors are as separated in time as say Chaucer and Yeats
were, and we would have grave trouble in trying to interpret
Chaucer through Yeats, though in some respects we are
doomed to do so. J is more original than Chaucer or Shakespeare, in that his central creation, Yahweh, had to undergo a
metamorphosis in the work even of the Priestly Author. The
prophets present a God who has more in common with P's
God than with J's, a process of progressive alteration that
culminated in the God of normative and rabbinical Judaism.

J's originality thus can be defined as another name for
his difficulty, for something in him that tradition never has
been able to assimilate. His uncanny Yahweh defies concep-
tualization and derives much of his literary and spiritual
authority from that defiance. If to begin is to be free, such
freedom in an originator like J becomes the freedom to rule
those who come later, and such freedom to rule is authority,
in a textual sense. Plato rose among the Greeks to contest the
authority of Homer, but among the Hebrews no one contested
the authority of J, except through the subtle techniques of
redaction, of joining oneself to J's text by interpolation and
addition, by adumbrations peculiarly interpretative.

Though the difficulties (and rewards) of reading J are
the largest in the Bible, there are few biblical texts, whatever
their authorship, that are not particularly difficult this late in
the history of Western culture. Christian, Jewish, or secular,
the contemporary reader has been nurtured by literary
suppositions that frequently are alien to the nature of the
ancient Hebrew text. It is mistaken to call J an epic writer, or

the maker of a saga, or a historian, or even an originator of prose fiction in something like the modern sense, though any of these is preferable to calling him a religious writer. Even calling J a storyteller is rather misleading. He chronicles the vicissitudes of an agonistic blessing and is therefore not only the first but still the most Jewish of writers, just as his Jacob, most agonistic of his characters, remains the most Jewish of all personages. But even the term "agonistic" is a Greek importation, and Greek, particularly Platonic, importations have been prevalent in Jewish interpretations from the days of Rabbi Akiba until now. The Judaism of Ezekiel, in the Exile, and of Ezra, in the Return, already had moved a considerable way from the doctrine implicit in J, but a partly Platonized Judaism, in Akiba and after, which we inherit, has little possibility of interpreting J accurately. Martin Buber was as little interested in his imprisonment by the brute contingency of tradition as more normative interpreters have been, but his impatience with the normative was a true advantage for him as a literary critic of the Bible.

J, the strongest of the Biblical writers, is also the most enigmatic from a normative stance. I hold to the odd formula I have expressed elsewhere, that J improbably is an amalgam of Tolstoy and of Kafka, as though Hadji Murad and the Hunter Gracchus could be accommodated by the same fictive universe. Despite his prevalent tendancy, so vigorously protested by Scholem, to reduce every Biblical text to an *I—Thou* confrontation, Buber at least puts J's uncanniness in the foreground and teaches the reader to distrust normative misreadings of J. Thus, Buber's account of "The Tree of Knowledge" is superb at seeing J's irony in the story of the "Fall," though odd in ascribing the irony to a theme of oppositeness rather than to J's rhetorical stance. Buber emphasizes play and dream rather than good and evil, an emphasis that restores the primal strangeness with which J recounts origins. J's Yahweh is without doubt the most bewildering representation in the world's literature. Whether or not J invented the Hebraic mode of the anti-iconic or developed it from tradition is beyond investigation, particularly since J, for all pragmatic purposes, simply *became* the tradition, even as Homer did. J, much more than Homer, shows us that tradition depends upon the processes, strong and weak, of misreading an overwhelming precursor. J's starkness is beyond assimilation, which is to say that reading J without crippling presuppositions is not possible, since prior readings of J, starting with the Elohist, the Priestly Author, and the Deuteronomist, have established all the available presuppositions concerning Yahweh and mankind and their relationships.

A careful reading of Genesis 3 might begin with the realization that Adam's wife (not yet named, until after Yahweh's curses) is in no way surprised by the talking, standing, shrewd serpent, whether in itself or in its message. J does not say the serpent was evil or even ill-intentioned but merely rather sly, a craftiness which in the Hebrew is connected to nakedness by a pun. Nor does J have the serpent lie; a half-truth is enough to encourage human catastrophe. The woman eats so as to gain wisdom and gains instead death and the knowledge of death, but only after Yahweh takes action. What she gains eventually, therefore, is the darkest of wisdoms, yet the immediacy of the supposed gain is the previously nonexistent consciousness of sexuality, through its sign of nakedness. What the serpent teaches must be called consciousness or a sense of nakedness, and it is the largest irony of J that his God Yahweh had created consciousness in the serpent but not in the woman or in Adam. J's saga begins not with the autumnal and cosmic harvest of the Priestly Author in Genesis 1, but with the harsh Judean spring of Genesis 2, a moment in the history of Yahweh's will when a lump of earth can be formed into an earthling. It is instructive that J's text, except for his part in the Book of Joshua, may end with Yahweh's return of his prophet, Moses, to an unmarked grave in the earth. Here, interpolated as Deuteronomy 34:6, are what may be J's concluding words about Moses:

> Yahweh buried Moses in the valley in the land of
> Moab, near Beth-peor; no one to this day knows his
> burial place.

From earth to earth is J's cycle while J's God Yahweh
goes from a first speech forbidding the tree of knowledge of
good and bad, lest man die, to a final speech forbidding
Moses to cross over into the land sworn to Abraham, Isaac,
and Jacob. The speeches have the same pattern, first giving,
but then taking away. "I have let you see it with your own
eyes," Yahweh says to Moses, and to Adam: "You are free to
eat of every tree in the garden," but the limitation or final
narrowing down of choice follows in each instance. Yahweh
is unconditioned; Moses and Adam must accept conditions.
Moses and Adam cannot will to be present wherever and
whenever they choose to be present. That power belongs to
presence itself.

Buber's essay, "Abraham the Seer," strongly reads
Genesis 12 to 25 as a mediation of presence, covering the gap
between Adam and Moses by way of a contrast between the
covenants of Noah and of Abraham with Yahweh. Buber's
Abraham is the first *nabi* or prophet of Yahweh, and so the
precise precursor of Moses, Elijah, and Isaiah. Buber's Noah
"has received no call that goes beyond his 'generations' and
no *historical* task," but Abraham matters because of "what
he does, and what he becomes." Tracing the seven revelations made to Abraham, Buber emphasizes the sixth and
seventh, respectively at Mamre and at Beersheba. The
Mamre episode is J almost at his uncanniest, giving us a
Yahweh so humanized as to make scholarly categories like
"anthropomorphism" laughably inadequate. A Yahweh who
sits upon the ground, devouring roast calf, curds, milk, and
rolls, and then is offended by an old woman's sensible
derision, is beyond all normative understanding. Buber
praises Abraham in this episode for "the boldest speech of
man in all Scripture," surpassing Job (though not, I would
say, surpassing the one bold outcry of Job's wife). What
Buber, like normative commentary, ignores is the peculiarity

of J's Yahweh, who is argued down stage by stage and with obvious recalcitrance. Buber's achievement here as an *esthetic* critic lies in his emphasis upon Abraham's *seeing*, particularly in the vision on Mount Moriah, a seeing that allows Isaac to be spared. The birth of prophecy, as Buber strikingly suggests, is a birth of a particular kind of sight: "The man sees, and sees also that he is being seen."

Buber's essay on "The Burning Bush," already glanced at in this Introduction, primarily meditates upon Yahweh as a name, yet in passing considers also one of J's greatest and most demonic incidents, Jacob's wrestling at the Jabbok with a nameless one from among the Elohim. In the powerful section on "Divine Demonism," placed directly after "The Burning Bush" in his *Moses*, Buber returned to wrestling Jacob in connection with J's weirdest passage, Yahweh's attempt to murder Moses (Exodus 4:24–26). By associating the two incidents, Buber in my judgment is far superior to any rivals at this point as a critic of J and of J's God:

It is part of the basic character of this God that he claims the entirety of the one he has chosen; he takes complete possession of the one to whom he addresses himself. It is told of him that once in the early days of the human race a human being (Enoch) was allowed to accompany him in his wanderings; this human being had then suddenly vanished, because the God had taken him away. Such taking away is part of his character in many respects. He promises Abraham a son, gives him and demands him back in order to make a gift of him afresh; and for this son he remains a sublime "Terror." His character finds even more direct expression when he first tells the son of that son to return from Aram to Canaan, and thereafter attacks him or causes him to be attacked and dislocates his hip while wrestling. At this point the tradition is not yet fully interested in ascribing everything to YHVH himself, and so the one who performs the action is "a man," but that the God stands behind cannot be doubted. Unlike the narrative of the attack on

Moses, the motif of the "dread night," which is merely hinted at there, is expanded in repeated keywords. By the nocturnal struggle with the divine being, by holding the "man" fast until a blessing is obtained, Jacob passes his test. His leading God had ordered him to wander, the same God who had once promised him: "See, I am with you, I shall protect you wherever you go, and shall bring you back to this land." And now that he had returned to this land, the wanderer had to face the perilous encounter before he enjoyed the final grace of God.

The strange episode in the Exodus story is associated and yet different. YHVH attacks the messenger whom he has just sent, clearly because the man's devotion to him after his resistance has been surmounted does not appear full enough. . . .

We know from the life of the founders of religions, and also from that of other souls who live in the deeps of faith, that there is such an "event of the night"; the sudden collapse of the newly-won certainty, the "deadly factual" moment when the demon working with apparently unbounded authority appears in the world where God alone had been in control but the moment before. The early stage of Israelite religion knows no Satan; if a power attacks a man and threatens him, it is proper to recognize YHVH in it or behind it, no matter how nocturnally dread and cruel it may be; and it was proper to withstand Him, since after all He does not require anything else of me than myself.

Only a few normative traces obscure Buber's insights here. For "the tradition," J should be substituted, and the text in itself does not justify Buber's conclusion that the devotion of God to Moses was not yet complete. J's abruptness is absolute. Yahweh has just spoken to Moses, instructing him on the message to Pharoah, and Moses has just taken the rod of God in his hand. Hastening to Egypt, Moses necessarily camps by night, and there and then Yahweh encountered him and sought to kill him. But these minor points aside, Buber has broken through thousands of years of pious misreadings, or at least he has begun the break. J's God, whether through a nameless "some man" among the Elohim (the Angel of Death?), who cripples Jacob, or in his own person, can behave in modes that almost might have been designed to render normative interpretation gratuitous. No moral meanings can be ascribed to this Yahweh, in our terms, that will not be weak misreadings. Buber's vision of a God who desires complete possession, the entirety of the elected one, restores to J much of his primal force as a writer.

This primal force again is placed in the foreground in the meditation, "Holy Event," excerpted in this volume from Buber's *The Prophetic Faith.* The Holy Event is the account in Exodus 19 to 27 of Yahweh's epiphany at Mount Sinai, but Buber resumes in it his own acount of divine demonism. Scholem's critique of Buber's "pneumatic exegesis" asserts that the specific and historical occurrences of revelation are subverted here by a purely personal mysticism. The issue, I think, is more problematic than Scholem makes it out to be. What Buber clearly does subvert is the normative tradition of reading, but Buber's own reading is again closer to the uncanniness of the Biblical text. Buber's obsession with the kingship of God helps him in conveying the super-mimetic force of the Sinai text.

"The Election of Israel: A Biblical Inquiry" continues this reading by juxtaposing Exodus 3 and 19 with aspects of Deuteronomy. "Election without obligation" is Buber's succinct formula, illuminating again the texts' own departures from normative conventions. Buber's personalism and religious anarchism are at the center of his account of "The Words on the Tablets," his reading of Exodus 20 in *Moses,* to which "What Are We To Do about The Ten Commandments" forms a coda. For Buber, the Decalogue is no catechism but an address to the "Thou." Here, perhaps, Scholem is vindicated again, since Buber's idealizings soften the text in ways that the normative tradition does not countenance and thus weaken Buber's truest justification for his own stance, which is the cleansing of the text from its more barren commentaries.

Much richer is the brief article on "The Prayer of the First Fruits," possibly because the text (from Deuteronomy 26) is so cunningly integrated by Buber with Jeremiah's great trope: "Israel was holy to the Lord, the first fruits of his harvest." Buber goes on to cite the Mishnah's report of the actual ceremony of the offering, with its vivid realization of the prayer's figurations. Halfway through this volume, we are thus given a graceful transition from the Pentateuch to the prophets and from the thematic concern with revelation to the adjacent problematics of redemption.

The brief examination of "Samuel and the Ark" enforces Buber's characteristic exaltation of prophet over priest by way of a questionable transmogrification of Samuel from judge to prophet. Yet Buber goes so far here as to add Deborah to the line of prophets. The operative definition of prophet, for Buber, is a proclaimer of the kingship of Yahweh against any other authority, priestly or royal. This persuasive definition allows Buber unquestioned insights, as when he points out that "Samuel is made to utter the first non-anonymous prophecy of doom in the Bible," or when he names Samuel as the *nabi* because he is "one who speaks also of his own accord, *unasked*, the message of revelation." These insights are more impressively set forth in the much earlier lecture, on "Biblical Leadership," which follows in this volume and represents Buber at his most eloquent.

Here Buber begins with the surprising assertion that the Bible is not concerned with character nor with individuality, but only with "persons in situations," and so not with the differences between persons, but only with the different degrees of success or failure in those situations. Palpably this is untrue, since we have an overwhelming sense of Jacob and of Moses, as J represents them, or of Jeremiah as he represents himself. Probably Buber means that *he* is concerned only with "persons in situations," and with their dialogical situation in particular. This personal stance on

Buber's own part causes him to exclude as biblical leaders "all those who are not called, elected, appointed anew, as the Bible says, directly by God," such as Joshua and Solomon, for these do not transcend both nature and history. Buber looks instead to "the younger sons who are chosen—from Abel, through Jacob, Joseph and Moses, to David." He looks also to Gideon, who deliberately reduces his army from ten thousand to three hundred, a reduction here interpreted as another incident in the struggle against merely natural and historical strength.

There is something impressively hyperbolical about Buber's emphasis, which is a kind of sublime trope of the thematics of his entire life and work. The reader is likely to be carried along when Buber asserts that Moses and David were somehow *failures,* an assertion that can only be judged a sublime misreading or creative misunderstanding on Buber's part. Yet, I would call Buber's vehement rhetoric and its effect here his greatest strength as a *literary* critic of the Bible. As criticism, Buber's figurative, hyperbolical language does the work of breaking down our preconceived response and restores the strangeness of the Bible. Here, it particularly stresses the problematic but authentic continuity between Moses and David as precursors, Isaiah and Jeremiah as latecomers *in the same spiritual grouping.* For Buber, the prophets find their essence in historical and natural failure:

> The prophet is the man who has been set up against his own natural instincts that bind him to the community, and who likewise sets himself up against the will of the people to live on as they have always lived, which, naturally, for the people is identical with the will to live.

Despite its eloquence, Buber's formulation is again vulnerable to Scholem's characteristic critique, which is that this is more Buber than it is Isaiah or Jeremiah. Buber himself was fated to become a prophet more accepted by the Gentiles than by the Jews. Certainly the anti-historical element in Buber's vision is never more vehement than in the peroration of this astonishing lecture:

The real work, from the biblical point of view, is the late-recorded, the unrecorded, the anonymous work. The real work is done in the shadow, in the quiver. Official leadership fails more and more, leadership devolves more and more, upon the secret. The way leads through the work that history does not write down, and that history cannot write down.

This *sounds* much more like a gnostic or kabbalistic point of view than like the biblical one. Even Buber's beautiful allusion to Second Isaiah (49:2) subverts the meaning of that lament, whose point is that the true prophet ought *not* to be concealed in the shadow and the quiver. Buber's personal darkening of the prophetic faith is in some ways intensified in his pages on "Plato and Isaiah," excerpted from his introductory lecture at the Hebrew University in 1938. In a contrast between Plato's failure to found a perfect state in Syracuse, through his pupil Dion, and Isaiah's failure to keep the kings of Judah from disaster, Buber insists that the prophet's failure is more fruitful. Plato's truth was timeless and so could never be realized in time, but paradoxically Isaiah's truth was timely, failed in its own temporal moment, and yet survives perpetually through and in that failure. A reader's puzzlement at Buber's judgment can be tested by contrasting these two Buberian lectures with "Jerusalem and Athens," two lectures given by Leo Strauss in New York City in 1967. Strauss also compares Plato and the prophets, or rather Socrates and the prophets, since Socrates has the call or mission, as Isaiah and Jeremiah did. For Strauss, neither Socrates nor the prophets are failures, paradoxical or otherwise, and more crucially their primary difference is not in the temporal nature of their work. In a fine discrimination, Strauss reminds us that Socrates expects the truth always to be knowable only to philosophers, whereas Isaiah chants of when "the earth shall be full of knowledge of the Lord, as the waters cover the earth." Like Kierkegaard, Socrates speaks to the single one, to a man who can be made to understand, but the *nabi* is a public orator. Isaiah and

Jeremiah sometimes speak to the king, but sometimes to all
the people of Jerusalem.

Shall we say that Strauss is the better scholar here, while
Buber is the more literary interpreter? Buber's pages on
"Redemption" in Isaiah and Second Isaiah emphasize the
way in which Solomon's temple becomes a Messianic trope, a
Zionist prophecy to which Buber himself can assent. Again
the reader is left uncertain as to the historical difference
between the two Isaiahs, a difference that Strauss would not
have voided. Something of the spirit of Strauss would have
been a useful corrective for Buber, as we can see by a further
contrast between these two sages. Buber considers Jeremiah
28 in "False Prophets," where he grants that the false
prophet Hananiah was an honest patriot but condemns him
nevertheless for supposed worship of success, unlike Jeremiah, who embraced failure. Strauss, in his lecture on Socrates
and the prophets, astutely traces Hananiah's downfall to
something subtler than the worship of success:

> The false prophets trust in flesh, even if that flesh is
> the temple in Jerusalem, the promised land, nay, the
> chosen people itself, nay, God's promise to the chosen
> people if that promise is taken to be an unconditional
> promise and not as a part of a Covenant. The true
> prophets, regardless of whether they predict doom or
> salvation, predict the unexpected, the humanly unfore-
> seeable—what would not occur to men, left to them-
> selves, to fear or to hope.

False prophecy, on this view, is a failure of imagination,
rather than a failure to accept the burden of temporal failure.
If Strauss is persuasive here, more than Buber, it is because
he is closer to literature this time or to the critical insight that
literature fosters and demands. But Buber is a formidable
theorist of prophecy, and even his obsession with prophetic
failure has links to his lasting achievement as an interpreter
of what he calls the prophetic faith.

Buber's central ideas on prophecy exist only in dialecti-
cal tension with his polemic against the apocalyptic. Presum-

ably Buber would have endorsed the formula that failed
prophecy becomes apocalyptic, while failed apocalyptic becomes Gnosticism. Scholem again identifies Buber's refusal
of the apocalyptic vision with Buber's insistence upon projecting his own dialogical spirituality into the prophetic
impulse. Even if true, this does not invalidate the intense
essay on "Prophecy, Apocalyptic, and the Historical Hour,"
where the true subject is individual freedom, and the telling
contrast is between Jeremiah the prophet and Karl Marx.
Jeremiah's crucial image is the double wheel of the potter, a
figure for God's making and unmaking of the house of Israel.
The immanent dialectic of Marx, substituting for Yahweh's
will, obliterates the will and the act of the individual, such an
obliteration representing, for Buber, the authentic stigma of
the apocalyptic. Buber, in my judgment, is never more
powerful as a critic than in his characteristic juxtaposition of
prophetic *voice* and apocalyptic *writing*, with its illuminating
preference for voice:

> The time the prophetic voice calls us to take part in
> is the time of the actual decision; to this the prophet
> summons his hearers, not seldom at the risk of martyr-
> dom to himself. In the world of the apocalyptic this
> present historical-biographical hour hardly ever exists.
> . . . The prophet addresses persons who hear him, who
> should hear him. He knows himself sent to them in order
> to place before them the stern alternatives of the hour.
> Even when he writes his message or has it written,
> whether it is already spoken or is still to be spoken, it is
> always intended for particular men, to induce them, as
> directly as if they were hearers, to recognize their
> situation's demand for decision and to act accordingly.
> The apocalyptic writer has no audience turned toward
> him; he speaks into his notebook.

Unquestionably powerful, this is also unquestionably
unfair to the apocalyptic, scorned here as mere literature.
Buber's animus against the apocalyptic is at one with his
polemic against gnosis; both are modes of self-absorption, of

the I obsessed with I, on this view. Persuasive as a rhetorician because of his own certainty as to what prophecy was or was not, Buber represses our authentic inability to know exactly where and how the prophetic voice edges into the apocalyptic. Yet he relies upon the literary experience that is increasingly our only authority for recognizing prophetic voice. The paradigm for this experience is unforgettably the abrupt entry of Elijah into the biblical text:

> Now Elijah the Tishbite, of Tishbe in Gilead, said to Ahab, "As the Lord the God of Israel lives, before whom I stand, there shall be neither dew nor rain these years, except by my word."

It is not that any material has been lost, as unimaginative scholars have insisted, but rather that nothing less in esthetic force could convey the ethos of this precursor of Amos and Hosea, Isaiah and Jeremiah. But it seems to me that scholarship has failed with the Hebrew prophets, even in the massive achievement of Gerhard von Rad or the sympathetic psychologizing of Abraham J. Heschel. Poets of action as well as of words, or overwhelmingly the exemplification of the range of meanings of *davar* (word, thing, deed), the prophets remain still to be read in all the difficulties of what a genuine reading would have to be. I know of no more difficult text than Jeremiah. He has in common with J a quality that defeats interpretation, and I suspect at last we must call the quality "originality." Buber's great virtue is that almost uniquely he does not underemphasize biblical originality, but as that is the burden of his last essay in this volume, I defer comment on this quality until my own conclusion.

The essay on prophecy and the apocalyptic does not mention Nietzsche, but the shadow of his Zarathustra is very dark as Buber moves towards closure:

> . . . only the unbelief remains in the broken yet emphatic apocalyptic of our time. It steps forward with a heroic mien, to be sure; it holds itself to be the heroic

acknowledgment of the inevitable, the embodiment of *amor fati*. But this convulsive gesture has nothing in common with real love.

I read this as Buber's unmastered anxiety of influence in regard to Nietzsche, who far more than Buber himself fulfilled Buber's program for prophecy as set forth in *The Prophetic Faith*:

> But the word of God . . . breaks into the whole order of the word world and breaks through. The aforementioned is an addition to rite, and is even nothing but rite in the form of language; whereas the other, the divine word, which suddenly descends into the human situation, unexpected and unwilled by man, is free and fresh like lightning. And the man who has to make it heard is over and over again subdued by the word before He lets it be put in his mouth.

Buber's reference is to the exemplary sufferings of Jeremiah, but Nietzsche, as Jeremiah's truest descendant, could be described here. It is from *The Prophetic Faith* also, Buber's finest single book, that the remarkable analysis of Job is excerpted in the present volume. The Book of Job has had Calvin, Blake, Kierkegaard, and Newman among its commentators, and it cannot be said that Buber rivals them, but then no biblical scholar does either. What Buber does uncover, with great clarity, is a pattern of four very diverse views of God's relationship to Job's sufferings. There is the "popular" view of the prologue, with a God too easily "enticed" by Satan. There is the "dogmatic" view of Job's "comforters": if sufferings, then sin. There is Job's own view, which became Buber's theology: the "eclipse" of God. But most powerfully, there is God's own view, his answer. As Buber phrases it, this is "not *the* divine justice, which remains hidden, but *a* divine justice, namely that manifest in creation." Buber cites Rudolf Otto here on the playful riddle of God's creative power. Karl Barth in his *Church Dogmatics* makes a nice point illuminating this riddle, which is that God shrewdly allows creation to speak for him:

He obviously counts upon it that they belong so
totally to Him, that they are so subject to Him and at His
disposal, that in speaking of themselves they will necessarily speak of Him.

Buber's Job is a "faithful rebel" and therefore a servant
of God. Perhaps toward this text Buber was not audacious
enough. A reader is likelier to remember the bitter irony of
Calvin on Job: "God would have to create new worlds, if He
wished to satisfy us"; or the more complex irony of Kierkegaard: "Fix your eyes upon Job; even though he terrifies you,
it is not this he wishes, if you yourself did not wish it." But
Buber is not Calvin nor Kierkegaard, Blake nor Kafka. If he
gentles Job, it is because as exegete he seeks consolation as
well as wisdom.

I judge Buber to be as valuable a commentator as the
wisdom Psalms have had, and "The Heart Determines," his
reading of Psalm 73, is without critical parallel. This intricate
exegesis defies summary, and so I restrict myself to indicating
its subtle technique of continuously undermining apparent
meaning until only the trope of the Psalmist's "nearness"
remains. Here Buber is at last wholly beyond Scholem's
strictures, for the interpretation is normative, in no way
"pneumatic," and yet wholly original.

Originality is the crucial concern of the address on
"Biblical Humanism," dating back to the fateful year 1933,
that fittingly ends this volume. When one seeks Buber's
central apothegm on the Bible, one finds: "The purity of the
Hebrew Bible's word resides not in form but in originality."
Buber's words, *Ursprunglichkeit,* relates in his view to "the
immediacy of spokenness." At the least, as a critic Buber
returns us to the uncanniness of J, of the court personage
who wrote of David, of Jeremiah, of the author of Job. These
writers are the spring of the longest normative tradition in
the West, yet that tradition has never subdued the strangeness of its origins, never overcome the originality of its God.
Buber's biblical criticism has the final virtue of being a kind
of threshold rhetoric, beckoning the reader on to the wan-

dering of further criticism. As a sustained body of work, Buber on the Bible is more vitalizing than any other critic has been. Kafka once complained of Buber that "no matter what he says, something is missing." One can hazard what Kafka missed in Buber by finding it in Kafka himself:

> The essence of Wandering in the Wilderness. A man who leads his people along this way with a shred (more is unthinkable) of consciousness of what is happening. He is on the track of Canaan all his life; it is incredible that he should see the land only when on the verge of death. This dying vision of it can only be intended to illustrate how incomplete a moment is human life, incomplete because a life like this could last forever and still be nothing but a moment. Moses fails to enter Canaan not because his life is too short but because it is a human life. This ending of the Pentateuch bears a resemblance to the final scene of [Flaubert's] *Education sentimentale*.

That final sentence is magnificently beyond audacity. Moses gazing at the land promised but not to be entered "resembles" two men thinking back to a Sunday of their adolescence, when first they entered but then too quickly fled a bordello, yet in recall seeing the incident as the happiest time they ever had. Even Kafka is more strangely studying the nostalgias than being ironic here. That splendor aside, the rest of the passage is simply the finest criticism I have read of J's saga of Moses, and of much else as well. Kafka, as I remarked earlier, is half of J; Tolstoy perhaps is the rest. So unlikely a writer may never find his adequate critic. Buber, though much indeed is missing in him, surely represents better than anyone else certain qualities that a true critic of the Bible will have to possess.

ON THE BIBLE

THE MAN OF TODAY
AND THE JEWISH BIBLE

BIBLIA, books, is the name of a book, of a Book composed of many books. It is really one book, for one basic theme unites all the stories and songs, sayings and prophecies contained within it. The theme of the Bible is the encounter between a group of people and the Lord of the world in the course of history, the sequence of events occurring on earth. Either openly or by implication, the stories are reports of encounters. The songs lament the denial of the grace of encounter, plead that it may be repeated, or give thanks because it has been vouchsafed. The prophecies summon man who has gone astray to turn, to return to the region where the encounter took place, promising him that the torn bond shall once more be made whole. If this book transmits cries of doubt, it is the doubt that is the destiny of man, who after having tasted nearness must experience distance and learn from distance what it alone can teach. When we find love songs in the Bible, we must understand that the love of God for His world is revealed through the depths of love human beings can feel for one another.

Since this book came into being, it has confronted generation after generation. Each generation must struggle with the Bible in its turn, and come to terms with it. The generations are by no means always ready to listen to what the Book has to say, and to obey it; they are often vexed and defiant; nevertheless, the preoccupation with this book is part of their life and they face it in the realm of reality. Even when gen-

erations negated the Book, the very negation confirmed the
Book's claim upon them; they bore witness to the Book in
the very act of denying it.

The picture changes when we shift to the man of today,
and by this I mean the intellectual of our time, the man who
holds it important that intellectual values exist, and admits,
yes, even himself declares that their reality is bound up with
our own power to realize them. But if we were to question
him and probe down to truth—and we do not usually probe
that far down—he would have to own that this feeling of his
about the obligations of the spirit is in itself only intellectual.
It is the signature of our time that the spirit imposes no obligations. We proclaim the rights of the spirit, we formulate
its laws, but they enter only into books and discussions, not
into our lives. They float in mid-air above our heads, rather
than walk the earth in our midst. Everything except everyday
life belongs to the realm of the spirit.

Instead of union, a false relationship obtains between
the spirit and everyday life. This relationship may shape up
as spurious idealism, toward which we may lift our gaze without incurring any obligation to recover from the exigencies
of earth; or it may present itself as spurious realism, which
regards the spirit as only a function of life and transforms its
unconditionality into a number of conditional characters:
psychological, sociological, and others. It is true that some
contemporaries realize all the corroding consequences of this
separation of two interdependent entities, a corrosion that is
bound to penetrate into deeper and deeper strata, until the
spirit is debased into a willing and complacent servant of
whatever powers happen to rule the world. The men of whom
I am speaking have pondered how this corrosion can be
halted, and have appealed to religion as the only power still
capable of bringing about a new union between spirit and
world. But what goes by the name of religion nowadays will
never bring about such a union. For nowadays "religion"
itself is part of the detached spirit. It is one of the subdivi-
sions—one in high favor, to be sure—of the structure erected
over and above life, one of the rooms on the top floor, with
a very special atmosphere of its own. But this sort of religion

is not an entity that includes all of life and, in this its present status, can never become one. It has lost its unity and so it cannot lead man to inner unity. It has adapted to this twofold character of human existence.

To exert an influence on contemporary man, religion itself would have to return to reality. And religion was always real only when it was free of fear, when it shouldered the load of concreteness instead of rejecting it as something belonging to another realm, when it made the spirit incarnate, and sanctified everyday life.

The so-called Old Testament constitutes the greatest document of such reality. Two traits—which are, however, interrelated—set it apart from the other great books of the world religions.

One trait is that in the "Old Testament" both events and words are placed in the midst of the people, of history, of the world. What happens does not happen in a vacuum existing between God and the individual. The Word travels by way of the individual to the people, so that they may hear and translate it into reality. What happens is not superior to the history of the people; it is nothing but the secret of the people's history made manifest. But that very fact places the people acted upon in opposition to the nations that represent—in their own eyes—an end in themselves, to groups concerned only with their own welfare. This people is called upon to weld its members into a community that may serve as a model for the so many and so different peoples. The historical continuity of "seed" and "earth" is bound up with the "blessing" (Gen. 12 ff.), and the blessing with the mission. The Holy permeates history without divesting it of its rights.

The second trait is that in the Bible the law is designed to cover the natural course of man's life. Eating meat is connected with animal sacrifice; matrimonial purity is sanctified month after month; man is accepted as he is, with all his urges and passions, and included in holiness, lest his passions grow into a mania. The desire to own land is not condemned, and renunciation is not demanded, but the true Lord of the land is God, and man is nothing but a "sojourner" in His midst. The Landlord makes a harmonious balance of property ownership, lest inequality arise, grow, and break the bond between the members of the community. Holiness penetrates nature without violating it. The living spirit wishes to spiritualize and quicken life; it wishes spirit and life to find the way to one another; it wishes spirit to take shape as life, and life to be clarified through spirit. The spirit wishes creation to attain perfection through itself.

The function of this book is to bear witness to the spirit's will to perfection and to the command to serve the spirit in its search for union with life. If we accept the Old Testament as merely religious writing, as a subdivision of the detached spirit, it will fail us, and we must needs fail it. If we seize upon it as the expression of a reality that comprises all of life, we really grasp it, and it grasps hold of us. But contemporary man is scarcely capable of this grasp any longer. If he takes any interest at all in the Scriptures, it is an abstract, purely "religious" interest, and more often not even that, but an interest connected with the history of religion or civilization, or an aesthetic interest, or the like—at any rate it is an interest that springs from the detached spirit with its numerous autonomous domains. Man of today is not like the generations of old, who stood before the biblical Word in order to hearken to or to take offense at it. He no longer confronts his life with the Word; he locks life away in one of many unholy compartments, and then he feels relieved. Thus he paralyzes the power that, of all powers, is best able to save him.

Before demonstrating in greater detail and by way of examples what power the Jewish Bible has to guide the life of the man of today, I must broach the basic question which the thoughtful reader is asking himself at this point: Even if this man of today—even if we were able to approach this whole book with our whole selves, would we not still lack the indispensable prerequisite to its true reception? Would we be able to believe it? Could we believe it? Can we do more than believe that people once did believe as this book reports and claims?

The man of today has no access to a sure and solid faith,

nor can it be made accessible to him. If he examines himself seriously, he knows this and may not delude himself further. But he is not denied the possibility of holding himself open to faith. If he is really serious, he too can open up to this book and let its rays strike him where they will. He can give himself up and submit to the test without preconceived notions and without reservations. He can absorb the Bible with all his strength, and wait to see what will happen to him, whether he will not discover within himself a new and unbiased approach to this or that element in the book.

But to this end, he must read the Jewish Bible as though it were something entirely unfamiliar, as though it had not been set before him ready-made, as though he has not been confronted all his life with sham concepts and sham statements that cited the Bible as their authority. He must face the Book with a new attitude as something new. He must yield to it, withhold nothing of his being, and let whatever will occur between himself and it. He does not know which of its sayings and images will overwhelm him and mold him, from where the spirit will ferment and enter into him, to incorporate itself anew in his body. But he holds himself open. He does not believe anything a priori; he does not disbelieve anything a priori. He reads aloud the words written in the book in front of him; he hears the word he utters and it reaches him. Nothing is prejudged. The current of time flows on, and the contemporary character of this man becomes itself a receiving vessel.

In order to understand the situation fully, we must picture to ourselves the complete chasm between the Scriptures and the man of today.

The Jewish Bible has always approached and still approaches every generation with the claim that it must be recognized as a document of the true history of the world, that is to say, of the history according to which the world has an origin and a goal. The Jewish Bible demands that the individual fit his own life into this true history, so that "I" may find my own origin in the origin of the world, and my own goal in the goal of the world. But the Jewish Bible does not set a past event as a midpoint between origin and goal.

It interposes a movable, circling midpoint which cannot be pinned to any set time, for it is the moment when I, the reader, the hearer, the man, catch through the words of the Bible the voice which from earliest beginnings has been speaking in the direction of the goal. The midpoint is this mortal and yet immortal moment of mine. Creation is the origin, redemption the goal. But revelation is not a fixed, dated point poised between the two. The revelation at Sinai is not this midpoint itself, but the perceiving of it, and such perception is possible at any time. That is why a psalm or a prophecy is no less Torah, i.e., instruction, than the story of the exodus from Egypt. The history of this people—accepting and refusing at once—points to the history of all mankind, but the secret dialogue expressed in the psalms and prophecies points to my own secret.

The Jewish Bible is the historical document of a world swinging between creation and redemption, which, in the course of its history, experiences revelation, a revelation *I* experience *if I am there*. Thus, we can understand that the resistance of the man of today is that of his innermost being.

The man of today has two approaches to history. He may contemplate it as a freethinker, and participate in and accept the shifting events, the varying success of the struggles for power, as a promiscuous agglomeration of happenings. To him history will seem a medley of the actions and deaths of peoples, of grasping and losing, triumph and misery, a meaningless hodgepodge to which the mind of man, time and again, gives an unreliable and unsubstantial semblance of meaning. Or he may view history dogmatically, derive laws from past sequences of events and calculate future sequences, as though the main lines were already traced on some roll which he need merely unroll; as though history were not the vital living, growing, of time, constantly moving from decision to decision, of time into which my time and my decisions stream full force. He regards history as a stark, everpresent, inescapable space.

Both these approaches are a misinterpretation of historic destiny, which is neither chance nor fatality. According to the biblical insight, historic destiny is the secret correlation inhering in the current moment. When we are aware of origin and goal, there is no meaningless drift; we are carried along by a meaning we could never think up for ourselves, a meaning we are to live—not to formulate. And that living takes place in the awful and splendid moment of decision—your moment and mine no less than Alexander's and Caesar's. And yet your moment is not yours, but rather the moment of your encounter.

The man of today knows of no beginning. As far as he is concerned, history ripples toward him from some prehistorical cosmic age. He knows of no end; history sweeps him on into a posthistorical cosmic age. What a violent and foolish episode this time between the prehistorical and the posthistorical has become! Man no longer recognizes an origin or a goal because he no longer wants to recognize the midpoint. Creation and redemption are true only on the premise that revelation is a present experience. Man of today resists the Scriptures because he cannot endure revelation. To endure revelation is to endure this moment full of possible decisions, to respond to and to be responsible for every moment. Man of today resists the Scriptures because he no longer wants to accept responsibility. He thinks he is venturing a great deal, yet he industriously evades the one real venture, that of responsibility.

Insight into the reality of the Bible begins with drawing a distinction between creation, revelation, and redemption.[1] Christianity withdrew from such insight—and thus from the grounds of the "Old Testament"—in its earliest theology, which fused the essentials of revelation and the essentials of redemption in the Christ. It was entirely logical for Marcion to dispute the value of a creation that from this point of view was bound to seem nothing but a premise, and to brand it as the blunder of another, inferior god. With that act, the essence of time, which was closely allied to the essence of our spirit, was abandoned; time, which distinguishes between past, present, and future—structures which in the Bible reach their most concrete expression in the three structures of creation, revelation, and redemption.

The only gate that leads to the Bible as a reality is the faithful distinction between the three, not as hypostases or manifestations of God, but as stages, actions, and events in the course of His intercourse with the world, and thus also as the main directions of His movement toward the world. But such distinction must not be exaggerated to mean separation. From the point of view of the Bible, revelation is, as it were, focused in the middle, creation in the beginning, and redemption in the end. But the living truth is that they actually coincide, that "God every day renews the work of the Beginning," [2] but also every day anticipates the work of the end. Certainly both creation and redemption are true only on the premise that revelation is a present experience. But if I did not feel creation as well as redemption happening to myself, I could never understand what creation and redemption are.

This fact must be the starting point for the recurring question, if and how the chasm between man of today and the Scriptures can be bridged. We have already answered the question of whether the man of today can believe by saying that, while he is denied the certainty of faith, he has the power to hold himself open to faith. But is not the strangeness of biblical concepts a stumbling stone to his readiness to do so? Has he not lost the reality of creation in his concept of evolution, that of revelation in the theory of the unconscious, and that of redemption in the setting up of social or national goals?

We must wholly understand the very substantial quality of this strangeness, before we can even attempt to show that there is still an approach or, rather, *the* approach.

And again we must begin with the center.

What meaning are we intended to find in the words that God came down in fire, to the sound of thunder and horn, to the mountain that smoked like a furnace, and spoke to His people? It can mean, I think, one of three things. Either it is figurative language used to express a "spiritual" process; or if biblical history does not recall actual events, but is metaphor and allegory, then it is no longer biblical, and deserves no better fate than to be surrendered to the approach of modern man, the historical, aesthetic, and the like approaches. Or it is the report of a "supernatural" event, one that severs the intelligible sequence of happenings we term natural by interposing something unintelligible. If that were the case, man of today in deciding to accept the Bible would have to make a sacrifice of intellect that would cut his life irreparably in two, provided he does not want to lapse into the habitual, lazy acceptance of something he does not really believe. In other words, what he is willing to accept would not be the Bible in its totality, including all of life, but only religion abstracted from life.

But there is a third possibility: it could be the verbal trace of a natural event, i.e., of an event that took place in the world of the senses common to all men, and fitted into connections that the senses can perceive. But the assemblage that experienced this event experienced it as revelation vouchsafed to them by God, and preserved it as such in the memory of generations, an enthusiastic, spontaneously formative memory. Experience undergone in this way is not self-delusion on the part of the assemblage; it is what they see, what they recognize and perceive with their reason, for natural events are the carriers of revelation, and revelation occurs when he who witnesses the event and sustains it experiences the revelation it contains. This means that he listens to that which the voice, sounding forth from this event, wishes to communicate to him its witness, to his constitution, to his life, to his sense of duty. It is only when this is true that man of today can find the approach to biblical reality. I, at any rate, believe that it is true.

Sometimes we have a personal experience related to those recorded as revelations and capable of opening the way for them. We may unexpectedly grow aware of a certain apperception within ourselves, which was lacking but a moment ago, and whose origin we are unable to discover. The attempt to derive such apperception from the famous unconscious stems from the widespread superstition that the soul can do everything by itself, and it fundamentally means nothing but this: what you have just experienced was always in you. Such notions build up a temporary construction which

is useful for psychological orientation, but collapses when
I try to stand upon it. But what occurred to me was otherness, the touch of the other. Nietzsche says it more honestly,
"You take, you do not ask who it is that gives." [3] But I
think that as we take, it is of the utmost importance to know
that someone is giving. He who takes what is given him, and
does not experience it as a gift, is not really receiving; and
so the gift turns into theft. But when we do experience the
giving, we find out that revelation exists. And we set foot
on the path that will reveal our life and the life of the world
as a sign communication. This path is the approach. It is on
this path that we shall meet with the major experience that
is of the same kind as our minor experience.

The perception of revelation is the basis for perceiving
creation and redemption. I begin to realize that in inquiring
about my own origin and goal I am inquiring about something other than myself, and something other than the world.
But in this very realization I begin to recognize the origin
and goal of the world.

What meaning are we intended to find in the statement
that God created the world in six days? Certainly not that He
created it in six ages, and that "create" must mean "come
into being"—the interpretation of those who try to contrive
an approach to the Bible by forcing it into harmony with
current scientific views. But just as inadequate for our purposes is the mystic interpretation, according to which the
acts of creation are not acts, but emanations. It is in keeping
with the nature of mysticism to resist the idea that, for our
sake, God assumed the lowly form of an acting person. But
divest the Bible of the acting character of God, and it loses
its significance, and the concepts of a Platonic or Heraclitean
system—concepts born from the observation of reality—are
far preferable to the homunculus-like principles of emana-
tion in such an interpretation.

What meaning, then, are we intended to find? Here
there can be no question of verbal traces of an event, because
there was none to witness it. Is access then barred to everyone who cannot believe that the biblical story of creation
is the pure "word of God"? The saying of the talmudic

sages[4] to the effect that the Torah speaks the language of men hides a deeper seriousness than is commonly assumed. We must construe it to mean that what is unutterable *can* only be uttered, as it is here expressed, in the language of men. The biblical story of creation is a legitimate stammering account. Man cannot but stammer when he lines up what he knows of the universe into a chronological series of commands and "works" from the divine workshop. But this stammering of his was the only means of doing justice to the task of stating the mystery of how time springs from eternity, and world comes from that which is not world. Compared to this, every attempt to explain cosmogony scientifically, to supply a logical foundation for the origin of all things, is bound to fail.

If then, the man of today can find the approach to the reality of revelation in the fact that it is our life that is being addressed, how can he find the approach to the reality of creation? His own individual life will not lead him straight to creation as it does to revelation, which he can find so readily because—as we have seen—every moment we live can in itself be its midpoint. Nevertheless the reality of creation can be found, because every man knows that he is an individual and unique. Suppose it were possible for a man to make a psycho-physical inventory of his own person, to break down his character into a sum of qualities; and now suppose it were possible for him to trace each separate quality and the concurrence of all back to the most primitive living creatures, and in this way make an uninterrupted genetic analysis of his individuality by determining its derivation and reference—then his form, his face, unprecedented, comparable to none, unique, his voice never heard before, his gestures never seen before, his body informed with spirit, would still exist as the untouched residue, underived and underivable, an entity that is simply present and nothing more. If after all this futile effort, such a man had the strength to repeat the question, Whence, he would in the final analysis discover himself simply as something that was created. Because every man is unique, another first man enters the world whenever a child is born. By being alive, everyone groping like a child back to the origin of his own self, we may experience the fact that there is an origin, that there is creation.

And now to the third, the last, and the most difficult problem: How are we to understand the concept that "in the end of days" everything in the world will be resolved, that the world will be so perfectly redeemed that, as it is written, there will be "a new heaven and a new earth" (Isa. 66:22)? Here again, two opposite interpretations must be avoided. We must not regard the tidings in the light of another world to come. They mean that this, our world, will be purified to the state of the Kingdom, that creation will be made perfect, but not that our world will be annulled for the sake of another world. Neither do the tidings refer to a more righteous order, but to righteousness, not to mankind grown more peaceful, but to peace.

Here, too, the voice we hear stammers legitimately. The prophet, who is overwhelmed by the divine word, can only speak in the words of men. He can speak only as one who is able to grasp from what and whence he is to be redeemed, but not for what and whither. And the man of today? Must not this he hears be strangest to him, exactly because it is closest to his fathomless yearning? He dreams of change, but does not know transformation. He hopes that if not tomorrow, then the next day things will be better, but the idea that truth will come means nothing to him. He is familiar with the idea of development and the overcoming of obstacles, but he can realize neither that a power wishes to redeem him and the world from contradiction, nor that because of the existence of this power it is demanded of him that he turn with the whole of his being. How can we mediate between this man and the biblical message? Where is the bridge?

This is the most difficult of all. The lived moment leads directly to the knowledge of revelation, and thinking about birth leads indirectly to the knowledge of creation. But in his personal life probably not one of us will taste the essence of redemption before his last hour. And yet here, too, there is an approach. It is dark and silent and cannot be indicated by any means, save by my asking you to recall your own dark and silent hours. I mean those hours in the lowest depths when our soul hovers over the frail trap door which, at the very next instant, may send us down into destruction, madness, and suicide at our own verdict. Indeed, we are astonished that it has not opened up until now. But suddenly we feel a touch as of a hand. It reaches down to us, it wishes to be grasped—and yet what incredible courage is needed to take the hand, to let it draw us up out of the darkness! This is redemption. We must realize the true nature of the experience proffered us: It is that our "redeemer liveth" (Job 19:25), that He wishes to redeem us—but only by our own acceptance of His redemption with the turning of our whole being.

Approach, I said. For all this still does not constitute a rootedness in biblical reality. But it is the approach to it. It is a beginning.

THE TREE OF KNOWLEDGE

(GENESIS 3)

T HE biblical account of the so-called fall of man (Gen. 3) may well be founded upon a primeval myth of the envy and vengeance of gods, of whose contents we have no more than an inkling: the story that has been written down and preserved for us has acquired a very different meaning. The divine being whose actions are here recorded is repeatedly referred to (with the exception of the dialogue between the serpent and the woman) by an appellation, alien to the style of the rest of the Bible, which is compounded out of a proper name—interpreted elsewhere (Exod. 3:14 f.) as He-is-there —and a generic term which is plural in form and corresponds most nearly to our "Godhead." This God is the sole possessor of the power both of creation and of destiny; He is surrounded by other celestial beings, but all these are subject to Him and without names or power of their own. Of course, He does not impose His will upon man, the last of His works; He does not compel him, He only commands, or rather forbids, him, albeit under a severe threat. The man—and with him his woman, who was not created till after the prohibition had been pronounced, but who appears to have become cognizant of it in some peculiar manner while still a rib within the body of the man—may give or withhold his obedience, for he is at liberty; they are both at liberty to accede to their creator or to refuse themselves to Him. Yet their transgression of the prohibition is not reported to us as a decision between good and evil, but as something other, of whose otherness we must take account.

The terms of the dialogue with the serpent are already strange enough. It speaks as though it knew very imprecisely what it obviously knows very precisely. "Indeed, God has said: You shall not eat of every tree of the garden . . ." it says and breaks off. Now the woman talks, but she too intensifies God's prohibition and adds to it words He did not use: ". . . touch it not, else you must die." As becomes manifest subsequently, the serpent is both right and wrong in denying that this will be the consequence: they do not have to die after eating, they merely plunge into *human* mortality, that is, into the knowledge of death to come—the serpent plays with the word of God, just as Eve played with it. And now the incident itself begins: the woman regards the tree. She does not merely see that it is a delight to the eye, she also sees in it that which cannot be seen: how good its fruit tastes and that it bestows the gift of understanding. This seeing has been explained as a metaphorical expression for perceiving, but how could these qualities of the tree be perceived? It must be a contemplation that is meant, but it is a strange, dreamlike kind of contemplation. And so, sunk in contemplation, the woman plucks, eats, and hands to the man, and now he eats also, whose presence has till then been revealed to us by neither word nor gesture—she seems moved by dream-longing, but it seems to be truly in dream-lassitude that he takes and eats. The whole incident is spun out of play and dream; it is irony, a mysterious irony of the narrator, that spins it. It is apparent: the two doers know not what they do; more than this, they can only do it, they cannot know it. There is no room here for the pathos of the two principles, as we see it in the ancient Iranian religion, the pathos of the choice made by the Two themselves and by the whole of mankind after them.

And nevertheless both of them, good and evil, are to be found here—but in a strange, ironical shape, which the commentators have not understood as such and hence have not understood at all.

The tree of whose forbidden fruit the first humans eat

is called the tree of the knowledge of good and evil; so does God Himself also call it. The serpent promises that by partaking of it, they would become like God, knowers of good and evil; and God seems to confirm this when He says subsequently that they have thereby become "as one of us," to know good and evil. This is the repetitive style of the Bible; the antitheses constantly reappear in fresh relationships with one another: its purpose is to demonstrate with superclarity that it is they we are dealing with. But nowhere is their meaning intimated. The words may denote the ethical antithesis, but they may also denote that of beneficial and injurious, or of delightful and repulsive; immediately after the serpent's speech the woman "sees" that the tree is "good to eat," and immediately upon God's prohibition followed His dictum that it was "not good" that man should be alone—the adjective translated by "evil" is equally indefinite.

In the main, throughout the ages, three interpretations have repeatedly emerged in explanation of what the first humans acquired by partaking of the fruit. One, which refers to the acquisition of sexual desire, is precluded both by the fact of the creation of man and woman as sexually mature beings and by the concept of "becoming like God," which is coupled with the "knowledge of good and evil": this God is suprasexual. The other interpretation, relating to the acquisition of moral consciousness, is no less contrary to the nature of this God: we have only to think of the declaration in His mouth that man, now that he has acquired moral consciousness, must not be allowed to attain aeonian life as well! According to the third interpretation, the meaning of this "knowledge of good and evil" is nothing else than: cognition in general, cognizance of the world, knowledge of all the good and bad things there are, for this would be in line with biblical usage, in which the antithesis good and evil is often used to denote "anything," "all kinds of things." But this interpretation, the favorite one today, is also unfounded. There is no place in the Scriptures where the antithesis meant simply "anything" or "all kinds of things"; if all those passages that are taken as having this significance are examined in relation to the concrete nature of the current situation and the current in-

tention of the speaker, they are always found to refer in actual fact to an affirmation or a negation of both good
and bad, of both favorable and unfavorable. The "be
it . . . be it . . . ," which is always found in this context,
does not relate to the whole scale of that which is, inclusive
of everything neutral, but precisely to the opposites and to
discrimination between them, even though knowing them is
bound up with knowing "everything in the world." Thus it is
stated, for instance, as of the angel as the heavenly, so of the
king as the earthly representative of God, that he knows all
things (II Sam. 14:20); but where it is said of him that he
discerns the good and the evil (14:17), this refers specifically
to the knowledge of the right and the wrong, the guilty and
the innocent, which the earthly judge, like the heavenly who
rules over the nations (cf. Pss. 82:2 and 58:2), receives from
his divine commissioner, so that he may give it practical realization. But added to this is the fact that the word sequence
"good and evil" (without an article)—which, apart from our
tale, only occurs on one other occasion, in a subsequent passage that is dependent upon this one (Deut. 1:39)—is given
an emphasis in the story of Paradise, by repetition and other
stylistic means, that does not permit us to suppose it a rhetorical flourish. Neither is it the case that "cognition in general" only came to the first humans when they partook of the
fruit: it is not before a creature without knowledge that, even
before the creation of the woman, God brings the beasts that
he may give them their appointed names, but before the
bearer of His own breath, the being upon whom, at the very
hour of creation, He had manifestly bestowed the abundance
of knowledge contained in speech, of which that being is now
the master.

"Knowledge of good and evil" means nothing else than:
cognizance of the opposites that the early literature of mankind designated by these two terms; they still include the for-
tune and the misfortune or the order and the disorder that
are experienced by a person, as well as that which he causes.
This is still the same in the early Avestic texts, and it is the
same in those of the Bible which precede written prophecy
and to which ours belongs. In the terminology of modern

thought, we can transcribe what is meant as: adequate awareness of the opposites inherent in all being within the world. And that, from the viewpoint of the biblical creation-belief, means: adequate awareness of the opposites latent in creation.

We can only reach complete understanding if we remain fully aware that the basic conception of all the theo- and anthropology of the Hebrews, namely the immutable difference and distance that exist between God and man, irrespective of the primal fact of the latter's "likeness" to God and of the current fact of his "nearness" to Him (Ps. 73:28), also applies to the knowledge of good and evil. This knowledge as the primordial possession of God and the same knowledge as the magical attainment of man are worlds apart in their nature. God knows the opposites of being, which stem from His own act of creation; He encompasses them, untouched by them; He is as absolutely familiar with them as He is absolutely superior to them; He has direct intercourse with them (this is obviously the original meaning of the Hebrew verb "know": be in direct contact with), and this in their function as the opposite poles of the world's being. For as such He created them—we may impute this late biblical doctrine (Isa. 45:7) to our narrator, in its elementary form. Thus He who is above all opposites has intercourse with the opposites of good and evil that are of His own making; and something of His primordial familiarity with them He appears, as can be gathered from the words "one of us" (Gen. 3:22), to have bestowed upon the "sons of God" (6:2) by virtue of their share in the work of creation. The "knowledge" acquired by man through eating the miraculous fruit is of an essentially different kind. A superior-familiar encompassing of opposites is denied to him who, despite his "likeness" to God, has a part only in that which is created and not in creation, is capable only of begetting and giving birth, not of creating. Good and evil, the yes-position and the no-position of existence, enter into his living cognizance; but in him they can never be temporally coexistent. He knows oppositeness only by his situation within it; and that means *de facto* (since the yes can present itself to the experience and perception of man in the no-position, but not the no in the yes-position): he knows it directly from within that "evil" at times when he happens to be situated there. More exactly: he knows it when he recognizes a condition in which he finds himself whenever he has transgressed the command of God, as the "evil" and the one he has thereby lost and which, for the time being, is inaccessible to him, as the good. But at this point, the process in the human soul becomes a process in the world: through the recognition of oppositeness, the opposites which are always latently present in creation break out into actual reality; they become existent.

In just this manner the first humans, as soon as they have eaten of the fruit, "know" that they are naked. "And the eyes of both of them were opened": they see themselves as they are, but now, since they see themselves so, not merely without clothing, but "naked." Recognition of this fact, the only recorded consequence of the magical partaking, cannot be adequately explained on the basis of sexuality, although without the latter it is, of course, inconceivable. Admittedly, they had not been ashamed before one another and now they are ashamed, not merely before one another, but with one another before God (3:10), because, overcome by the knowledge of oppositeness, they feel the natural state of unclothedness in which they find themselves to be an ill or an evil, or rather both at once and more besides, and by this very feeling they make it so; but as a countermeasure they conceive, will, and establish the "good" of clothing. One is ashamed of being as one is because one now "recognizes" this so-being in its oppositional nature as an intended shall-be; but now it has really become a matter for shame. In themselves, naturally, neither the concept of clothed- and unclothedness, nor that of man and woman before one another, has anything whatsoever to do with good and evil; human "recognition" of opposites alone brings with it the fact of their relatedness to good and evil. In this lamentable effect of the great magic of the becoming like God the narrator's irony becomes apparent; an irony whose source was obviously great suffering through the nature of man.

But does not God Himself confirm that the serpent's promise has been fulfilled? He does; but this most extreme expression, this pronouncement, "Man is become as one of us, to know good and evil," is also still steeped in the ironic dialectic of the whole, which, it here shows most clearly, does not emanate from an intention freely formed by the narrator, but is imposed upon him by the theme—which corresponds exactly to his suffering through the nature of man—at this stage of its development. Because man is now numbered among those who know good and evil, God wishes to prevent him from also eating of the tree of life and "living forever." The narrator may have taken the motif from the ancient myth of the envy and vengeance of gods: if so, it acquired through him a meaning fundamentally different from its original one. Here there can no longer be any expression of fear that man might now become a match for the celestial beings: we have just seen how earthly is the nature of man's knowledge of "good and evil." The "like one of us" can be uttered here only in the ironic dialectic. But now it is the irony of a "divine compassion." [1] God, who breathed His breath into the construction of dust, placed him in the garden of the four rivers and gave him a helpmate, wanted him to accept His continued guidance; He wanted to protect him from the opposites latent in existence. But man—caught up in demonry, which the narrator symbolizes for us with his web of play and dream—withdrew at once from both the will of God and from His protection and, though without properly understanding what he was doing, nevertheless with this deed, unrealized by his understanding, caused the latent opposites to break out at the most dangerous point, that of the world's closest proximity to God. From that moment on, oppositeness takes hold of him, not indeed as a must-sin—of that, and hence of original sin, there is no question here— but as the ever-recrudescent reaction to the no-position and its irredeemable perspective; he will ever anew find himself naked and look around for fig leaves with which to plait himself a girdle. This situation would inevitably develop into full demonry, if no end were set to it. Lest the thoughtless creature, again without knowing what he is doing, long for the fruit of the other tree and eat himself into aeons of suffering, God prevents his return to the garden from which He expelled him in punishment. For man as a "living soul" (Gen. 2:7), known death is the threatening boundary; for him as the being driven round amid opposites, it may become a haven, the knowledge of which brings comfort.

This stern benefaction is preceded by the passing of sentence. It announces no radical alteration of that which already exists; it is only that all things are drawn into the atmosphere of oppositeness. When she gives birth, for which she was prepared at the time of her creation, woman shall suffer pains such as no other creature suffers—henceforth a price must be paid for being human; and the desire to become once more one body with the man (cf. Gen. 2:24) shall render her dependent upon him. To the man work, which was already planned for him before he was set in the garden, shall become an affliction. But the curse conceals a blessing. From the *seat,* which had been made ready for him, man is sent out upon a *path,* his own, the human path. That this is the path into the world's history, that only through it does the world have a history—and a historical goal—must, in his own way, have been felt by the narrator.

ABRAHAM THE SEER

(GENESIS 12–25)

HERE I shall speak not of what is behind the biblical story of Abraham, but of what is in it.

The nineteenth century was convinced that there must be something quite different behind it; perhaps the myth of a god told as the story of a man, or the history of a tribe personified in an individual destiny. Since then people have begun to feel how absurd it was to think that this story about the life of a man with human weaknesses and needs, with the relationship of that man to an unconditionally superior God as its basic theme, could have originated in a myth about the exploits of a god. And they began to feel, further, how absurd it was to think that this story about the life of a wandering shepherd, clearly meant for the origins of a tribe, could have been an embroidered report of tribal conquests. The nineteenth century was sure, in any case, that the story of Abraham could not be based on one thing, that is, a family tradition about a tribal patriarch. It was believed that no people preserved such stories. But we know today that among the Arabic tribes in Moab, for instance, each one not only derives its origins from a tribal father, but has also preserved a traditional account of him; a legendary one, to be sure, but not necessarily imaginary for all that. And the Jewish people happens to be, it seems, the one example of a people that, in becoming a nation, did not give up or forget its tribal character, but remained tribal at the core, and retained the tribal memory along with the tribal character. The nineteenth cen-

tury was convinced that the account of the Fathers had originated in much later times, because there were no literary
documents of the earlier times in Palestine; and it did not
consider that with some oriental peoples word-of-mouth tradition maintains itself for hundreds of years. Furthermore,
paleographers investigating the mythological texts discovered
in the North-Syrian Ugarit are inducing from various circumstances that the nucleus of the patriarchal histories must
have been written down much earlier than had hitherto been
assumed. In brief, the nineteenth century excluded the possibility that the man Abram or Abraham could have been a
real historical person.

But when we look into what is being written today by
scholars, whether they be archeologists, philologists, or his-
torians, we find that what they have in common is precisely
the opinion that, as the archeologist Leonard Woolley, the
discoverer of the culture of Ur, puts it in his book about
Abraham, the story as originally told contains a considerable
substratum of literal truth; or, as the Dutch linguist and historian Franz Böhl formulates it more cautiously, "the assumption of a historic basis appears to be the scientifically
better grounded hypothesis." Some see Abraham as a sheik
in the early primitive times of a half-nomadic tribe, while
others see him as the founder of a cult and the leader of a
religious community; a duality of conception where the Jewish traditional double image of "the father of the nation" and
"the father of the world" reappears in scientific guise. But
everyone sees again what the former century had failed to
see, a living person.

At this point in the investigation, and from the perspective of this modern realism, the question must be put anew:
in what way does biblical history itself, in its blending of
both of these conceptions into a perfect unity, really understand this person, and how does it wish him to be understood? We are not given a historical reality, to be sure, but
a document of its reflection. What might be behind the biblical story, science, lacking other evidence, will only be able
to surmise. But what is contained in it is something we are
permitted to deduce from the text itself.

One might object that no unified conception can be gained from the biblical story since it is known to have been put together from numerous fragments of various books, the so-called "sources" coming out of different periods and determined by different tendencies. But even this theory, so dear to the eighteenth and nineteenth centuries, has been badly shaken. It appears that a book like the Book of Genesis could not have been put together like a cheap newspaper, with the help of scissors and paste. Many expressions and turns of phrase formerly thought to be characteristic of one or another "source" increasingly reveal their meaning and their intent within a well-ordered whole. Such a rounded unity is not necessarily the finished work of a single early author. My ear, too, distinguishes a variety of voices in the chorus. Even the most ancient memories are likely to have been preserved from a variety of motives and will accordingly have been rendered in a variety of tones. Later chroniclers and scribes are even more likely to differ from one another in their treatment of the material and their style of representation: prophets differ naturally from court officials in their way of telling a story, as their motives differ, while a prophet with an official position at court will develop a different manner from that of an independent prophet, and a priest, insofar as priests took part in telling this story, is something else again.

And yet this story has an amazingly homogeneous character, although the homogeneity did not exist from the beginning, but developed in time. For all the chroniclers, i.e., all the custodians of the tradition, regardless of any particular tendencies or peculiarities of each individual, inhabit a common spiritual atmosphere which I would like to designate as the proto-biblical, that is, the biblical atmosphere that existed before the Bible. All who contributed something to the history of beginnings—the beginning of the world, of the human race, of Israel—were ultimately concerned, each in his own way, with one thing: to show the people how their God prepared the goal and the road for them, even before they were yet a people. The court officials may have intended this as an encouragement to the people to persist in their

wars, as warriors of their God; the prophets, to call them to
an inward return to their God and to His commandment of
the righteous life. What was decisive was what they had in
common: each desired to have a share in this common good,
this growing Bible, each knowing of it as much as had already taken shape, and taking it openly or covertly as his
point of departure. And lastly, there came the men usually
referred to as the compilers, probably out of the circle of the
chroniclers themselves, and I believe that for the Book of
Genesis they came no later than the final period of the kingdom of Solomon. They are great men, inspired by the proto-
biblical unity of vision, and they—or that one man—go to
work to express this unity in the multiplicity of the traditional
stories. And now story is entwined with story, insofar as this
had not yet been done, not infrequently by means of words
rare in their context but recurring in the different narratives,
and all fitted together in an almost symmetrically articulated
architectonic structure, as is the story of Abraham. Only the
realization of this tectonic unity, the achievement of an im-
age-making religious composing on a large scale, enables us
to see in what way the Bible wants Abraham to be understood. In order to arrive at this realization, we must first ask,
what is the position of the story of Abraham in the structure
of the history of beginnings, and secondly, what is the structure of the story itself. Here, we will find matter of primary
importance which cannot be derived from the treatment and
formulation of the traditional accounts, but only from the
tradition itself. The Bible tells us its conception of Abraham;
but at the core of this conception, there is something remembered.

The Book of Genesis intends to relate *toledot,* generations. It is concerned with deriving the *toledot* of the nation
Israel from the *toledot* of the human race; and these, from
the generations of the heavens and the earth. The cosmogony, the origin of the world, is related for the sake of the
ethnogony, the origin of the people. We are to trace the
meaning of the people's origin back to the meaning of the origin of the world, and back to the intention of the Creator for

His creation. To be sure, the Bible does not present us with theological statements about this intention and this meaning; it presents us with a story only, but this story is theology; biblical theology is narrated theology. The Bible cannot be really comprehended if it is not comprehended in this way: as a doctrine that is nothing but history, and as a history that is nothing but doctrine. The history of the world comes to us as the history of Israel; and in this, and only in this and not outside of it, do we receive the teaching as to the purpose of the world and the purpose of Israel, both in one.

The Book of Genesis begins with two accounts of the creation which, no matter when and how the one or the other originated, complement one another perfectly, like nature and mind, and like man's sense of living at the fringe of the cosmos as a latecomer, and man's sense of being at home in the center of his world, as one of its first-born. The first account of the creation ends with a double blessing: a blessing upon the first human beings and a blessing upon the Sabbath. The second account ends with a double curse: a curse upon the first human beings, and a curse upon the ground. Between the two stands sin. The blessing inaugurates natural man, the curse inaugurates historical man, and both together inaugurate the double nature and the double destiny of man.

The first race of mankind, thus launched into the world and into the world's history, fails. But not because of the sin against God. The sin against God led only to the expulsion from Paradise. It is the sin of men against each other, the way of strife, beginning with fratricide and ending by filling the earth with "violence"; it is the wickedness of men "corrupting" the earth itself that leads to the Deluge. Once more the waters rise above the earth, as in the beginning. Preserved from those waters, the second generation of men is set upon the earth. It receives the same blessing as the first, the blessing of natural fecundity, of the *toledot,* of historical growth by way of nature. But now the blessing, in contradistinction to the first, is made contingent upon the commandment to do no acts of violence. Man is told directly what he formerly knew only as a story: that he was created in the image of God, and that he injures this image by his acts of violence.

And now the second race of men also fails; this time, by sinning against God. The strangest thing about this sin is that it is the outcome of an intention the precise opposite of that which had constituted the first sin. The first race of men instead of clinging together had divided man from man, beginning with the murder of brother by brother. The second race of men wants to join together—in the wrong way. The first had missed its aim to become an undivided humanity by an act of violence; the second wants to remain together in its city to avoid dispersal, to work together, to be united in a common humanity—by rising up against God. The shared work centers in the tower, its spire pointing to heaven, against heaven. That this is their intention becomes clear through the "Come let us . . . !" with which the heavens reply to their war cry of "Come let us . . . !" (Gen. 11:4 and 7). The punishment speaks the language of the sin. Adam and Eve had atoned for their sin against the tree of knowledge by being barred from access to the tree of life. Their progeny was punished for having destroyed one another by being destroyed, and since they had "corrupted the earth" the flood came to "corrupt the earth." The second race of men suffers precisely the fate it had sought to prevent without having been actually threatened by it: the fate of dispersal. There is no further destruction, for the earth had been promised immunity from destruction in God's covenant with "all living things."

But now, as punishment for the perverse kind of unity, comes the dispersal. In answer to their "lest we be scattered" comes the reiterated "scattered them" which reports God's action. The passage, built up to that magnificent juxtaposition of the above and the below, beginning with "all the earth," ends with the refrain, repeated three times to drum its meaning into the awareness of hearer and reader: "upon the face of all the earth." The preceding chapter, the Table of Nations, had already announced four times what would happen, using three verbs: first, that "they were divided," then "they were spread abroad," then "were sundered" and then again "were divided." The humanity which was none because it sought union *against* God is "scattered" into nations; the one earth is broken up into countries, and the one language ("lip") into languages ("tongues"). The most explicit symbol of the new situation is that now no one understands the other. And in the midst of the transformed human world, the world of nations, there stands the unfinished, unfinishable city, Babel, city of "confusion." Such is the state of the humanity into which Abram is born, in which he and his kindred wander toward Canaan, and in which he now receives the call of God. We can understand the meaning of that call only out of the meaning of that state, the meaning of Abraham's blessing only out of the outcome of the first and second blessing; that third blessing which follows upon the call, and sounds so different from the first two, which read almost alike.

The basic assumption is this: after men had in two successive ages thwarted, time and again, the Lord's intention that they grow into one human community of their own free will and free obedience, a third beginning is to be made. But this third beginning cannot, like the two previous ones, mean placing the responsibility on a single tribe out of which the human community is to arise or renew itself, for there is to be no more annihilation that would extirpate all the guilty and unusable ones. Moreover, there no longer exists a single homogeneous human community, but a multiplicity of peoples. The new effort can begin only with this as a starting point. The aim can no longer be an undivided humanity, but only one that will overcome its division and achieve a unity beyond peoples, a joining of the peoples into a new human community, a people of many peoples. But how is this aim to be reached? In order that the multiplicity of people may become the one people of peoples, they must first be shown what a real people, a unity made up of the various many, is like. This cannot be shown by the world, but only by life itself—the life of a true people made up of many peoples. But none among the existing products of disintegrations is fit to serve as a model. A new people must arise, one that will come not only out of the natural begetting of generations but will be helped into being by the revelation, the promise, and the commandment from above. Its beginning must include its goal, so that it may fulfill its mission with regard to the ultimate goal of mankind. And this is what happens.

The man Abram is singled out, and sent out. He is brought forth from out of the world of peoples and must go his own way, which means an ever-new separation for him and his progeny. As he goes out of his father's house, he is still accompanied by relatives; the fact that he takes leave of them actually means that they wish not to separate themselves from the other peoples, but to fuse with them. In the next generation, division occurs among his own kin, and so again in the next; and above each stands the word of God. Then at last there is a generation in which no further division need occur. But this very generation is cast into a new "iron furnace" (Deut. 4:20; I Kings 8:51) out of which it must be led, "a people from out of the midst of another people" (Deut. 4:34). As the tribal father came out of one of the two river empires between which Israel's national history was to play itself out, so this people has come out of the second empire, in order, first of all, to become that which alone will enable it to fulfill the prophecy: "Lo, the people shall dwell alone and shall not be reckoned among the nations" (Num. 23:9). This entire history of the road from Ur of the Chaldees to Sinai is a consequence of choices and partings, events of history—tribal history and national history. But above them stands revelation and gives them their meaning, points out to them their goal. For the end of all these partings is a future community of all men.

The prophets have something to report about this goal. But even the story of the beginning of the way, of the singling-out of Abraham, has a strange affinity to the crucial experience of the prophetic man as such, his own experience of being taken out of his natural environment. When Abraham says to Abimelech, "When God caused me to wander away from my father's house," we think of Amos answering the priest: "YHVH took me as I followed the flock." Yet Abraham's speech sounds so much *earlier!* Indeed, it is strange that in the same passage, and only in this passage, Abraham is called a *nabi,* i.e., a vocal mediator between heaven and earth. An early prophet, belonging possibly to the springtime of the kingdom of Greater Israel, may be responsible for this figure of the story. But we would be thoroughly mistaken if we believed him to be merely projecting his being and his experience into the earliest times. Regardless of when the *concept* of the prophet arose, the *existence* of prophets is as old as Israel itself. This sort of thing does not appear suddenly in the midst of a community's history, but is in its original, spontaneous form as old as that history itself. And without the archaic experience of the being-singled-out, being taken out—that is, without the certainty of a man of primitive times that what he is doing springs not of his own will but from the will of God—the faith of Israel would not exist.

I have pointed out that the story of Abraham is to be understood only in relation to its place in biblical history, between the story of the failure of the first human race and the story of the growth of the people Israel under the shadow of the call and the promise. This place, in this connection, determines the choice of subject and the interpretation of the subject, the composition and the style, the imagery and the choice of words. Scripture does not state its doctrine as doctrine but by telling a story, and without exceeding the limits set by the nature of a story. It uses the methods of story-telling to a degree, however, that world literature has not yet learned to use; and its cross references and interconnections, while noticeable, are so unobtrusive that a perfect attention is needed to grasp its intent—an attentiveness so perfect that it has not yet been fully achieved. Hence, it remains for us latecomers to point out the significance of what has hitherto been overlooked, neglected, insufficiently valued.

The place held by the story of Abraham within the sequence of the biblical history requires this story to fulfill a threefold task. It must first of all make visible its relation to its own past, to show how Abraham appears as a new beginning for the people as such, in relation to the old, fallen, nationless humanity. It must, secondly, measure out the road and let us, the readers, follow the road taken by the divine call and the promise, throughout the life of Abraham from

Haran to Mount Moriah; and it must, in passing, luminously
forecast the road to be followed till they shall become people
and shall receive the second call and promise directed to that
new people: the road from Beersheba through Egypt to
Mount Sinai. Thirdly, it must present, through the imagery of
the events in Abraham's life, "symbolically," the history of
the nation Israel. For as his personal mission foreshadows
the national mission of Israel, so his biography is the pattern
for the history of the people and must be presented as a living
prophecy, as it were. The first of these tasks Scripture fulfills
by making reference, in content and language, to the story of
Noah, the father of the second race of men. The second task
is met by the architecturally composed account of the seven
revelations to Abraham. The third is accomplished by the
way in which the story of the events of Abraham's life, apart
from the revelation, gives intimations of the existence and
history of a people.

I shall begin with the retrospective part.

Scripture does not need to juxtapose Abraham with the
first human race which perished in the Deluge, but only with
the second, in the midst of which he lives. Abraham must be
related only to this second beginning because it alone, like
the third, is based upon election. The juxtaposition is accomplished by comparing Abraham with that other chosen man,
Noah. Abraham, the second chosen man of God, is compared
with the first; his character is viewed against the character of
Noah, and the revelation made to him against that made to
the former. But this comparison is not given as such, not
didactically; it uses the means offered by the vocabulary itself, those images and other expressive resources of the language requiring only our attention. It addresses itself not to
our discursive understanding, but to our contemplation.

Noah is the first person in Scripture to whom epithets
are attached. He is said to have been "righteous" (*zaddik*)
and "whole" (*tamim*) in "his generations," i.e., in the generations encompassed by his life span. Both concepts are
concepts of agreement: the first, of agreement between
"within" and "without," between a "truth" and a "reality,"
between the rightness of a cause and its recognition, between

conviction and behavior. The second indicates a harmony
among the parts and qualities of a man, a unity of being, and
a perfection of being. The archetype of the first concept is
the verdict that declares a man's innocence in court, establishing agreement between the true facts of the case and their
outward significance. The type of the second concept is the
hale, unblemished sacrificial animal, the creature that "is
whole." Scripture itself clarifies the first concept by the parallel "which keeps faithfulness" (Isa. 26:2), the second by
the commandment to "be whole with your God" (Deut. 18:
13). Both of these epithets are applied to Noah in a simple
declarative statement; but to these is joined a third, the information that "Noah walked with God." We already know
this expression (Gen. 5:22, 24) from Enoch, Noah's fore-
bear, who until his end "walked with God" but then, instead
of dying like his fathers and his progeny, mysteriously vanished, "for God took him." The expression, occurring only
in relation to these two men, is not a metaphor for a pious
way of life pleasing to God. In those early stories especially,
images from the religious sphere do not generally signify
moral concepts. God's participation in the destinies of the
human world is seen in the image of a movement, from the
walking of God or the voice of God in the Garden of Eden
(Gen. 3:8) to the walking of God in the midst of the camp
of Israel (Deut. 23:15). The community of men with God
in that nationless, primitive time, men who had no function
extending beyond their own life, is seen in the image of their
accompanying God in this movement.

The three words "righteousness," "wholeness," and
"walking with God" turn up again in the story of Abraham,
and just as Noah is characterized only by those three, no
others are joined to them in the description of Abraham. But
here they reappear in a strangely altered way. They are not
used here, as in the previous instance, to characterize the
man in a single statement. We find the first word in the middle of the seven revelations, the one that serves as crux.
Here Abraham's belief in the Lord is counted to him "for
righteousness"; i.e., it is not said of Abraham, as it was of
Noah, that he was a righteous man; only a single character-

istic or attitude of his makes him appear righteous in the
eyes of God (Gen. 15:6).

The second word in association with the third stands
here, again not in the form of a statement, but in that of a
command. God seems to command Abraham to become
that which Noah was by nature! This does appear to reverse
the order of rank of the two men. This riddle has been
searched before, and the Jewish tradition was on the right
track when it found the solution to it in the words "in his
generations." Noah, accordingly, was righteous and whole
not in the absolute sense but only in relation to the corrupt
or questionable generations of his time. That Scripture, at
this point, really attempts to explain itself is made apparent
in that the statement made in the story (6:9) about Noah is
varied at the decisive point in the Lord's addresses to Noah
(7:1): "for thee have I seen righteous before me in this
generation." Such repetitions in Scripture often are a signal
to take note, and to begin to understand. But the insight into
the right interpretation must be deepened further still. For
Noah is truly one who is bound up with his "generations"—
despite the fact that as a "husbandman" (9:20) he renews
agriculture and frees the soil from the curse. He has received
no call that goes beyond his "generations" and no *historical*
task. Even the prohibition against shedding blood which is
addressed to him is meant for all; of him nothing is demanded that he, and he alone, must accomplish for future
generations; nor does he, like Abraham, prefigure with his
life the life of the people destined to become the model community for the nations of mankind.

With Abraham what matters is not his character as God
finds it, so to speak, but what he does, and what he becomes.
His faith, which the Lord counts to him for righteousness, the
fact that he trusts in God *before* God has fulfilled the promise,
is thus significantly contrasted with the very different "faith"
of the people who trust in God only after Moses has given
them signs (Exod. 4:31), and then again after they have
been led through the Sea of Reeds and the Egyptians have
been drowned in it (14:31). That the people falls short of
Abraham in that respect in which Abraham had pointed

the way makes us feel in a quiet, but unsurpassably forceful way the failure of the people before its task. Significant, too, is that second self-elucidation of Scripture. The commandment to Abraham: "Be thou whole," at the beginning of the passage where he is offered the sign of the covenant to distinguish Israel from other peoples, recurs as a commandment to the people: "Thou shalt be whole with the Lord my God" (Deut. 19:13). The latter passage contrasts the dignity of the prophet with the "abominations" of magic practices among the peoples of paganism. These two times only does this adjective occur in Scripture in a personal commandment, and so the second occurrence of it seems to be referable to the first. It may be surmised that in such cases the compilers purposely avoided retaining other instances of this usage, so as not to obliterate the impression of mutual reference between these two passages.

A stronger mutation is undergone by the third of the three characteristic words in the story of Abraham. "And Noah walked with God," was the way it was put there. But now we hear the commandment to Abraham: "Walk before me!" How important this is we discern in that Abraham expresses his achievement of his mission, having gone through his ordeal and proved himself, in just this way (Gen. 24: 40): that he walked before God. Jacob, speaking of his forefathers, puts it the same way (48:15). But even this image is not to be understood as a metaphor for "being devoted to God," but in a more concrete and precise sense. If "walking with God" means accompanying Him, then "walking before Him" has another sense. When a leader says to the led, as Samuel says to Israel (I Sam. 12:2), that he had walked before them, and now the king whom he anointed was walking before them, then we see an army on the march and a general at its head. But when the relationship is reversed, as when God says to Eli (I Sam. 2:30, 35) that whereas the men of the House of Eli had hitherto walked before Him, but since they have fallen away from Him, He would now appoint a faithful priest who would walk before the anointed of God, then we see an image of the ruler at peace sending a herald ahead to announce his coming and prepare the way for a visit in person to a city in his realm. Precisely this is Abraham's office.

But we must understand even more accurately the true nature of his task. We are told that, traveling throughout the land, he builds altars at Shechem and at Bethel and proclaims there the name of the Lord: and that later on he goes to Beersheba and calls out the name of the Lord. This is not to be understood as a prayer, and certainly not as a sermon to the heathen; there is no evidence for the latter interpretation, but even the first is not the original meaning, as indicated by the fact that in Scripture, God proclaims His own name in the same way (Exod. 33:19; 34:5). As we know it, from the time of the establishment of the kingdom, from Abraham to Gideon, often in connection with the building of an altar and sometimes as the calling out of a *new* name (Gen. 21:23; 33:20; Exod. 17:15; Judg. 6:24), it means just that: *a proclamation.* He who conquers a city has his name proclaimed over it, as we know from a statement of Joab's (II Sam. 12:28). A somewhat difficult passage in Psalms (49:12) is to be explained by the fact that the names of the owners are proclaimed over their estates. We are told about the Lord that His name is proclaimed over the place and the community where He dwells as Lord: over the Ark (II Sam. 6:2); over the Temple (I Kings 8:43); over Jerusalem (Jer. 25:29); over all Israel (Deut. 28:10). As the herald of the Lord, Abraham goes before Him, the King of the future Israel, making his way throughout the province of the Lord which He will some day make His dwelling place, and proclaims it as God's property and residence by calling out His name.

Noah appears against the background of several generations of a nationless humanity; Abraham before the backdrop of all the generations of a people that has been commanded, as "God's Chosen People," to bring all the nations to the mountain of the Lord, that they might here join together in the community of mankind (Isa. 2:1–5). Noah stands in his place in nature, as one who has been saved from the Deluge, a "husbandman"; Abraham is the first to make his way into history, a proclaimer of God's dominion.

The seven revelations to Abraham are precisely and significantly related both to one another and to the stories with which they are interspersed. Each one of the revelations and each one of the other stories has its particular place in the pattern, and could not stand in any other. The revelations appear as stations in a progress from trial to trial and from blessing to blessing; not one of them can be transposed without disrupting the whole. No theory of sources can explain this structure, which is so manifold in character and style and yet held together by a uniformly great vision. If, for example, one attributes the two so radically different accounts of the making of the covenant, Gen. 15 and 17, to separate scriptural sources, this hardly serves, any more than the two accounts of the creation, to clarify how the two came to complement each other so perfectly. For each contains the essential motifs lacking in the other, and the second, quite active one, which contains the change of name and the conferring of the sign of the covenant, can appear nowhere else but after the first, purely visionary one, with its vision of the stars and vision of history, and the appearance of fire among the pieces of the sacrifice. Only these two together provide the perfect counterpart to the covenant with Noah: in both, beast and bird are offered in sacrifice, but in the one case it is a covenant with all living things, in the other, with a future people; in both, the preservation of life in the future is promised, but the first is a promise of general preservation, with the most public of signs, the rainbow, while in the second it is national preservation, with the most intimate of symbols, circumcision; in the first, the whole earth is meant, in the second, the begetting of Israel.

This is no mere compilation, but a composition of the greatest kind. And this kind of thing cannot be done with excerpts from various sources but only with the entire, rich, and plastic material of the narrative tradition. And this is true also of the interrelationship among the individual revelations and the interspersed stories. Abraham's intercession on behalf of Sodom in the sixth revelation, for example, and the story of his sojourn with Abimelech are attributed to two different sources. But it is precisely this intercession that motivates God's saying about Abraham: "he is a prophet, and he shall pray for thee" (Gen. 20:7). By this daring intercession, Abraham has risen in God's view to the stature of the prophet who mediates between the upper and the lower world as well as between the lower and the upper. God has, as it were, recognized that "indeed, the man has become a prophet," and now He states it. This is not an interpretation after the fact; it is the primary content of the self-elucidation in the biblical composition. The great prophetic compositor is saying that it is by virtue of a man's compassion, and his fearless intercession in the face of God for the object of his compassion, that prophecy came to be. And he says it by choosing the appropriate subject matter out of the traditional material about the patriarch, and by ordering it in the necessary way. But what enabled him to do this? The fact that the tradition itself offered the material in such a way that it was possible to bring out this meaning by means of selection and arrangement.

The seven revelations are seven stations on the way of a man from the beginning of the mutual relation between this man and God until its completion.

In the first revelation (12:1–3), God sends this man out of his house into the land He will "let him see"; so sending him on his mission, He promises to make a people of him and blesses him on his way.

The second (12:7) comes in the new land to which Abraham has already come in his wanderings. While promising him the land He is showing him now for the first time ("this land"), God also "lets him see" Himself. Abraham is the first man in Scripture to see God. This, too, is clarified by Scripture itself, where the prayer of Moses to God to let him see the Lord in His glory is granted by God's proclaiming before Moses those divine attributes that are directly concerned with the behavior of men.

The third revelation (12:14) comes after Abraham has separated from Lot, so that henceforth no alien tendency in the relationship of other nations to his own might disturb Abraham. Again "seeing" is mentioned, and now it is a matter of seeing the entire land, as now for the first time

Abraham is promised "the entire land" throughout which he
will have to wander in order to take possession of it for his
people. This is how Joshua phrases the words of God, in just
that sense, when he speaks before the assembly of the tribes
at Shechem, Abraham's first dwelling place in Canaan: "I
led him throughout all the land of Canaan" (Josh. 24:3).
And in the third revelation it is entirely a matter of land, of
"earth," that even "the dust of the earth" necessarily becomes a metaphor for the increase of population; it is only
in connection with this land that the people will be able to
fulfill their task.

The fourth revelation (15:1), the central one, is coupled with the preceding story of Abram's campaign against
the kings by a pun, by the homophony of the word *miggen*
(delivered up) in the final part of the story (Gen. 14:20)
with the word *magen* (shield) in the beginning of the revelation (15:1)—two words that appear only this once in the
Book of Genesis, and the first of which appears only three
times in Scripture. The purpose of this coupling comes to
light when one considers that the simile in the third revelation is based on the seeing of the land, just as the simile in
the fourth revelation is based on the seeing of the heavens.
In the narrative between these two, God is designated, in
the speech of Melchizedek and in the reply of Abram, as the
"originator of heaven and earth."

In this central revelation of the seven, the "seeing"
which recurs in the three first revelations is raised to prophetic "sight," just as the entire passage is kept in the style of
prophetic vision. Now for the first time the promise of an
heir is given outright to the aged Abraham, and now for the
first time the covenant is announced symbolically by the
passing of the flame among the pieces of the sacrificial animal. But between these two episodes, and only here within
the story of Abraham, do we get a foreshadowing of a certain
period of the national history—the Egyptian exile. And in
connection with this, the full meaning of the beginning of the
patriarch's way is revealed here for the first time. Haran was
not the first place out of which God's call brought Abram;
God took him out of Ur, without Abram's realizing it, to

bring him into the land. And this bringing forth is significant
as a harbinger of Israel's being brought forth out of the Egyptian exile. The word of God that it was He who had "led"
this man out of the world of nations points to the beginning
of the Decalogue, where God says to the people that it was
He who had "led" them out from among another people. In
the announcement of the exile, it was stated that the Egyptians—who are not named—would "afflict" Israel; in the
following passage it is related that the "Egyptian bondserv-
ant" is "afflicted" by Sarah. The word, which does not
otherwise appear in the narration, occurs three times in
order to impress upon us the connection between the stories
of the fathers and the history of the people. The fleeing maid,
sent back home by the messenger of the Lord—she is the
first human being in Scripture sought out by such a messenger—calls upon God by a new name, a name that occurs only
here. Because she gazed "after Him"—at this point one inad-
vertently thinks of Moses who saw God's "back parts" when
God revealed His attributes (Exod. 33:23)—she calls Him
the God of Seeing. This word root occurs here four times.

It also leads us to the beginning of the next, the fifth,
revelation (17:1), where God allows Himself "to be seen"
for the second time by Abraham, now on the threshold of his
hundredth year. He gives him, at last, the command to go
before Him as His herald, and to be whole in so doing. And
now God names him anew, by casting a letter from His own
name into the midst of the original name of the man. Now
He makes the all-encompassing promise: that Abraham shall
become the father of many nations. This was understood
long ago[1] to refer not to Israel but to the future humanity of
many peoples that is to develop through Israel. But that
Israel is the way to this goal is affirmed by the sign of the
covenant, which sanctifies procreation and the growth of the
people through procreation.

And once more an act of "seeing" ("letting him see")
begins the story of the sixth revelation (18:1). The meeting
of God and man, coming more strongly to the fore as we go
on, is now presented to us in the most intimate image of all
biblical narration. Three men come to Abraham, he looks up

and sees that they are "standing by him" (18:2), he invites them into the house, they eat at his table while he "stands by them" (18:8), they speak to him, not saying "we" but "I," as though God alone were speaking. And so they promise Abraham the birth of his son in that year. The men—two of the three, it seems—go away. Abraham accompanies them. The Lord, who had remained behind, speaks to Himself, and then comes His conversation with Abraham. But between the soliloquy and the conversation, there is set up a relation that raises the meeting between God and man to the correspondence between God and man. In His soliloquy, God says that He knows Abraham will enjoin his sons to keep the way of the Lord; and this again is no metaphor. "The way of God" means the actual movement of God throughout the history of the world. Israel is expected, as the Torah and the prophets repeatedly insist, to follow the Lord's footsteps on this road. The nature of the road is characterized by God, in this passage, as doing "justice and righteousness" (18:19), and in the conversation, Abraham utters the boldest speech of man in all Scripture, more bold than anything said by Job in his dispute with God, greater than any, because it is the word of the intercessor who is moved by the purpose of his intercession to lose even the awe of God. He fearlessly risks his own person: "Shall not the Judge of all the earth do justice?" (18:25). Through the recurrence of this word combination—this too is found only in this one passage in the Book of Genesis—the correspondence between God and the just man, the community of the way, is brought to its strongest expression. Now the path to the status of prophet is accomplished; and now Abraham can be raised by God to the rank of a prophet.

But this does not as yet complete the way of revelation, the way of the ordeal and of the blessing, the way of the relation of this man to this God. The story of the birth of Isaac is followed first by the expulsion of Ishmael, sanctioned by God for the sake of Israel's mission. Just as the parting of Abraham from Lot is necessary, so is the parting from Ishmael necessary. Lot is destined to form marriage ties with Sodom; Ishmael's hand will be against all men. What is left

to be told is now the story of the founding of Beersheba, the
place of the seventh revelation (22:1), from which Abraham
will be sent on to Mount Moriah, there to undergo the greatest ordeal and to receive the highest blessing.

The *active* surrender of Abraham, which begins to be
evident after the fourth revelation, as if to actively atone for
that moment of doubt in the midst of trustfulness ("by what
shall I recognize?"), here reaches its apex. On the other
hand, God does not here allow Himself to be seen at the beginning as He did at the beginning of the two preceding revelations, and here for the first time He is called not YHVH but
Elohim: it is the *hidden* God who will reveal Himself only
then. At the same time, this is the second column of a great
architectonic structure. At its base are the same motives as
in the first column. Both in the first and the last of the revelations, God—the as yet unknown God in the first, and the
familiar one in the last—sends Abraham out with the same
command: "Get thee . . ." (22:2). This phrase occurs
only on these two occasions in the entire Bible. In the one
instance the demand, at the beginning of his trials, is that he
separate himself from the past, from the world of the Fathers;
in the second instance, at the end of his trials, that he separate himself, despite the promise given him by that same
God, from the future, from the world of the sons. Both times
God does not tell the man where He is sending him. Later,
while he is on the road, God will show him the land that is
his goal, will tell him the name of the mountain that is his
goal. Out of the life of memory, God sends man into uncertainty, out of the life of expectation, into uncertainty; except
that the man knows, in the first instance, that he is going into
fulfillment of the promise, and, in the second instance, that
he is going into what is, as far as he can see, the cancellation
of the promise and this, moreover, by his own act, the inhu-
man act he must accomplish at the Lord's bidding. But this
time, as before, Abraham answers this demand not by a
word, but by a deed. This time as before, it is written: "and
he went."

And now the theme-word "to see," which has accompanied us through all the stations of the way of God and man,

opens up for us in all its depth and meaningfulness. It appears here more often than in any previous passage. Abraham *sees* the place where the act must be accomplished, at a distance. To the question of his son, he replies that God will provide ("see to") the lamb for the burnt offering. In the saving moment he lifts up his eyes and *sees* the ram. And now he proclaims over the altar the name that makes known the imperishable essence of this place, Mount Moriah: YHVH Will See. The narrator is actually making reference to a common expression of his own day, "on the mountain where YHVH lets Himself be seen. . . ." God sees man, and man sees God. God sees Abraham, and tests him by seeing him as the righteous and "whole" man who walks before his God, and now, at the end of his road, he conquers even this final place, the holy temple mountain, by acting on God's behalf. Abraham sees God with the eye of his action and so recognizes Him, just as Moses, seeing God's glory "from behind," will recognize Him as Gracious and Merciful. Even the Egyptian bondwoman had praised God, who sees her and "after whom" she looked. But now the reciprocity of seeing between God and man is directly revealed to us. The mutual relationship of the one making the demands, who makes them only in order to bless, and of the one making the sacrifice and receiving the highest blessing in the moment of greatest readiness to sacrifice, here appears as the reciprocity of seeing. God sees the innermost reality of the human soul, the reality He has brought out by testing the soul; and man sees the way of God, so that he may walk in His footsteps. The man sees, and sees also that he is being seen.

If the gift of mediation between the above and the below, and between the below and the above, is the one great attribute of the prophet, then such *seeing* is the other. And now, at the end of the road, with its stations where the earth and the heavens and God Himself are seen, we are shown the perfection of seeing: as a seeing and a being-seen in one.

"The prophet of our day was formerly called a seer," we read in the story of Samuel and Saul (I Sam. 9:9). In its meaning, too, the "seer" is the older of the two concepts. Abraham *becomes* a prophet, but a seer is what he was from

the very first moment when God "let Himself be seen"—the
very first time He let Himself be seen by any man in Scripture. As a seer, Abraham now goes on to achieve the perfection of seeing. Now that we have reached the end of the way
with him, the symbols of this "seeing" in all the stories become united for us in one mighty theme-word, not stated in
Scripture precisely because it is so fundamental that we are
expected to read it between the lines: Abraham the Seer.

Three things in the Bible are traced back to Abraham.
The first, overtly, is the origin of the people; the second, by
connection with the people's past history, is the mission of
the people to become a community of nations; the third,
by the indications of the story itself, is the birth of prophecy.
Three traditions seem to be merged in the story of Abraham:
the tradition, preserved among the people, of a family of an-
cestors; the tradition, preserved by the Torah, about a divine
revelation at the beginning concerning the road for the future; and the tradition, preserved by the prophets, about the
historic origin of the prophetic gift.

THE BURNING BUSH

(EXODUS 3)

THE section that deals with the Revelation at the Burning
Bush (Exod. 3:1–4, 17) cannot be regarded as a compilation from varying sources and documents. All that is
needed is to remove a few additions, and there appears before us a homogeneous picture; any apparent contradiction
can be accounted for by the fact that the text has not been
fully understood. The style and composition of this section
show that it is the fruit of a highly cultivated dialectic and
narrative art; but certain of the essential elements of which
it is composed bear the stamp of early tradition.

Moses, tending the flocks of his father-in-law, leads
them out of the accustomed steppe on one occasion: just as
we hear of the Bedouins of the same district moving with
their flocks into the hills, where the animals find pastures
that are still green. There Moses suddenly finds himself at
the "Mountain of God," Mount Horeb or Sinai. "Mountain
of God" (or "of gods") had been its name since time untold,
presumably because mysterious phenomena, either of volcanic or other character, take place on it and local tradition
therefore claims that divine beings reside there.[1] Here Moses
sees the "burning bush." Just as the mountain is described
as "*the* mountain of God," that is, the mountain known as
"a god-mountain," * so is the bush described as "*the* thornbush," that is, the specific bush that is known to grow upon

* Only after the revelation to the people in Numbers 10:33 is
it called "the Mountain of YHVH."

Sinai. The name *seneh* which is peculiar to it (no other kind
of bush is called so) echoes the name of the mountain, which
is omitted of set purpose at this point. The word *seneh* repeated three times in the same sentence suggests the name
Sinai, which is used only (16:1) when the nation reaches
the mountain in order to receive the revelation.

The bush burns, the blaze flares up, and in the blaze
the "messenger of YHVH" is seen by Moses. Such "messengers" (which we call "angels") are always recorded in the
earlier Scriptures without personal names, and, so to say,
without personal character. They are nothing save the perceptible intervention of God in events, which is sometimes
made even more plain by the fact that they and YHVH Himself are alternately named as speakers.

The flame does not consume the bush. This is not a
consuming fire that nourishes itself on the material it has
seized, and is itself extinguished in the destruction of that
material. The bush blazes but is not consumed: and in the
blaze shining forth from it, Moses sees the "messenger."

Certain scholars take the story to mean that "on Sinai
there was a holy thornbush which was considered by the
residents of the region to be the seat of the mountain divinity," and they draw the conclusion that YHVH "is also regarded here as a tree god." [2] They find support from the fact
that in the "Blessing of Moses" (Deut. 33:16) the god is
designated *shokhni seneh,* which is translated as "He who
dwells in the thornbush." The verb, in question, however,
did not originally mean to dwell but to take up residence; to
sojourn, no matter how temporarily. Further, the apparition
is seen not in the plant but in the fire; and accordingly the
voice that calls Moses "from the midst of the bush" (Exod.
3:4) should be understood as coming from the fire which
blazes throughout the entire bush. YHVH, to be sure, can just
as little be regarded here as mountain god—He who attacks
Moses on the way to Egypt (4:24) and orders Aaron in
Egypt (4:27); and in our story He already states the deeds
He would perform there in support of Moses. All these are
characteristics the like of which are not reported of any of
the mountain gods, and which (apart from the fact that

YHVH Himself says [3:8] that He has "come down" from heaven) speak against the view that Moses had "discovered the seat of YHVH."

There are some who tend to "draw a distinction in principle" between the calling of Moses, which commenced with this apparition, and the calling of the prophets; "for whereas the latter undergo a psychological experience which takes place in dream or vision, there is a mythical event in the case of Moses, since the Divinity appears to him corporeally." [3] This is a distinction in categories which finds nothing in the Bible text to support it. Isaiah says (Isa. 6:5), apparently in a memorial written many years after the event reported, that his eyes had seen "the King YHVH of Hosts"; which is not less but rather more corporeal than the apparition described in the story of the summoning of Moses. For it is made perfectly clear here that Moses saw no form. After the messenger permitted himself to be seen "in the blazing fire," what Moses sees is expressly stated: "and there, the bush was burning with fire, but the bush was not consumed." That it was this he saw and nothing else is also stressed by the fact that he says to himself: "Let me go across, and see this great sight—why the thornbush is not burnt up." Nobody who had seen a divine form in the fire could talk in that way. Moses actually sees the messenger *in* the blaze; he sees nothing other than this. When he sees the wondrous fire he sees what he has to see. No matter how we explain the process as being natural, this at least is what the narrative tells us and wishes to tell us; and whatever this may be, it is clearly not "mythology."

As against this the difference between the literary categories of saga and prophecy is indicated in scholarly quarters, and the explanation is given[4] that literary history must "*ab initio* protest at the obliteration of the saga-like character"; no scientific investigator, it is claimed, would even dare "to derive the legends of Hellenic heroes, whose eyes so often saw divinities, from psychological experiences." Yet with all the deference to literary categories, their scientific dignity is not great enough to decide the character and dimension of the content of truth in an account of a revelation; it is not even enough to ensure the correct formulation of the question. Instead of the legends of Greek heroes let those of Greek thinkers be taken—say that of Pythagoras, which appears to have influenced the late Alexandrian version of Moses' life story[5]—and it will immediately be seen that we are face to face with the problem of a transmitted nucleus of personal experience contained in it—naturally without even thinking of being able to extract that nucleus. How much more so when it comes to a vision so singular, so characteristic, despite certain external analogies, as that of the Burning Bush, followed by such a conversation as the one that follows. It compels us to forsake the pale of literature for that singular region where great personal religious experiences are propagated in ways that can no longer be identified.

YHVH sees Moses approach to look; and "God" (here of set purpose not "YHVH" appears as the acting one, as previously, but "God"), in order to establish the connection with the "messenger," calls to Moses from out of the bush. It has correctly been remarked [6] that such a calling by God from a specific place occurs only three times in the story of Moses, and that each of them is made from a different one of the three sites of revelation: once, in our text, from the bush, once (Exod. 19:3) from the mountain, and once (Lev. 1:1) at the Tent of Meeting. The biblical work of redaction indeed shows wisdom and art of a rare kind. The passage now under consideration differs from the others by the fact that Moses is called on by name. That is the fashion in which divinity establishes contact with the one chosen. The latter, not conscious yet aware of the One whose voice is calling him, places himself at the service of the God by his words "here I am"; and the God first orders him not to come closer (the restriction on the "approach" to the Divinity is one of the basic provisions of biblical religion) and to remove the sandals from his feet. The reason may possibly be because, being holy ground, it should not be trodden by any occupying and therefore possessing shoe (cf. Ruth 4:7).[7] It is only now that God tells him who He is; He who communicates with him, Moses, here in strange parts, is none other than the god of his forefathers, the God of the Fathers; and hence, as we may suppose, the God of whom Moses must have heard yonder in Egypt when he went forth every day "unto his brethren."

The favored "Kenite" hypothesis explains that YHVH was unknown to Israel until then, being a mountain, a fire, or maybe a volcanic god and simultaneously the tribal god of the Kenites (who are often assumed to have been wandering smiths) and that Moses had "discovered" this god at His seat of worship on Sinai. This hypothesis is unfounded.[8] There are not the faintest indications that any god of the name was ever honored in that district. No more than suppositions are possible with regard to the character and qualities of a, or the, putative Kenite god. For this reason the hypothesis has not unjustly been described [9] as "an explanation of *ignotum ab ignoto*." We know of YHVH's connection with Sinai only from the Bible; and what we know is that at the time of the exodus of the Children of Israel from Egypt YHVH had selected Sinai as the seat for His manifestation. The Song of Deborah, which is referred to (Judg. 5:5), does not bring YHVH, as is supposed, from Sinai to the Galilean battlefield; it only ascribes the name "a Sinai" to Mount Tabor, from which (4:6) the God who had come in storm clouds out of the south revealed Himself in the glorious victory over His foes. And Elijah, who is thought to have made a pilgrimage to Sinai when he wished to "speak personally to and seek an audience of YHVH," [10] really wandered defeated and weary of life to the mountain in order to lay himself down and perish in "the cave" (I Kings 19:9), that is, in yonder cleft in the rock (Exod. 33:22), familiar to the wanderers, from which Moses had once seen the God passing by. YHVH never appears in the tales of His revelations to Moses and Israel as "fixed" on Sinai; He only comes down thither on occasion, descending from heaven to do so (Exod. 3:8; 19:18, 20). Comparative religion, too, is familiar with mountains not merely as the divine seat, but also as the place where gods manifest themselves.

And just as this does not make Him a mountain god, so the fact that in the course of the revelation He often makes use of the element of fire, the heavenly origin of which is fre-

quently referred to in the Bible, does not convert Him into
a fire god. For our purpose, however, the most important
fact is not the traits of the nature gods that He has absorbed
(criticism of these particular characteristics is offered in the
story of the Sinai revelation to Elijah; cf. I Kings 19:11 f.)
but what He is to begin with. Is He an alien god whom Moses
meets, and through Moses, Israel, and who is made the national god of Israel by Moses? Or is He a "God of the Fathers"?

The Bible permits us to ascertain this. All we have to
do is to compare the peculiarities of the God of Moses with
those of the God of the Fathers. More precisely, it is our
concern to reveal the peculiar divine likeness, first in the con-
stituents of our tale which, beyond all question, lead back to
early tradition, and then in the corresponding elements of the
other, a likeness, that is to say, that it is impossible simply
to classify by some type or other of the pre-Mosaic religious
history of the Ancient East, for despite all its relationships
with one or another of these types, it shows a character differing from them all. Thereafter we must compare the two divine likenesses with one another.

If the material in the Bible is subjected to such an examination, the two likenesses will be found to differ in a
special manner; namely, just as a clan god in non-historical
situations might be expected to differ from a national god
in a historical situation. Yet at the same time it can be observed that both depict the identical god. To begin with the
former, the clan god: we immediately observe two main
characteristics which are both demonstrated in his relation
to the men chosen by him. One is that he approaches these
men, addresses them, manifests himself to them, demands
and charges them and accepts them in his covenant; and the
second, closely connected with the first, that he does not remain satisfied with withdrawing them from their surrounding
world and sending them on new paths, but wanders with
them himself and guides them along those new paths; meanwhile, however, remaining invisible insofar as he does not
"make himself seen" by them. Taken both together, these
cannot be compared with the attributes of any other divinity

in the history of religion, despite certain analogies of detail. The prerequisite assumption for both is that this god is not bound to any place, and that the seats of his manifestations do not restrict him; above them open the gates of heaven (Gen. 28:17), through which he descends and returns to his inaccessible realm.

We find all this once more in the second likeness, in the national god; but here it has the vivid color of a historical driving force. The new and supplementary characteristics, striking as they may appear, nevertheless seem peripheral to us when compared with the central power of the common element. Once again the God makes His great demands of His men, commanding and promising, establishing a covenant with them. But now He no longer turns to single persons but to a people, and that people too He leads forth and Himself conducts along the new way. Once again the invisible One becomes manifest from time to time. Once again heaven and earth are joined, and the God utters His words from heaven unto earth (Exod. 20:22).

This is no alien god "discovered" by Moses on Sinai; it is the God of the Fathers. And yet it is in his eyes none other than the God of whom his wife's kinsfolk may have told him, saying that He dwells on this mountain. When Moses came to the Midianites, he entered the range of life of the Fathers; and he senses the apparition he now sees as being that of the God of the Fathers. As YHVH had once gone down with Jacob to Egypt (Gen. 46:4), so has He now gone from Egypt to Midian; possibly with Moses himself, who was obviously under His protection like Jacob of old. At all events Moses perceives who it is that appears to him; he recognizes Him. That was what had happened in the days of the Fathers too. Abraham had recognized YHVH in the El 'Elyon of Melchizedek, YHVH had permitted himself to be seen (16:7, 13) by Abraham's concubine, the Egyptian maid Hagar, as the spirit of a desert spring—seemingly one of those divinatory springs at which something can be "seen" during sleep. What happens here, as it had happened there, is, from the point of view of religious history, an identification. The God brought with and accompanying a man is identified with the one known as previously to be found at this spot; He becomes recognized in him. From Babylonian and Egyptian religious thought we know the tendency to give full expression to the faith in the supremacy of a single god by interpreting the other gods as his forms of manifestation. But with the exception of the short-lived imperialistic theology of Amenhotep IV, no serious attempt in this direction was or could be made in the great pantheons. Only in the religious atmosphere of a solitary exclusive God outside the pantheons, claiming and leading His own men, could any such identification become a living reality.[11]

Attention deserves to be given to the fact that YHVH addresses Moses not merely as the God of the Fathers, but first as the God of his (i.e., Moses' own) father. Later on this was, at times, no longer understood, as can be seen in the text of the Samaritans which knows only of a "God of thy fathers." But the biblical narrative lets Moses (Exod. 18:4) say when naming a son: "the God of my father was my aid." Only Jacob before him in the Bible spoke of himself both personally and yet in relation to past generations (Gen. 31:5, 42; 32:10). Nobody spoke in that way after him. Here too can be felt the peculiar relation with the world of the patriarchs. And, whatever may be the position in disentangling the sources, the redactor knew well what he was doing when he introduced those passages, in which the man who had grown up in his own father's home is shown to be conscious of his God as the God of his own father.

After the God tells His chosen one who He is, He reveals the cause and purpose of the message with which He wishes to entrust him. The sentence with which this partial address begins and that with which it ends balance one another like the members of a building, through the two key words *ammi,* my people, and *Mitzraim,* Egypt. These are repeated in both, and denote the subject and the aim of the act: "I have indeed seen the sufferings of my people who are in Egypt," and "lead out my people the children of Israel from Egypt." To attribute the two sentences, as is so often done, to different sources constitutes a misunderstanding of the entire form and sense of the speech. With this repeated "my people" at the commencement and close of the passage, YHVH recognizes Israel in a fashion more powerful and unequivocal than would have been possible by any other verbal means. To be sure, He has not yet designated Himself their God. He will become the God of Israel as a people solely through the revelation to the people; now He wishes to be known only as the God of their forefathers, to whom He had once promised the land whither He would lead Israel. But since He so stresses the naming of Israel as His people, He shows that the bond uniting them had been established of old. No new, no alien god talks in such a way. This likewise indicates the hopelessness of the attempt sometimes made to attribute this first speech, which refers to the patriarchs, to some later stratum of the text. Try to insert at this point the phrase assumed to have been in the original, namely "I am the god," i.e., "I am the god of this mountain," and the message, flaming with historical revelation and historical faith, shrinks, one might well say, to a private remark that conveys nothing.

And now begins the great duologue in which the God commands and the man resists. As we have it before us, it is clearly disfigured by supplements, inserted by editors, which should not be considered as sections of a source. To begin with, something is introduced between the two first objections of the resisting man, namely his inadequacy and his inability to tell the people what they would demand to hear of the name and hence of the character of the God, on the one hand; and the final passage which returns once again to his inadequacy, on the other. In the interpolated passage Moses asks how he can demonstrate the reliability of his message to the people and is instructed to perform wonders. Here later narrative motifs are introduced in evidence, largely in order to link the story of the revelation with that of the negotiations with Pharaoh; but by this both sections are impaired. The style differs here from that in the undoubtedly genuine parts of the narrative of the Burning Bush; it is more loose, more expansive, more wordy. Here necessity does not hold sway as it does there; the purposeful repetitions are replaced by casual ones; and finally a rhetorical note is to be heard. The hard rhythm has become a thin absence of rhythm, the firm composition has become negligent; even the structure of the sentences is careless. The contents do not resemble those of the genuine parts; questions and answers move at a lower level. In the genuine part every reply gives some essential information as to the will and work of the God; but here there is, so to speak, a technical atmosphere. The clearest sign of the difference, however, is that the word "sign" is used here in a sense differing entirely from the one in which it is used there. In the genuine parts it is used in accordance with prophetic terminology. (For instance, compare Isaiah 20:3, where the prophet's nakedness appears as a sign, or Ezekiel 4:3, where the erection of an iron wall which separates the prophet from the city of Jerusalem has the same function.) It is a symbolization, a sensory presentation of a manifested truth, a perceptible reality which, no matter whether it is more or less "wondrous," always reminds people once again of that truth. In the same sense, after Moses says (Exod. 3:11): "Who am I that I should go to Pharaoh and that I should lead the children of Israel out of Egypt?" YHVH provides the assurance "Indeed I shall be present with you," and He promises Moses a "sign" which at first seems strange to us: that the people would come to this same mountain, where they would engage in the service of their God; and this is what must serve Moses as a sign that it is this same God who has sent him. We have to understand this as meaning: what is now only existent in words will then take on real existence. Then Moses will experience the mission of this God as an expression of His being; not as a spiritual mission, as now, but as a reality apparent to the senses. Unlike this, the word "sign" in the supplement (4:8 f.) appears as a proof of reliability produced by way of supernatural arts, which have no inner relationship with the truth intended; a meaning that is alien to the prophetic sphere. (The case of Isaiah 8:8, 11, for example, is not concerned with a proof; the "sign" proposed there is not a proof.)

If we omit this supplement, however, together with the seven final verses of chapter 3, all written in a later and rhetorical style (reminiscent of the late parts of Deuteronomy),

which were also clearly introduced in order to link the passage with the following events, we are left with a narrative
religious document of almost incomparable purity, in which
every word is evidence of its derivation from the hands of an
early prophet, who worked up elements offered to him by
tradition in the light of his own basic experience. The resistance offered to the mission, which was opposed to all the
natural tendencies of the one charged, and the breaking down
of this resistance by the divine power, belong, as shown us
by the autobiographical notes of Jeremiah and the paradig-
matic little book on Jonah (the nucleus of which may derive
from the eighth century B.C.),[12] to the most intimate experience of the prophetic man.

The first objection, that of his own smallness compared
with the vast task, corresponds precisely, after eliminating
the supplements, to the third (4:10), in which Moses stresses
his difficulty of speech. And once again, after YHVH responds
that He, the God of Creation,[13] makes the mouth of man to
speak or be dumb, and therefore made Moses himself as he
is, and sends him just as he is, YHVH continues: "Go, I myself shall be present with your mouth and shall instruct you
what you should say." Here ends the original wording of the
narrative. (Verses 13–16, repeating the motif "I shall be
present with you" once again, but without inner necessity,
are formed on a variant to 7:1, and have clearly been inserted in order to introduce Moses' brother Aaron, "the Levite," the forefather of the priesthood, at this early point, as
fellow carrier of the divine will. This complement actually
has a later stamp than the original tale, but an earlier one
than the supplements. Verse 17 derives from the author of
the second supplement.)

It is necessary to bear in mind the two promises of the
speaking God that begin with the word *ehyeh,* "I shall be,"
I shall be present, assuring that He would remain present
amid His chosen, in order properly to understand the central
part of the duologue, the central question and the central response, framed by these two pillars.

The point at issue here is not Man but God, the name of
God. The words of Moses are generally taken to mean that

he wished to learn the answer he would have to give the people if they asked him to tell them the name of the God whose message he brought. Understood in this sense, the passage becomes one of the chief supports of the Kenite hypothesis, since it is scarcely possible to imagine that any people would not know the name of the God of their fathers. If you wish to ask a person's name in biblical Hebrew, however, you never say, as is done here, "What (*mah*) is his name?" or "What is your name?" but "Who (*mi*) are you?" "Who is he?" "Who (*mi*) is your name?" "Tell me your name." Where the word "what" is associated with the word "name," the question asked is what finds expression in or lies concealed behind that name.

When the "man" with whom Jacob wrestled at the ford of Jabbok asks him "What is your name?" (Gen. 32:28), the point at issue is that this name can be given the reproach of an interpretation as "heel-sneak" (cf. Gen. 27:36 and Hos. 12:4). Now, however, the new name Israel is intended to take away the reproach of the old: "Not Jacob, Heelsneak, should any longer be uttered as your name." That is the change which is to be introduced through the mention of the old name by the one who bears it. In simpler form, and without dialogue, this takes place again when God fulfills the promise (Gen. 35:10).

The phrase "What is His name?" appears once more in a gnomic saying (Prov. 30:4); but here the question asked is certainly not the name of the One who "has established all the ends of the earth." The speaker is presumably well aware of that; the subject of the question is not sound but mystery. Moses expects the people to ask the meaning and character of a name of which they have been aware since the days of their fathers. Which name? From the answer of the God it can be seen that the question refers to YHVH.

In a later manifestation (Exod. 6:3), YHVH informs Moses that He was seen by the forefathers "in El Shaddai," that is, in the quality of a Shaddai God; but "by my name YHVH I did not make myself known to them." What Shaddai is can only be guessed from the word and the circumstances under which it is used in the stories of the patriarchs; yet the name clearly means the Divinity as Power; and, as seems to be indicated by five of the six passages in Genesis where the name is found, as the power making the human clan fruitful. Therefore the term can be taken to imply the power founding the tribe. Here, indeed, the issue is the biological development of Israel, which is understood as a divine work. The name YHVH, it is true, is introduced only once in the Genesis narrative in the form of a direct revelatory speech placed in the mouth of the God (Gen. 15:7), and in the identical form of phrase with which the revelation to the people begins (Exod. 20:2). But Abraham proclaims the name when he comes to Canaan as might a herald, at one spot after another (which should not be understood as a calling in prayer),[14] and his clan knows the name. Is it likely that the author of Exodus 6:3 did not know this? Here, however, what is said is not that the patriarchs made no use of the name of YHVH, but only that they did not know him in the quality characterized by this name; and that this had now been discovered. What can that mean?

Of all the various suppositions regarding the prehistoric use of the name YHVH there is only one[15] the development of which makes all this understandable without contradiction. To the best of my knowledge it was first expressed nearly half a century ago by Bernhard Duhm in an (unpublished) lecture at Göttingen: "Possibly the name is in some degree only an extension of the word *hu*, meaning he, as God is also called by other Arab tribes at times of religious revival—the One, the Unnamable." The Dervish cry *Ya-hu* is interpreted to mean "O He!" and in one of the most important poems of the Persian mystic Jelaluddin Rumi,[16] the following occurs: "One I seek, One I know, One I see, One I call. He is the first, He is the last, He is the outward, He is the inward. I know no other except *Yahu* (O He) and *Ya-man-hu* (O-He-who-is)." The original form of the cry may have been *Ya-huva*, if we regard the Arabic pronoun *huwa*, he, as the original Semitic form of the pronoun "he" which, in Hebrew as well as in another Arabic form, has become *hu*. "The name *Ya-huva* would then mean O-He! with which the manifestations of the god would be greeted in the cult when the god became perceptible in some fashion. Such a *Ya-huva* could afterwards produce both *Yahu* and *Yahveh* (possibly originally *Yahvah*)." [17] Similar divine names deriving from "primitive sounds" are also known in other religions, but in, say, the Dionysos cult the cries developed into corresponding nouns, whereas the Semites preserved the elemental cry itself as a name. Such a name, which has an entirely oral character and really requires completion by some such gesture as, for example, the throwing out of an arm, is, to be sure (as long, at least, as the undertone of the third person still affects the consciousness of speaker and listener) more suitable for evocation than for invocation. As an invocation it appears in the story of the patriarchs only in a cry (Gen. 49:18) which strangely interrupts the continuity of the blessings of Jacob. This may also explain why during the pre-Mosaic period scarcely any personal names are recorded as having been formed with this divine name. The only known exception, as it would appear, is the name of Moses' mother, Yochebed, which apparently means "YHVH is weighty." If so, it might possibly be regarded as a sign of some specific family tradition, which prepares the way for a new relation to the divine name.

Certainly it is more typical that in the course of the ages, particularly at an epoch of increasing religious laxity, as the Egyptian period appears to have been for Israel, the element of excitation and discharge connected with the calling of the name did not merely ebb away, but the name itself degenerated into a sound simultaneously empty and half forgotten. Under such conditions an hour might well come when the people would ask this question of a man bringing them a message from the God of their fathers: "How about His name?" That means: "What is this God really like? We cannot find out from His name!" For as far as primitive human beings are concerned, the name of a person indicates his character.

But there is also something else included in the question, namely the expression of a negative experience that the enslaved people had had with this God of theirs: "After all, He never troubled about us all this while! When the

Egyptians require their gods, they invoke them by uttering their 'true' names in the correct fashion, and the gods come and do what is necessary. But we have not been able to invoke Him, we cannot invoke Him. How can we be certain of Him, how can we bring Him into our power? How can we make use of His name? What about His name?"

The "true" name of a person, like that of any other object, is far more than a mere denotative designation, for men who think in categories of magic; it is the essence of the person, distilled from his real being, so that he is present in it once again. What is more, he is present in it in such a form that anybody who knows the true name and knows how to pronounce it in the correct way can gain control of him. The person himself is unapproachable, he offers resistance; but through the name he becomes approachable, the speaker has power over him. The true name may be entirely different from the generally familiar one that covers it; it may also, however, differ from the latter only in the "correct" pronunciation, which would also include the correct rhythm and the correct attitude of the body while engaged in the act of pronouncing it; all things that can only be taught and transmitted personally. And since the true name phoneticizes the character of the object, the essential thing in the last resort is that the speaker shall recognize this essential being in the name, and direct his full attention upon it. Where that happens, where the magical work requires an aiming of the soul at the being meant, that is, when the "person" aimed at is a god or a demon, the fuel is provided into which the lightning of a religious experience can fall. Then the magical compulsion becomes the intimacy of prayer, the bundle of utilizable forces bearing a personal name becomes a Thou, and a demagization of existence takes place.

As reply to his question about the name, Moses is told: *Ehyeh asher ehyeh*. This is usually understood to mean "I am that I am" in the sense that YHVH describes Himself as the Being One or even the Everlasting One, the one unalterably persisting in His being. But that would be abstraction of a kind that does not usually come about in periods of increasing religious vitality; while in addition the verb in the biblical language does not carry this particular shade of meaning of pure existence. It means: happening, coming into being, being there, being present, being thus and thus; but not being in an abstract sense. "I am that I am" could only be understood as an avoiding of the question, as a "statement which withholds any information." [18] Should we, however, really assume that in the view of the narrator the God who came to inform His people of their liberation wishes, at that hour of all hours, merely to secure His distance, and not to grant and warrant proximity as well? This concept is certainly discouraged by that twofold *ehyeh*, "I shall be present" (Exod. 3:12; 4:12), which precedes and follows the statement with unmistakable intention, and in which God promises to be present with those chosen by Him, to remain present with them, to assist them. This promise is given unconditional validity in the first part of the statement: "I shall be present," not merely, as previously and subsequently, "with you, with your mouth," but absolutely, "I shall be present." Placed as the phrase is between two utterances of so concrete a kind, that clearly means: I am and remain present. Behind it stands the implied reply to those influenced by the magical practices of Egypt, those infected by technical magic: it is superfluous for you to wish to invoke me; in accordance with my character I again and again stand by those whom I befriend; and I would have you know indeed that I befriend you.

This is followed in the second part by: "That I shall be present," or "As which I shall be present." In this way the sentence is reminiscent of the later statement of the God to Moses: "I shall be merciful to him to whom I shall be merciful" (33:19). But in it the future character is more strongly stressed. YHVH indeed states that He will always be present, but at any given moment as the one as whom He then, in that given moment, will be present. He who promises His steady presence, His steady assistance, refuses to restrict Himself to definite forms of manifestation; how could the people even venture to conjure and limit Him! If the first part of the statement says: "I do not need to be conjured for I am always with you," the second adds: "but it is impossible to conjure me."

It is necessary to remember Egypt as the background of such a revelation: Egypt where the magician went so far as to threaten the gods that if they would not do his will he would not merely betray their names to the demons, but would also tear the hair from their heads as lotus blossoms are pulled out of the pond. Here religion was in practice little more than regulated magic. In the revelation at the Burning Bush religion is demagicized.

At the same time, however, the meaning and character of the divine name itself changes; that is, from the viewpoint of the narrator as well as from that of the tradition given shape by him, it is unfolded in its true sense. By means of the introduction of an inconsiderable change in vocalization, a change to which the consciousness of sound would not be too sensitive, a wildly ecstatic outcry, half interjection half pronoun, is replaced by a grammatically precise verbal form which, in the third person (*havah* is the same as *hayah*—to be—but belongs to an older stratum of language), means the same as is communicated by the *ehyeh:* YHVH is "He who will be present" or "He who is here," He who is present here; not merely some time and some where but in every now and in every here. Now the name expresses His character and assures the faithful of the richly protective presence of their Lord.

And it is the God Himself who unfolds His name after this fashion. The exclamation was its hidden form; the verb is its revelation. And in order to make it clear beyond all possibility of misapprehension that the direct word *ehyeh* explains the indirect name, Moses is first instructed, by an exceptionally daring linguistic device, to tell the people "*Ehyeh,* I shall be present, or I am present, sends me to you," and immediately afterwards: "YHVH the God of your fathers sends me to you." That *ehyeh* is not a name; the God can never be named so; only on this one occasion, in this sole moment of transmitting His work, is Moses allowed and ordered to take the God's self-comprehension in his mouth as a name. But when, shortly before the destruction of the

Northern Kingdom of Israel, the prophet Hosea, in order to give concrete expression to the impending crisis in national history, calls his newborn son *Lo-ammi,* not my people, he justifies this name with the divine word: "you are not my people and I am not *ehyeh* for you" (Hos. 1:9). One expects to hear: ". . . and I am not your God," but what is said is: "For you I am no longer *ehyeh,* that is, 'I am present.'" The unfaithful people lose the presence of their God, the name revealed is concealed from them once again. Just as the *Lo-ammi* refers to the *ammi* of the Burning Bush episode, so does this *ehyeh* refer to that.

Again and again, when God says in the narrative: "Then will the Egyptians recognize that I am YHVH," or "you will recognize that I am YHVH," it is clearly not the name as a sound, but the meaning revealed in it that is meant. The Egyptians shall come to know that I (unlike their gods) am the really present One in the midst of the human world, the standing and acting One; you will know that I am He who is present with you, going with you and directing your cause. And until the very close of the Babylonian Exile, and later, sayings such as "I am YHVH, that is my name" (Isa. 42:8), or even more clearly, "Therefore let my people know my name, therefore on that day, that I am He who says 'Here I am'" (Isa. 52:6), cannot be otherwise understood.

However, it appears that the message of the name never became actually popular in biblical Israel. It seems that the people did not accept the new vocalization. The interpretation, to be sure, hovers around the name in their consciousness; but it does not penetrate it. In the innermost nucleus it remains the dark, mysterious cry, and there is evidence in all periods until the days of the Talmud that an awareness of the sense of the pronoun "he" hidden in it was always present. The prohibition against pronouncing the name only raised an ancient reluctance, which was rooted in the resistance against rationalization, to the power of a taboo. Nevertheless a tremendous vitalization in the relation of the people to the name clearly took place on Sinai; the boys are given names containing it, and just as its proclamation combines

with the moving and stopping of the crowd, so it also finds
place in the life of the tribe and in that of the individual;
the certainty of the presence of the God as a quality of His
being began to possess the souls of the generations. It is
impossible properly to grasp such a process independently of
the actually unaccepted yet so effective message contained in
the meaning of the name.

The meaning of the name is usually ascribed to the "Elohist," to whose source this section of the narrative is attributed. But quite apart from the fact that there was no Elohist
in this sense and that, as has been said, if we eliminate complements and supplements, we find a uniform and firmly
constructed narrative—such discoveries or conversions are
not born at the writing desk. A speech like this *ehyeh asher
ehyeh* does not belong to literature but to the sphere attained
by the founders of religion. If it is theology, it is that archaic
theology which, in the form of a historical narrative, stands
at the threshold of every genuine historical religion. No matter who related that speech or when, he derived it from a
tradition that, in the last resort, cannot go back to anybody
other than the founder. What the latter revealed of his religious experience to his disciples we cannot know; that he
informed them of what had happened to him we must assume; in any case, the origin of such a tradition cannot be
sought anywhere else.

At his relatively late period Moses did not establish the
religious relationship between the Bnei Israel and YHVH. He
was not the first to utter that "primal sound" in enthusiastic
astonishment. That may have been done by somebody long
before who, driven by an irresistible force along a new road,
now felt himself to be preceded along that road by "Him,"
the invisible one who permitted Himself to be seen. But it
was Moses who, on this religious relationship, established a
covenant between the God and "His people." Nothing of
such a kind can be imagined except on the assumption that
a relation which had come down from ancient times has been
melted in the fire of some new personal experience. The
foundation takes place before the assembled host; the experience is undergone in solitude.

HOLY EVENT

(EXODUS 19–27)

W E KNOW nothing of Israel's religious situation in the
Egyptian age, and we can only conjecture on the basis
of scattered disconnected phrases (e.g., Ezek. 20:7 f.) that
it was out of a state of religious decay that Moses stirred them
up. We can proceed only by putting the period of the Exodus
alongside that of the Fathers.

When we pass from the atmosphere of the patriarchal
tradition, as we have tried to picture it hypothetically, and
enter the atmosphere of the Exodus tradition, we are confronted at first glance with something new. But it is quickly
manifest that this does not mean a change in the deity, but a
change in men. We have already seen that the deity is in
essence no other than the primitive deity. Against this the
human partner is essentially changed; therefore, the situation
common to the two is entirely different; and with this the
sphere in which the deity acts is so different that one may
easily think the very character of this activity to be changed,
and one does not recognize the identity of the agent. The new
thing from the human side is that here we have "people,"
not "a people" in the strictest sense, but at all events the
element people. That is to say, this collection of men is no
longer a company assembled around the recipients of revelation and their kinsmen as in the patriarchal age, but a
something that is called "Israel" and which the deity can
acknowledge to be "His people"—again it is not of decisive
importance whether this people comprises all the tribes of

Israel, or only some of them, the rest having been left in Canaan or having returned thither before this. We do not know whether "Israel" originally was the name of a people or the name of a "holy confederacy," to which the tribes were gathered together by the leadership of Moses,[1] and gave themselves, after their sacred call, the name "Israel," the meaning of which probably is not "God strives," but "God rules." [2]

But if this is the original explanation of "Israel," then this community has already, in consequence of the special historical conditions, reached, at the moment of the Exodus —i.e., at the moment when we are able to perceive them historically—that stage of self-evident unitedness, so that we are justified in applying to them the name "people," even though they do not yet possess all the marks reckoned as belonging to this concept. And if "Israel" was already in origin the name of a people, then it is only at this point, at the exodus from Egypt, not in Egypt itself, that the people comes into actual existence, and only at this point is the name "Israel" perfectly manifest as "the visible program of God's sovereignty." [3] And the deity now acts historically upon this people seen by Him as an absolute unity, the same deity whom the Fathers discovered as the guardian God accompanying them. The change that we think we perceive in Him as we now advance in time is nothing but the transformation of the situation into a historical one, and the greatness of Moses consists in the fact that he accepts the situation and exhausts its possibilities. No external influence is to be found here. Indeed it is vain to attempt to find here a Kenite ingredient; YHVH has taken over nothing from the Egyptian god Aton, who is brought into the picture as "monotheistic"; and other things which may have approached Him have not touched His nature. This God has become manifest as a God of history, because He became the God of Israel, this Israel that only now came into being, that only now He was able to "find" (Hos. 9:10), and because this Israel only now has entered the realm of history. He reveals Himself to it: what was hidden in prehistoric time is made historically manifest. Our path in the history of faith is not a path from one kind of deity to another, but in fact a path from the "God who hides Himself" (Isa. 45:15) to the One that reveals Himself.

If we look at the first of the writing prophets, Amos, and examine the traditions that he handles concerning this activity of YHVH, and ask: what are the reminiscences that he knows to be common to all his hearers, these two appear before us: the leading from Egypt through the desert (Amos 2:10; 3:1; 9:7), and the appropriation the deity expresses in a word reminiscent of the marriage union (Gen. 4:1) but later uses to indicate the primal mission of the prophet (Jer. 1:5), "you have I known" (Amos 3:2). The first of these two, talked over by everyone and thought to be understood by all—"I have brought you up" (2:10)—Amos shows (9:7) to be something that is in no way peculiar to Israel, but the fundamental fact of the historic contact of this leader God with the peoples. It is with set purpose that record is here kept of the names of the two neighboring peoples who fought most mightily with all Israel or Judah, the one in early times, the other in the immediate past. In these instances, very painful as they are to you—this is the force of the prophet's words —you see that this God of yours, of whose historic dealing with you you boast, deals historically with other peoples as with you, leading each of them on its wanderings and singling out its lot. The second thing, not familiar to the people as to its expression and sense, but corresponding in the people's memory to the events of revelation and covenant making, he lays bare as the *suprahistorical election* to be bound absolutely, peculiar "only" to Israel alone among all the peoples: "therefore"—and now comes the iron word from the Decalogue—"I will ordain upon you all your iniquities." YHVH has not revealed Himself to any other family of "the families of the earth" save only to this Israel, and to them He has revealed Himself really as the "zealous God." And in the mouth of Amos' contemporary, Hosea, who presupposes no general thought or teaching, but expresses directly the things of the heart, YHVH illustrates His zealousness by His experience with Israel in the desert: I loved (11:1) and they betrayed me (9:10; 11:2; 13:6).

Those Semitic peoples who call their tribal deities by

the name *malk,* meaning originally counsellor, arbitrator, leader, and only afterwards receiving the meaning of king, appear to have expressed by this name not the oracle power of the settlement but the leadership in primitive wanderings and conquest. These are nomad gods, leader gods of the tribe which, through the political change of meaning of the word, become afterwards "kings"; the type of this tribal god, although not the name, we find in the message of Jephthah to the king of the "Ammonites" (or more correctly the king of Moab), where he tells him that Chemosh his god "disinherited" other peoples even as YHVH had done, in order to give a land to the people led by him (Judg. 11:23 f.). Amos' saying about the bringing up of the Aramaeans disposes of such a notion: the peoples do not know who is their liberator, they each call him by a different name, each one thinks to have one of its own, whereas we know the One, because He "has known" us. This is the *national* universalism of the prophetic faith.

The Mosaic age does not possess this religious view of the history of peoples, but it does have the fundamental religious experience that opens the door to this view. What is preserved for us here is to be regarded not as the "historization" of a myth or of a cult drama, nor is it to be explained as the transposition of something originally beyond time into historical time[4]: a great history-faith does not come into the world through interpretation of the extrahistorical as historical, but by receiving an occurrence experienced as a "wonder," that is, as an event that cannot be grasped except as an act of God. Something happens to us, the cause of which we cannot ascribe to our world; the event has taken place just now, we cannot understand it, we can only believe it (Exod. 14:31). It is a holy event. We acknowledge the performer (15:1, 21): "I will sing unto YHVH, for He has verily risen, the horse and its rider He has cast into the sea." [5]

In this undeniably contemporary song the deliverance is asserted as a holy event. A later song, which nevertheless is very ancient in form, vocabulary, and sentence construction, the song framing "the Blessing of Moses," praises in its first half (the second half tells of the conquest of the land) a series of divine appearances in the wilderness,[6] beginning with the appearance at Mount Sinai. From the difficult text it can be understood that the "holy ones" of the people collect around YHVH, when they camp "at His feet" (cf. Exod. 24:10); that later the people receive from the divine words the "instruction" (*torah*) which Moses "commands"; that so "the congregation of Jacob" becomes YHVH's "inheritance"; and that finally the heads of the tribes gather together and proclaim YHVH to be king over them. What is recorded here of the holy event can only be reconstructed incompletely out of the exodus story. The fact that the proclamation is lacking here is probably to be explained by the fear they felt for the influence, combated by the prophets, of the *melekh* cult of the neighboring peoples, that is to say, for the penetration of child sacrifice into Israel. Isaiah is the first (6:5) directly to give YHVH the title *melekh,* king, after forcibly demonstrating the uncleanness of the people over against Him. But we still have preserved for us another echo of the proclamation, namely the last verse of the Song of the Sea (Exod. 15:18), which although it is not so near in time to the event as the opening of the Song, yet clearly is "not long after the event about which it tells." [7] Here proclamation is made triumphantly that the divine kingdom will stand forever. This is to be understood not in the light of the state concept of kingship, nor on the basis of the later idea of a cosmic-cultic kingdom of God, but only as the recognition by wandering tribes of their divine leader: the sovereignty of this leader over His people is proclaimed.

Thus over against the two sayings of Amos we have before us two series of events. The first comprises the deliverance from Egypt and the leading through the wilderness to Canaan, the second comprises the revelation, the making of the covenant and the setting up of an order of the people by the leadership of the divine *melekh.* That is to say, the first series exists for the sake of the second. So we are to understand the words "unto me" in the first Sinai message (Exod. 19:4), which still precedes the revelation in the thunderstorm.[8] YHVH bears the people, as the eagle from time to time bears one of its young on its wing (a late form of the picture is found in Deut. 32:11), to the place of revelation: if the people hearken to the voice that now speaks to them, they will become for YHVH, whose is all the earth, a "peculiar treasure" among all the peoples that are His: they will become for Him, the king, a "king's realm" (cf. II Sam. 3:28), surrounding Him near at hand and serving Him directly, a circle of *kohanim,* that is "foremost ones at the king's hand" (so I Chron. 18:17 calls the office, while II Sam. 8:18 gives it the name *kohanim,* meaning those who minister to the king), a "holy" (i.e., hallowed, set apart for Him) *goy* (i.e., body of people). The saying dates apparently from the time before the division of the Israelite kingdom,[9] and it is already influenced by the political changes of meaning in the concept *melekh;* but it is clear that a traditional basic view of the meaning of the events, the Exodus and the making of the covenant, became crystallized in it. YHVH acts as *melekh* in the sense of sovereign. So through a holy event there comes into existence this category, decisive from the point of view of the history of faith, of the "holy people," the hallowed body of people, as image and claim; at a later time, after the people had broken the covenant again and again, this category changed and was replaced by the Messianic promise and hope.

Both series of events are blended together in a most noteworthy way in the great holy object, indeed the greatest of all holy objects created by the "nomadic faith," the faith of a people seeking a land and believing in the divine leader, who brings them to it, namely the Ark.[10] It clearly cannot be dated any later; for there is to be found in it all the incentive and motive force of the holy adventure, all its symbol-begetting power. And in spite of the many parallels in the history of religion to one or other aspect of the ark,[11] it can hardly be maintained that the ark is borrowed from anywhere, for its nature lies precisely in the unity of these different aspects. It carries the cherub throne of the Lord who, seated thereon, guides the wandering and the battle (here both are still absolutely interconnected the one with the other); and together with this is the ark proper containing the tablets. These are called "the testimony," because it is by them that the cove-

nant is always attested anew, and so the ark is also called
"the Ark of the Covenant." Neither of the two could be wanting. This holy object is a visible unity of the two divine activities: the activity of the leader, who now, in the historic
situation, has become also "a man of war" (Exod. 15:3),
and the activity of the revealer, whose revelation, once it
had taken place, is never more to be concealed and hidden,
but must remain carved on stone or written on a scroll. At
the same time even this characteristically is not attached to
a place: the tablets are fixed in the ark, but the ark is by
nature mobile, moving in the tent and outside it, for it is forbidden to remove the poles (25:15). Even after the ark
stands compact in the temple in Jerusalem, they are not removed (I Kings 8:8); but this means only reverence for tradition and symbolism, and not any longer a direct notion of
the leader deity. The double call, originating in the wilderness (Num. 10:35 f.), to the Lord of the ark, who travels
and halts with the camp, "rise up YHVH" and "return YHVH"
and the "*melekh* shout" because Israel's God is "with him"
(23:21), is no more heard. His special name "YHVH of hosts"
(i.e., the host of the people and the host of heaven, concerning both of which the Song of Deborah speaks) is still in the
mouth of the people, but its real meaning is no longer really
known—until Amos comes and expounds it again.

The paradox on which the sanctity of the ark is based
(every "holy" thing is founded on a paradox) is this: that
an invisible deity becomes perceptible as One who comes
and goes. According to tradition, as far as we can still recognize it, the ark must be brought into the "tent of meeting"—
not the tent that is described in all its parts in Scripture, and
which really cannot be conceived in the wilderness, but the
tent of the leader ("the tent" of Exod. 33:7 ff.)—after atonement for sin had been made. The image of the calf, which
has no other design than to be a likeness of that very God
"who brought you up from the land of Egypt" (32:4), was
put up to make the leadership permanently perceptible. In
the hour of forgiveness God grants (33:14, 17) that His
"face" will go with the people. The meaning of this is that a
visibleness is conceded which in fact is none; that is to say,

not the visibleness of an "image" or a "shape" (20:4), but as in the vision of the ancients (24:10) the visibleness of a *place*. This is the hour in which the holy object is born. Later, men attempted to render the principle, which could no longer be reconstructed in its reality, more conceivable by means of a concept of the *kabod,* that is, the fiery "weight" or "majesty" of the God radiating from the invisible, which now "fills" again and again the "dwelling" of the tent (40:34), just as it had "taken dwelling" upon the mount (24:16). In truth this idea of a filling of the tent, so that Moses "cannot come into the tent of meeting" (40:35), contradicts its character and purpose. The true tent—formerly Moses' leader tent, and now that of the leader deity—is characterized by just this: that Moses enters it for the sake of "meeting" the deity, and that "everyone who seeks YHVH" (33:7) can hand over his petition to Moses, who will talk it over with the deity. It is of the essence of the leadership that there is the divine word in dialogue: informative and initiative speaking. The informative function passes afterwards from the divine speech to the oracle vessels called *Urim and Tummim,* and from the *nabi*—for as such the former writing prophets know Moses from tradition (Hos. 12:13)—to the priest. Whereas the initiative speech, the genuine speech of the leader which is no answer but a commission and a command, is henceforth also spoken only to the *nabi,* whom "the hand" seizes and sends. Kings rule, priests minister in their office, while the man of the Spirit, without power or office, hears the word of his leader.

Besides the movable divine abode, yet another feature of the nomadic period has entered into the life of the settled community, and so deeply that it persisted long after the age of the settlement and shared the subsequent wanderings of the people in all ages and generations, becoming almost a perpetual renewal of the first event: the feast of the Passover.[12] A nomadic feast, as it certainly was in primitive times, it was transformed by the holy event into a feast of history; but that which recurs in the festival is the act of going forth, the beginning of the journeyings; the nomadic feast, without any historical character, becomes the historical feast. With loins girt, with feet shod, and with staff in hand, in the haste of departure they eat the sacrifice (Exod. 12:11). The Israelites do what was done formerly, not only performing the action, but in the performance doing it. Through the length and breadth of history, in every new home in a strange land, on this night the stimulus of the God-guided wanderings is active again, and history happens. The Israelites recount the story of the feast, this story that "cannot be the literary product of a later source," but which "contains facts," "solid tradition, springing from the ground of historic events." [13] But it is not the purpose to recount only what happened there and then. On the night of the Passover "the assembled company is fused together in every year and in all the world with the first cult confederates and attains that unity, which existed formerly at the first occasion in Egypt." [14] As they who keep the covenant in life know it to be the covenant that "YHVH our God made with us in Horeb," "not with our fathers," but "with us our very selves here this day, all of us being alive" (Deut. 5:2 f.), so telling the story of God's leading they experience His historic deed as occurring to themselves. In His footsteps they are wakeful through the night, which was a night of watching for YHVH and is now a night of watching for all the children of Israel in their generations (Exod. 12:42).

Berith, covenant, between YHVH and Israel denotes an expansion of the leadership and the following so as to cover every department of the people's life. The fundamental relationship represented perceptibly, that the deity—and it is the same in whatever form (pillar of fire, etc.) or even in no form (ark, "face")—goes before the company of wanderers and they follow after Him, and know in their heart that His way is the right way, this relationship is now taken as an all-embracing relationship founded as an everlasting bond in the making of the covenant. Here the mutual character of this relationship is announced, but the people feel already that a covenant with such a deity as this means no legal agreement, but a surrender to the divine power and grace. The most sublime expression of this is given in two sayings of YHVH (3:14 and 33:19), which by their sentence structure are shown to belong to each other (two similar verbal forms linked by the word *asher,* meaning "whoever," "whomever"). The first says that indeed the deity is always present but in every given hour in the appearance that pleases Him; that is to say, He does not allow Himself to be limited to any form of revelation and He does not limit Himself to any of them. And the second says that He bestows His grace and mercy on whom He will, and lets no one order a criterion for Him nor Himself orders any. But connected with this is that element called YHVH's "demonism," [15] the dread of which overcomes us whenever we read about YHVH meeting Moses, His chosen and sent one, and "seeking to kill him" (4:24). This is no survival, no "primitive fiend" that has entered, as it were, by mistake from earlier polydemonism into this purer sphere, but it is of the essential stuff of early biblical piety, and without it the later form cannot be understood. The deity claims the chosen one or his dearest possession, falls upon him in order to set him free afterwards as a "blood bridegroom," as a man betrothed and set apart for Him by his blood. This is the most ancient revelation of grace: the true grace is the grace of death, a gracing; man owes himself to the deity from the beginning. And here too, as with Jacob (Gen. 32), the event is significantly linked with a journey ordered earlier: the wanderer has to go through the dangerous meeting, in order to attain the final grace of the leader God.

The idea of following the deity raises itself—no longer in the Mosaic but still in an early biblical age—to the idea of imitating the deity, notably in the interpretation of the greatest institution set up by Moses, the Sabbath. It appears that the Sabbath too was not created *ex nihilo,* although its origin is not yet clear.[16] It is certain that the material used for this institution was adopted by a mighty force of faith, recast and molded into an indestructible creation of the life of the faithful. It is impossible to think of an age later than that of Moses in which this could have happened. Many think the "ethical Decalogue" (Exod. 20) to be later than the "cultic" (34), but the latter with its harvest and pilgrimage feasts presupposes an agricultural usage, whereas the former is yet "timeless," not yet stamped with any particular organized form of human society[17]; the "cultic" is seen after detailed examination to be a "secondary mixture," whereas the "ethical" in its fundamental core is known to have a primary, "apodictic" character.[18] The Sabbath ordinance contained in it, in the original shorter version—beginning apparently with the word "remember" and continuing as far as "thy God"—is the ordinance of setting apart the seventh day for YHVH (that is to say, a day not ordered for cultic reasons, but freed of all authority of command except that of the one Lord). On this day men do not do, as on other days, "any work"; the meaning of this for the nomad shepherd, for the shepherd who cannot neglect his flock, is that he puts off all "jobs which he can do today or leave to tomorrow," that he interrupts the cultivation of land in the oasis, that he does not journey to new places of pasture, and so on.[19] It is only in the age of the settlement that the Sabbath becomes a strict day of rest. Among the established and illustrative sayings that come up for consideration (we find in the Pentateuch seven variants of the ordinance), two are of special importance: Exod. 23:12, and 31:12 ff. It is customary to connect them with different "sources" from different periods, but a very rare verb (which is only found elsewhere in the Bible once, in the apparently contemporaneous story of Absalom, II Sam. 16:14), meaning "to draw one's breath," links the two, the "social" and the "religious" motives, in true biblical repetitive style, referring to one another and explaining one another. The one says that the purpose of the Sabbath ordinance was that the beast might rest and that men whose work is obligatory (that is to say, the slave and the hireling sojourner), who *must needs* work all the week, might draw breath. The other passage, which sets out the Sabbath ordinance in the most solemn form and imposes the death penalty upon those who transgress it, belongs in the original core of its first part (verses 13–15 in a shorter version) to the species of ordinances in the "apodictical style" of which A. Alt writes.[20] Having examined them fundamentally in their typical difference from all the rest of the later Canaanite-influenced "casuistical" forms, he rightly says "that the rise of this species was possible when the bond-relationship to YHVH and the resulting institution of making and renewing the covenant with Him came into being." But to this part of the ordinance is added a second, obviously a later expansion, in which the Sabbath is designated as an "everlasting covenant" and a "sign for ever," "for in six days YHVH made the heaven and the earth, and on the seventh day He rested and drew breath." The crass anthropomorphism binds together the deity and the tired, exhausted slave, and with words arousing the soul calls the attention of the free man's indolent heart to the slave; but at the same time it sets up before the community the loftiest sense of following the leader. Everyone that belongs to the essence of Israel—and the servants, the sojourners included, belong to it—shall be able to imitate YHVH without hindrance.

"The sayings in the apodictic form," says Alt,[21] "mostly have to do with things with which casuistic law did not deal at all, and by its secular nature could not deal. For the question is here on the one hand the sacred sphere of the contact with the divine world . . . and on the other hand holy realms in men's life together . . . religion, morals, and law are here still unseparated together." And again,[22] "in Israel's apodictic law an aggressive, as yet quite unbroken force operates, a force which subjects every realm of life to the absolute authority claim of YHVH's will for His people, and therefore cannot recognize any secular or neutral zone." These words fit our view that YHVH as "God of Israel" does not become the lord of a cultic order of faith, shut up within itself, but the lord of an order of people including all spheres of life, that is to say a *melekh,* and a *melekh* taking his authority seriously—unlike the gods of other tribes. I do not at all mean to go too far beyond Alt's carefully weighed thesis and to connect with Sinai the whole series of these sayings, rhythmically constructed in order to engrave them upon the memory of the people, among which there recurs again and again the "I" of the speaking God, and the "thou" of the hearing Israel; but in those too that bear the distinct scent of the field about them, we feel that the fiery breath of Sinai has

yet blown upon them. They are fragments of a people's order
subject to the divine sovereignty.

As with the term "divine sovereignty" the meaning here
is not a specialized religious authority but a sovereignty op-
erating on all the reality of the community life, so with the
term "people's order" the meaning is not the order of an indefinite society but of a completely definite people. To what
is called in the Song of Deborah and in other ancient passages of Scripture "people of YHVH" a secular concept can
approximate, namely the concept of "a true people," that is,
a people that realizes in its life the basic meaning of the concept *am*, "people," of living one *im*, "with," another; it ap-
proximates to it although, to be sure, it does not actually
reach it. The "social" element in the apodictic laws is to be
understood not on the basis of the task of bettering the living
conditions of society, but on the basis of establishing a true
people, as the covenant partner of the *melekh*, according as
the tribes are a people as yet only by God's act and not by
their own. If, for example, it is ordered (Exod. 22:21) not
to afflict the widow and orphan, or (22:20; 23:9) not to
oppress the sojourner—here there is word about individuals
dependent on others, lacking security, subject to the might of
the mighty; but the aim of such commands is not the single person, but the "people of YHVH," this people that shall
rise, but cannot rise so long as the social distance loosens the
connections of the members of the people and decomposes
their direct contact with one another. The *melekh* YHVH does
not want to rule a crowd, but a community. There is already
recognizable here, as in a network of roots, the widespread
prophetic demand for social righteousness, which reached its
highest peak in the promise of the union of the peoples in a
confederacy of mankind through the mediation of the "servant" from Israel (Isa. 42:1–6).

Hence we see that the agricultural statute with its ordinances for the periodical interruption of the families' privilege of eating the fruits of their allotted ground, the remission
of debts in the sabbatical year, and the leveling of all possessions in the year of Jubilee, is only late with regard to the lit-

erary setting before us (Lev. 25), whereas with regard to its contents it presents "a transposition of the patriarchal conditions of the wilderness age to the agricultural conditions of Palestine," and is designed so that "the absolute coherence of the people" will live on in the consciousness of the common possession of land.[23] This common ownership is by its nature God's property, as we know from ancient Arabic parallels,[24] and the undeniably early saying "Mine is the land, for you are sojourners and settlers with me" (verse 23) expresses the ancient claim of the divine leader on the ways of land-seeking and land-conquest, His claim to all the land of settlement.[25] We have already seen above how in the patriarchal story the divine name was called as of their true owner upon the places occupied beforehand in Canaan, as the names of their owners are called upon the great estates (Ps. 49:12). The divine ownership of the ground and the whole people's possession of it originate in a unity meant to last forever, whereas the rights of the individual are only conditional and temporary.

Within the ancient people's order, as we can deduce it from the apodictic laws, we find the sacred sphere of contact with the divine world substantially "only in the sense of keeping away all practices directed to gods or spirits other than YHVH, or implying a misuse of things belonging to Him and therefore holy, as for example His name or the Sabbath." [26] Only a single short sacrificial statute (Exod. 20, 24 ff.) can be cited here in its original form, purified of additions.[27] The words, "in every place, where I cause my name to be remembered, I will come unto thee and bless thee" come from the true character of the ancient nomad deity who does not allow Himself to be kept to any mountain or temple. Sacrifices were apparently not customary in the wilderness apart from the nomadic offering of the firstborn of the flock (13: 12; 34:19), except in extraordinary situations (the joining of Kenites, the ratification of the Sinai covenant). And there appears to have been no fixed sacrificial cult with special sacrificial rules; Amos was probably following a reliable tradition in this connection (5:25), although he gave it an extreme interpretation.

But there is one more feature belonging to this *melekh* covenant between God and people, this leading and following, and that is the person of the mediator. The revelation, the making of the covenant, the giving of the statutes, was performed by the "translating" utterance of a mortal man; the queries and requests of the people are presented by the internal or external words of this person; the species of man that bears the word from above downwards and from below upwards is called *nabi*, announcer. So Hosea (12:14) calls Moses. In the earlier parts of the Pentateuch Moses is not so designated directly; in a remarkable story (Num. 12) an ancient verse inserted in it (6b–8a) sets Moses apparently above the *nebiim*: for they only know the deity by visions, whereas to Moses, "His servant," He speaks "mouth to mouth" (not mouth to ear, but really mouth to mouth "inspiring"; cf. also Exod. 33:11, "face to face as when a man speaks to his neighbor"), and moreover not in riddles, which a man must still explain, but so that the hearing of the utterance is itself a "sight" of the intention. And this just fits the concept of the *nabi*, known also in a later verse of the Pentateuch (Exod. 7:1; cf. 4:16), where the "god" who speaks into a person is, so to say, dependent on the *nabi* who speaks out. It is relatively unimportant when this term came into existence, but it is important that the thing is as old as Israel. In the story, composed out of the saga material in a strictly consistent form, we are told in a particularly manifold repetition of the roots *ra'ah, hazah* (to see) (Gen. 12:1, 7; 13:14, 15; 15:1; 17:1; 18:1, 2a, 2b), of the series of visions Abraham saw, until he became the mediator between below and above, an undismayed mediator, pleading with God (18:25), who now declares him to be a *nabi* (20:7); in this story the prevailing view in prophetic circles of the antiquity of prophecy is obviously expressed. The temporary sequence seer-prophet recalls an ancient note on word changes, which tells us more than mere word history (I Sam. 9:9). At all events no age in the history of early Israelite faith can be understood historically without considering as active therein this species of man with his mission and function, his declaration and mediation. Whatever else Moses is and does, his prophecy, his ministry of the word, is the crystal center of his nature and work. It is true, he does not "prophesy," the prophetic mission in the strict sense belonging to a later and different situation between God and people, but he does everything a prophet should in this early situation: he represents the Lord, he enunciates the message, and commands in His name.

Here we meet a problem, which historically, both in the spiritual and the political sense, is singularly important.[28] The divine *melekh* leads the *qahal,* the assembly of the men,[29] by means of the one favored and called by Him, the bearer of the "charismatic" power, the power of grace. This power, however, is not based, as with oriental kings, upon the myth of divine birth or adoption, but upon the utterly unmythical secret of the personal election and vocation, and is not hereditary. After the man's death it is necessary to wait until the *ruah,* the stormy breath ("spirit") of the deity, rushes into another man. (Of the transmission of the visible charisma, the "splendor," or part of it, to a man "in whom there is spirit" Scripture speaks only once, that is concerning the transmission by Moses to "his servant" Joshua, Num. 27: 15 ff. The doubtful character of this passage increased later considerably with the insertion of the *Urim* as a determining power of leadership, 21 f.) Because of this, the commission and therefore the actual leadership discontinues, a break that in the time of the conquest served the seminomads ill, for even without this they were given to unlimited family and tribal particularism, loosening the YHVH confederation and weakening "Israel's" power of action. Joshua's attempt to secure the continued unity of the people, by getting rid of the family idols and by founding a tribal amphictyony[30] around a cult-directed center only, succeeded but partially, as can be seen from the Song of Deborah. The divine *melekh,* who wishes to determine the whole life of the community, is not content to be substituted by a cult deity, to whom it is sufficient to offer sacrifice at the yearly pilgrimages. The Sinai enthusiasm for the absolute God grows again and expresses itself in the activity and song of the Deborah circle. But the increasing difficulties of accomplishing the as yet incomplete

conquest and of strengthening a position against the hostile
neighbors arouse in opposition to this theopolitical ardor a
"realist-political" movement, aimed at establishing the hereditary charisma known to Israel from the great powers, the
dynastic securing of continuity. The opposition of the faithful to the *melekh* arises especially strongly in the days of
Gideon, whose refusal to accept the royal crown may be regarded as historically true.[31] But already his son Abimelech
stands in the opposite camp. And a national catastrophe,
which the people may be inclined to see as a defeat of the
leader God Himself, occurs; on the battlefield of Ebenezer
the victorious Philistines capture the Ark of the Covenant
which went at the head of the Israelite host (I Sam. 4). This
hour represents the turning point in the history of Israelite
faith.

THE ELECTION OF
ISRAEL: A BIBLICAL INQUIRY
(EXODUS 3 AND 19; DEUTERONOMY)

I N THE prophecies of Amos, the man who under the clear
historical skies of Samaria forecast a devastating storm,
we find two passages (3:2 and 9:7) that seem to contradict
each other. Biblical scholars have therefore preferred to designate one of the two as not genuine—despite their manifestly authentic and common language. At times they have
also explained the first verse as a question—despite its unequivocally declarative form. In reality, the verses complement one another: each of the two gains its truth only in
connection with the other.

Interpretation must begin with the second. "Are ye not
as the children of the Ethiopians unto me, O children of Israel? Have not I brought up Israel out of the land of Egypt,
and the Philistines from Caphtor, and Aram from Kir?" As
a historical people, Israel enjoys no precedence over any
other. Like Israel, the other peoples were all wanderers and
settlers; they all came "up" from a land of want and servitude into their present homeland. The one God, the Redeemer and Leader of the peoples, strode before all of them
upon their way—even the hostile neighboring peoples—protecting them by His might. He guided their steps, gave them
power, let them "inherit" the soil of a people that had been
ruined by its sins and abandoned by history.[1] Some of them
may have felt the guiding force and addressed it in prayer
by the name of a tribal god while others became only dimly
and uncertainly aware of what was happening to them. Yet

during that early period they shared a common formative destiny. The *national* universalism of the first of the literary prophets teaches that, historically, Israel enjoys no precedence over the others.

But:

"You only have I known of all the families of the earth; therefore I will visit upon you all your iniquities." "Know" (*yada*), in its precise biblical sense (only as a result of which the verb can be used to designate a union of love between a man and a woman), means that the knowing being draws the known out of the abundance of creatures and that a particular and exclusive relationship is established between the two of them.[2] The kind of relationship that is here intended is told us by the second part of the sentence beginning with "therefore": its content is established by just this relationship. "Visit upon" (*paqad*) in its precise sense means that someone is given what he deserves—either good or ill, reward or punishment. Israel alone has God set into such a relationship with Him that it can fail in this relationship and that all its failings are judged and punished in accordance with this relationship. As we learn from the great speech of rebuke (1:3–2:3), the other peoples must also atone for the historical iniquities they have committed in their national lives. But *their* faithlessness (*pesha*) consists in their pridefully doing evil to *one another* when they were put into their new lands to live together peacefully. Israel alone can at the same time offend against *God* by repudiating His teaching (Torah), for Israel alone has received it (2:4). Only Israel, during its wanderings, learned through revelation that its guiding power was not *its* God but *God:* the "God of hosts" (nine times in Amos), who guides the hosts of the cosmic powers as He guides the hosts of Israel, who as Creator also creates the spirit of man and as Revealer tells him what His intention is (4:13). However, this revelation did not befall Israel as a noncommitting announcement of the state of things, but as entry into a *berith* with this God, into a covenant, a bond, an unconditionally committing union with Him. Historically, Israel enjoys no precedence over the others; superhistorically, it has precedence over them in this covenant, this subjection, this unconditional commitment in all commissions and omissions. In consequence thereof: any offense against the *berith* is "visited upon" it. That is the election of Israel. Only the call to a new generation leads out of the unconditionality of the judgment on the heaped-up offense: "Hate evil, and love the good, and establish justice in the gate; it may be that the Lord, the God of hosts, will be gracious unto the remnant of Joseph" (5:15).

When God addresses the shepherd Moses from out of the burning thornbush of Sinai (Exod. 3),[3] He first reveals to him that He is the God of the Fathers (verse 6). But then He begins the speech in which He sends Moses forth with the words: "I have surely seen the affliction of *my people* (*ammi*) that are in Egypt" (verse 7), and He finishes it with the words: ". . . That thou mayest bring forth *my people* the children of Israel out of Egypt!" (verse 10). Repetition at the beginning and end of a speech calls special attention to the significance of a word as a "key word." [4] For the first time since the promises to the Fathers, Scripture has God speaking here about the people, and for the very first time about it as something already existing. The covenant has not yet been made, the people has not yet come "to Him" (18:5), the encounter has not occurred; and yet, in anticipation, He already calls it His own, He already binds Himself to it.

But the dialogue at the thornbush continues, and the first key word, *ammi,* is followed by a second, which is brought into much sharper prominence than the first. In reply to Moses' objection that he is too weak and insignificant for such a mission (verse 11), God answers: *"Ki ehyeh imakh,* certainly I will be there with thee" (verse 12). This *ehyeh im,* as assurance of God's direct support, recurs in two places (3:12 and 4:15), and between them (3:14) the word *ehyeh* is spoken another three times to reveal the meaning of the mysterious name of God.[5] He who speaks the *ehyeh* to you, who promises you He will be there with you, who is with you wherever you are—He is the God of the Fathers, whose name Abraham called out throughout the land of Canaan when he built his altars there.

But the assurance is decisively limited so that no security can be gained from it. *Ehyeh asher ehyeh* is what it says: "I shall be there as whom [or: however] I shall be there," God will be there, but He reserves to His will the manner and the action of His presence at any given time. You, my people, need not despair, God announces to Israel, for I am with you. But you may not forget your responsibility and rely on your being my people and on my being with you. For as soon as you do that, you are already no longer my people and my being with you will turn into consuming fire. Thus it happens, in fact, after each transgression of the people. And immediately after the first, the sin of the golden calf, it happens in a piercingly clear pronouncement. No longer "my people," says God in His remonstrance to Moses (32:7–10),[6] rather "your people" (verse 7), and, scornfully, "this people" (verse 9): it is no longer His people, and the divine presence henceforth means destruction (verse 10). Only when Moses pleads with God to remember His oath of promise and repeats "your people" (verses 11 and 12), does God let Himself be moved to partial forbearance (verse 14, cf. verse 35), and the narrator may once again call Israel the people of God (verse 14).

And again it is the prophet—the interpreter of the great dialogue between the divine and the human which is called history—who expresses the message in its complete form. The marriage that Hosea is commanded to enter into with a harlot figuratively represents the marriage of God with "the land" (Hos. 1:2). The last child of that union is called *lo ammi,* "not my people," for the word of God which commanded the giving of the name sounded thus: "You are not my people and I am not *ehyeh* to you." The statement refers to the two key words of the thornbush speeches. Their *ammi* is voided by this *lo ammi,* their *ehyeh* by this *lo ehyeh:* you are no longer my people and so my non-voidable being-there is no guiding and protecting being-with-you, no longer a standing-by-you. In the divine response to the enormous offenses of the people, God's *ehyeh,* His bond, is dissolved and rendered inoperative by His *asher ehyeh,* his awful freedom.

And yet, even Hosea—like Amos—ends with an (unquestionably genuine) promise of redemption. Amos closes with "I will *turn* the captivity of my people Israel" (9:14); and Hosea: "I will heal their *turnings* away" (14:5). The crucial presupposition is stated by Hosea: *"Turn* to Him!" (14:3).

The designation "my people" is not the most exalted we find. Again it is a prophet who announces the significance of the story of the exodus: "Out of Egypt I called my son" (Hos. 11:1).

This divine word, too, refers to one in the exodus story itself: "My first-born son is Israel" (Exod. 4:22).

What does this birthright mean? If one wants to picture the peoples as God's children, then Israel surely cannot count as first-born since it was not even in existence when the peoples were divided after the Tower of Babel. Therefore, only an act of divine favor can be meant. For not only can God elevate a person to be His "son" by an act of divine adoption (II Sam. 7:14; Ps. 2:7), He can also make him His "first-born" (Ps. 89:28), with special duties and privileges—and so likewise His people. But once again: What does this act mean in relation to Israel? What duties and privileges does it confer upon it?

For this, too, we have a prophetic explanation. Jeremiah says: "Israel is the Lord's hallowed portion [*qodesh,* selected for God], His first fruits of the increase! all that devour him shall be held guilty, evil shall come upon them" (Jer. 2:3). The offering to God of the earliest yield of corn, wine, and oil is called "first fruits," *reshit.* It is something selected out of the whole for a sacred purpose, a hallowed portion. What is meant by the prophet's designating Israel as such?

To understand it properly we must peer into the depths of the picture. God receives whatever has been harvested first, and that is Israel. Why does it count as having been harvested first? There must be some special significance. If something is harvested first, it would no doubt be for the special reason that it ripened first. But had Israel already ripened in the early period of which the prophet is speaking?

Was there already in the world of nations—for only this world can be the whole increase, the fruits of which are mentioned—a part that was worthy of being presented to God? The whole story of the exodus is evidence to the contrary. The designation of Israel as *qodesh*, as *reshit*, manifestly cannot be based on the past, but only on the destiny that was announced to it in its early period. On account of its destiny (which thus far it has not attained) Israel is sanctified first fruits; God has chosen it for that purpose.

This election, however, did not occur for the first time at Horeb. Like Jeremiah in his mother's womb, so Israel was "known" by God before it had yet been born. The time in which it was planted is the period after the division of the nations (Gen. 11). At that time it was planted in order to become *reshit*: beginning and preparing to fulfill the purpose of the human seed. At that time the as yet unborn Israel was elevated to become the "first-born son," with an office and a privilege. We can now move ahead to an understanding of what this office and this privilege were.

Endowed with the divine image as sign of his delegated authority, man in the beginning was set upon the earth to rule it and all living things in the name of God (Gen. 1:27 f.). The gift of the *zelem* (God's image, 1:27) and the delegation of the power to govern [*statthalterliche Gewalt*] belong together. God desires to rule over the earth through man; the second creation story presents this when it has man, not God, give the animals the proper names which express and establish their essence (2:19 f.). But man is disobedient and faithless and he is expelled from his seat as a "delegate." And yet his office is not taken away from him; the path of toil upon which he is sent (3:17 ff.) should manifestly guide him in learning to fulfill it. But mankind in exile fails the second precondition of the office as well: harmony with one another. The story of the exile begins with fratricide, and the earth is filled with iniquity (6:11). The Flood washes away this generation; from those that are saved a new humanity is to arise—but it fails like the first. To be sure, men now combine, but only for defiance and rebellion against the Lord who had intended for them the office of ruling in His stead. What they want is clear: not to serve as delegated governors upon earth, but to take their places in heaven—and themselves, through magical power (that is the meaning of "name" in 11:4), rule the world. This, their perverse harmony, is now destroyed; this united multitude is severed into nations of different languages and thus scattered over the face of the earth. No longer is a single humanity possible. Just as human history began with the fratricide, so the history of nations began with the Tower of Babel; humanity can now be composed, if at all, only of nations, no longer of individual men. Even now man is not divested of his office, but he will be able to fulfill it only when the nations, preserving their irrevocable division, yet bind themselves together in a single humanity, which realizes God's dominion upon earth through power delegated to man.

How shall this new situation come about? One people must set an example of harmony in obedience to God for the others. From a mere nation, from the biological and historical unity of a *goy* (cf. *geviyah:* corpse, body), it must become a community, a true *am* (cf. *im:* joined to . . . ; *umma:* side-by-side) whose members are connected not merely by origin and common lot, but are also bound to one another by just and loving participation in a common life. But it can do this only as an *am elohim,* a people of God, in which all are bound to one another through their common tie to a divine center. A pseudo-community which lacks the center (Gen. 11:6) must fall apart. For men become brothers only as they become children of one Father. That fratricide and that building of the Tower can only be atoned for and overcome together.

But this people, which is to be a living example to the other peoples, cannot be one of those that was dispersed; none of them is fit for the new task. A new people must arise.

In the cosmic hour after the Tower of Babel God calls to the man Abram (Gen. 12:1) and brings him forth from his land, his kindred, and his father's house, from all ties to people and national life, into a new land that he may there beget a new people. Its task is told to him when the people he is to engender is addressed in his, Abram's, name: from the blessing with which it is blessed is to come a blessing. "Be thou a blessing!" (12:2). This unprecedented imperative, which is compassed about by the fourfold recurrence of the same verbal stem and upon which God's blessing depends, confronts us as an enigma; but in God's monologue the enigma is solved. God, who "knows" Abraham, is aware that Abraham will bid the people he begets to adhere to the way of the God who strides before them by its practice of righteousness and its proof of worth (18:19). The principle of the imitation of God is here established decisively for all time. This is what becoming a blessing for the other peoples means: setting a living example of a true people, a community. At the turn of the epoch the prophet reflects upon the overwhelming imperative. Israel has not yet become a blessing. But he, Isaiah, does not repeat the imperative. Whatever he may demand of the people, the fulfillment of becoming a blessing he expects from grace. "In that day" little Israel, between the two world powers, will become "a blessing in the midst of the earth" (Isa. 19:24).

In a later, postexilic hour the stirring memory of that command to Abraham again seizes a prophet. Israel has not become a blessing but a curse among the nations. Yet the election must be fulfilled. The word of God breaks out from the prophet's lips: "so will I save you, and ye shall be a blessing!" (Zech. 8:13).

Jewish faith knows no "salvation by works alone." It teaches the mysterious *meeting* of human repentance and divine mercy.

With the words from the Burning Bush, "My people— I will be with thee," God confirms His covenant with the Fathers as progenitors of the people that has now come to be. At one time, in the last of His manifestations to the Fathers—in the last one to Jacob—He had promised: "I will go down with thee into Egypt, and I will also surely bring thee up again!" (Gen. 46:4). This, too, was spoken to the people *in* Jacob; only now is it to become reality. Now Israel is to be brought from Egypt and come to "this mountain." Here, with the sealing of a final covenant, it is to "become of service to God" (Exod. 3:12); it is to quit the service (*abodah*) of the oppressor and enter the service (*abodah*) of the Redeemer.

Israel camps at Sinai, opposite the mountain (19:2). God and His people stand opposite one another. Moses "goes up to God" (19:3). And now God calls out to him the all-embracing message. Thus He commands him to say to "the house of Jacob": "Ye have seen what I did unto the Egyptians, and how I bore you on eagles' wings, and brought you unto myself. Now therefore, hearken unto my voice indeed, and keep my covenant, then ye shall be mine own special treasure from among all peoples; for all the earth is mine, but ye shall be unto me a royal dominion of *kohanim,* a holy *goy*" (19:4 f.).

An explanation of some of the vocabulary in the passage is indispensable[7]: 1. "Unto myself" (*elai*) does not mean "to my abode" (that would be expressed differently), rather: to meeting with me; God was indeed present in Egypt with Moses (cf., e.g., 5:22), but the meeting with the *people* was to follow only at Sinai. 2. Special treasure (*segulah*) is a possession set apart from the common property of the tribe for special disposition and use. 3. *Mamlakhah* does not mean "kingdom" let alone "government," but rather designates the unmediated sphere of the king's dominion, in which he announces his will. 4. *Kohanim* here does not mean "priests," rather (as, for example, II Sam. 8:18; I Kings 4:5) the servants who "stand ready" to carry out the orders of the king, his adjutants through whom he announces his will.[8] 5. The peoples are here spoken of, not in a biological sense but in a sociological one, as *ammim,* for in *this* sense Israel is chosen from among them. But Israel is to be holy (*qadosh*) as a *goy,* i.e., with its whole biologically-determined corporeality. (For this reason Franz Rosenzweig was even inclined to translate here: "a holy body," which, however, might have aroused alien associations.) Where, later, the text proceeds from this point (as often in Deuteronomy), it avoids the ambiguity of the mystery and says "*am qadosh.*" 6. For *qadosh* it is necessary to proceed from the passages dealing with the imitation of the holiness of God (Lev. 11: 44 f. *inter alia*). Here it designates a withdrawal which must not, however, be understood as a separation: as God is withdrawn from the world and yet is present and active in it, so is Israel to be in its relation to the surrounding nations; it is to be a *berakhah,* a "blessing" to them.

After the completed redemption, Israel had acclaimed God, the Redeemer, as its eternal King (Exod. 15:18). Now this message at Sinai is His royal proclamation. He proclaims: I am the King of the world, but I have chosen you for myself as my *unmediated* royal dominion. Therefore you shall establish my kingdom over you—but as my messengers and helpers—in order thus to begin the preparation of humanity for my kingdom. For such disposition and use have I selected you unto me from my world-possession as a special treasure. But you are that only when and as long as you hearken to my voice and keep my covenant. Only those are royal messengers who hearken to the voice of the King. When my people betrays my covenant, I am no longer covenanted to it.

The Book of Deuteronomy, in particular, has assumed the task of elucidating the eagle passage in the powerful ancient *midrash* the Bible presents. In four sermons and introductions to laws (4:1–40; 7:1–11; 14:1 f.; 26:16–19) it interprets the passage and especially the concept of "special treasure": it is a unique and incomparable thing, it says, that God has brought you forth unto Himself, has torn this people (*goy*) out of the bowels of a people (*goy*), out of the midst of the peoples; has brought you out of the iron furnace of Egypt where you were smelted into suitable metal, and has now taken you as the people of His possession[9] and set you under His law. But not on account of your eminence and importance has He chosen you—for you are of little consequence (7:7)—rather out of gracious love. He has raised you unto Himself as sons; you are plighted to Him and He to you; He has entrusted you with high office as a people (that, and not rank, is meant by *'elyon* in 26:19 and 28:1). But all of this depends upon your walking in His ways—your following after Him.

Toward the end of the book, however, a song tells (32: 11 f.) how the being borne "on eagles' wings" should be understood. The newly fledged eaglets, as yet not daring to fly, huddle together in the eyrie. Then the eagle rouses his nest, stirs his young to flight, with gentle flapping of his wings hovers over them—the God-eagle over the peoples, as once at the beginning of creation His spirit hovered[10] over the face of the waters. But then he spreads his wings and sets *one* of the young upon his pinion, carries it away, and, by throwing it into the air and catching it, teaches it to fly freely. Why the one? Why else but that it may fly ahead, leading the way for the others!

Election without obligation appears only in two places in the Bible—and they are connected with each other in content. In imagery and language both are so closely related to several of the previously mentioned passages in Deuteronomy that it seems natural to relate them to each other. In fact, the other way around, the latter should be considered a Deuteronomic, supplementary correction of the former, since the elimination of everything that refers to commandment and law is all too unlikely.

God sends Nathan to David to explain to him why he has not been called upon to build the Sanctuary in Jerusalem. One of the most remarkable things about Nathan's speech (II Sam. 7)—one of the strongest and most important speeches of God in Scripture—is that it (and it alone) takes up again, together, the two key words of the thornbush speech: "my people" and "I will be with thee" (*ammi* three times: 7:10 and 11; *ehyeh imkha:* 7:9). In his direct answer to God, David takes up the matter of the threefold *ammi* with threefold *amkha* (verses 23 f.) and exclaims: "Who is like Thy people (*am*), like Israel, a nation (*goy*) one in the earth, whom God went to redeem unto Himself for a people (*am*)! . . . Thou didst establish to Thyself Thy people Israel to be a people unto Thee forever!" (II Sam. 7:23 f.). This untroubled royal glorification of the people gives not a word to the acceptance of obligation at Sinai and to the binding character of the *berith*.

The building of the Temple is complete; the Ark has been brought into the Sanctuary in a great procession. Solomon (I Kings 8:22–53) utters the broadly encompassing prayer in which he entreats God's response to all, even to the strangers who shall at some time pray turned toward this house; but, finally, also for Israel when, at some future time,[11] the anger of God shall bring about its defeat and, in complete, heartfelt repentance, it will pray from its exile, turned toward this land and toward this house. And he concludes with the plea to God that He then forgive the people. "For they are Thy people, and Thine inheritance (*nahalah*), which Thou broughtest forth out of Egypt, from the midst of the furnace of iron. . . . For Thou didst set them apart from among all the peoples of the earth, to be Thine inheritance, as Thou didst speak by the hand of Moses Thy servant, when Thou broughtest our fathers out of Egypt, O Lord God!" (I Kings 8:51 ff.). The Solomonic speech—unlike the Davidic—recognizes as well the sinfulness of the people, "all their transgressions, wherein they have transgressed against Thee" (verse 50); but that does not imply the people's breaking the covenant between God and people, rather only general and unavoidable human sinfulness, "for there is no man that sinneth not" (verse 46).

The fourth chapter of Deuteronomy, in particular, answers both speeches, providing significant correction and completion. At first it sounds like an antiphony to David's prayer: "For what great nation (*goy*) is there, that hath God so nigh unto them, as the Lord our God is whensoever we call upon Him!" (Deut. 4:7). But immediately thereafter we have what is missing in the king's speech: "And what great nation is there, that hath statutes and ordinances so righteous as all this law." Then a Solomonic motif appears: "But you hath the Lord taken and brought forth out of the iron furnace, out of Egypt, to be unto Him a people of inheritance" (4:20). But here, too, there follows the corrective completion: "Take heed unto yourselves, lest ye forget the covenant of the Lord your God, which He made with you!" (4:23). And again it sounds like an antiphony to David's prayer: "Or hath God assayed to go and take Him a nation from the midst of another nation . . . according to all that the Lord your God did for you in Egypt!" (4:34). But again what is missing there is here expressed: "thou shalt keep His statutes, and His commandments!" (4:40). There is no security in the covenant if it is not fulfilled; God is a devouring fire (4:24). Israel is chosen only when it realizes the election by its life as a community.

Here, too, it is a prophet who expresses the message in its ultimate, historically true form. The time is after the fateful battle at Megiddo; the leaders comfort the people by reference to the Temple as unconditional security for the life of the people. Jeremiah, who on other occasions was accustomed to preach in the marketplace, enters the court of the Temple on a solemn holiday and delivers his speech against the Temple to the surprised people and priesthood (Jer. 7:1–15; cf. 26:1–6). They come to the Sanctuary from all their wicked dealing and trust in the fact that God's name is called upon this house—thus certainly no evil can befall them! But God grants no security. If the house wherein His name dwells has become a robbers' den and there is no repentance, then it will be given over to destruction, as once in the days of the Judges, at a time when sin was ripe, He gave the sanctuary of Shiloh over to destruction: "And I will cast you out of my sight" (Jer. 7:15). Only He who has chosen can thus cast away. Soon the cry will resound: "Is the Lord no longer in Zion? Is her king no longer in her?" (Jer. 8:19). God, the King of Israel, leaves His throne and abandons it to destruction because Israel has not taken His kingdom seriously. It has known only the King's protective power and not submission of its own lived communal life to the truth of the King's covenant. But Israel is elected only when it realizes its election.

And yet—this is the consoling paradox of our existence —the Rejector can never cease being the Elector. One day God will make a new covenant with the house of Israel which will overcome the contradiction of their stubborn or indolent hearts. "I will put my law in their inward parts, and in their heart will I write it; and I will be their God, and they shall be my people" (Jer. 31:33).

THE WORDS ON THE TABLETS

(EXODUS 20)

C ERTAIN excerpts from a "Theosophia," presumably written by an Alexandrian of the fifth century A.D.,[1] have come down to us. In these we are told, among many other memorabilia, that Moses had actually written two decalogues. The first and hence older of them reads, "For their altars ye shall smash, their pillars ye shall break, their sacred poles ye shall cut down," and so on. This refers, of course, to Exodus 34:13–26, out of which it would be possible to construct ten commandments, though with a certain amount of difficulty. The second is the Decalogue of tradition, Exodus 20:2–17. To give this view expression in modern scientific terminology, it means that Moses preceded his "ethical" decalogue with an earlier, "cultic" one, which starts polemically and then goes on to various prescriptions. That the commencement proposed by the author, which begins with "their" and refers to the peoples already mentioned, cannot be any real commencement, was apparently not noticed by him.

In a dissertation on the Tablets of Moses, prepared with "indescribable toil," which the University of Strasbourg rejected, Goethe undertook to prove "that the Ten Commandments were not actually the covenantal laws of the Israelites." A year and a half later he returned to this thesis in a little paper entitled "Two important and hitherto unclarified biblical questions thoroughly dealt with for the first time by a country priest in Swabia." In this paper he has his country priest offer a view largely identical with that finding expres-

sion in the "Theosophia," which was unknown to Goethe. He
begins, however, with the sentence "Thou shalt worship no
other God," which might indeed be the starting-point for a
decalogue. Goethe sets out to overcome the "troublesome
old error" that the covenant "by which God pledged Himself
to Israel" could "be based on universal obligations." What
is regarded by us as the Decalogue is only "the introduction
to the legislation" which, in the view of the Swabian village
pastor, contains doctrines "that God presupposed in His people as human beings and Israelites." Behind this, however,
lies Goethe's actual idea, though not without some contradiction of what has been said: that the history and doctrine of
the people of Israel had a particularist and not a universal
character until the time when Christianity was grafted on to
its stem. Some decades later, in his Notes and Studies to the
West-Oestlicher Diwan, Goethe declared that he had endeavored to separate "what would be fitting to all lands, to
all moral people" from that "which especially concerns and
is binding on the people of Israel." He did not specify this
separation in any greater detail; in any case, however, his
views as they find expression in his early work remain a pace
behind those of his masters Johann Georg Hamann and
Herder, who recognized in that particularism the earthly ve-
hicle without which nothing universal can achieve earthly life.

A century after the "Two Questions" Julius Wellhausen, who was long followed and in wide circles still is followed
without restriction in critical Bible study, undertook to prove
the priority of the "Goethean Law of the Two Tablets" by
means of a comprehensive critical analysis of sources. Exodus 20 and 34, he held, are diametrically opposed. "There
the commandments are almost only moral, here they are exclusively ritual." [2] And obviously, in accordance with a view
still prevalent in our own days, the ritual one must be older
and in fact original. The Decalogue of Exodus 20 accordingly appears to be influenced by the prophetic protest
against ritualism, whereas that of Exodus 34 would mirror
the primitive pan-sacralism of the Moses epoch, though after
a fashion conditioned by the setting actually found in Canaan.

If we consider this so-called "cultic" decalogue without

prejudice, we find that it is not a complete whole in itself like the "ethical" one, but consists of a compilation of appendices and complements; chiefly, further, such as would comprehensibly derive from a transition to regular agriculture and the civilization associated therewith. Most of them, supplements almost exclusively, are also to be found in the same or an analogous form in the so-called "Book of the Covenant" (Exod. 20:22–23:19). The complements, on the other hand, in no case refer to the laws of this book, but only to those which are found either in the "Ethical Decalogue" itself or else in prescriptions to be found earlier in the text. Thus the provisions for the sacrifice or redemption of the animal first-born (13:11 ff.) are extended to horned cattle (cf. 22:29). Two characteristic complements to Exodus 20 are provided: the prohibition of images, which in that context has as its subject only such as are hewn and carved (this still remains to be shown), is extended there to molten images (34:17), while the commandment of Sabbath rest is rendered more stringent by being made applicable even to the seasons of ploughing and harvesting, the times of most pressing work in the fields. From all this it may reasonably be concluded that this compilation was younger than the Decalogue in its original form. It has therefore been justly described more recently as a "secondary mixed form" [3]; save that it may certainly be considered as older than the redaction of the "Book of the Covenant" in our possession, since it assuredly did not borrow the doublets from the latter. Still, the selection was clearly made in accordance with a specific attitude, so that we may well assume to have before us the "House-book of a Palestinian Sanctuary," [4] prepared from old material.

Critical research of the Wellhausen school has for the greater part not, or only inadequately, recognized the real character of this composition. In general it has not ceased to stress its "great age" and the "influence of the foundation of the religion of Moses" [5] that finds expression in it; as against which the date of the Decalogue was shifted into ever later times, until the assumption was made that it could belong only to the exilic or postexilic age[6]; and must in fact constitute the catechism of the religious and moral duties of Israel in exile[7]; and that as such it must be "a product of the religious needs of Israel in exile." [8] Supporters of a more moderate point of view still found it necessary to explain that the Ten Commandments were "both impossible and superfluous for archaic Israel." [9]

As against this negative self-certainty, the past three decades have seen the emergence of the feeling that it is necessary to examine the situation once again, and irrespective of all preconceptions and theories.

For the greater part the argument had been conducted on the basis of single commandments, which were held to be incompatible with the social and cultural, moral and literary conditions of the early period; to which the protagonists of the Mosaic origin of the Decalogue had replied by characterizing the passages that were questionable in respect of content and language as later supplements, and in turn laid bare an incontestably original decalogue. Now, however, the stress is being shifted to an increasing degree from the parts to the whole.

The thesis of the impossibility of such high ethical standards in those days lost its force when the publication and translation of Egyptian and Babylonian texts led to the dissemination of information regarding, and appreciation of, a reality in the history of the human mind which has received the name of the Ancient Oriental Moral Code, but which might rather be regarded as the ancient oriental tendency to commingle cultic prohibitions and postulates with those of a moral kind. In those texts that have become best known and are also most characteristic, a confession of the dead before the Judges of the Dead found in the Egyptian "Book of the Dead" (deriving from the period in which the exodus from Egypt took place), and a "catalogue of sins" from the Babylonian conjuration tablets, the moral part is the greater by far[10]; and this fact is quite sufficient in itself to break down the general assumption that cult necessarily preceded ethics. But even if we turn our attention to the so-called primitive races and read, say, the tribal lore of an East African tribe,[11] which the elders pass on to adolescents about to be admitted into the community, we observe that their real concern is with the correct relations between the members of a family, the members of a clan; and furthermore the important fact of the repeated stressing that this is the will of the god, of the "Heaven Man." The most thoroughgoing opponents of a Mosaic origin for the Decalogue therefore no longer reject the possibility that Moses may have proclaimed moral commandments such as those to be found in the Decalogue. "The moral commandments of the Decalogue," says one of these opponents,[12] "belong to those basic laws with which even the most primitive of societies cannot dispense."

So the question at issue is now held to be whether Moses could have regarded the moral commandments "as the totality of the basic prescriptions of religion," and whether he really presented "the *collection* of these commandments as the religious and moral norm par excellence," which, however, "would appear improbable and unthinkable in the highest degree, according to the evidence of the sources." "The question," says another critic,[13] "is not whether Moses could have established certain individual religious and moral demands with this content, but whether Moses, taking into consideration all that we otherwise know of his religious attitude, can be believed to have been capable of compressing the basic demands of religiousness and morality in this Decalogue, while excluding from it all the other motives which at the time were of importance in religious and moral life; whether he can be supposed to have done this with a genius which would find its parallel only in Jesus and which, indeed, would needs have been far greater in the case of Moses, who stands at the beginning of religious development, than in that of Jesus."

What is meant by the words "all that we otherwise know of his religious attitude" in this context is explained as follows: from the material of the most ancient sagas we received quite a different picture of the personality of Moses than that which we must assume in order to comprehend the Decalogue as having been his work. "Moses the sorcerer, the healer, the dispenser of oracles, the Faustian magician is a different figure from the man who summarized the essence of piety and morality in the few lapidary sentences of the Decalogue." But quite irrespective of the basic problem, regarding which it is possible to hold very different views, as to which, namely, are the oldest sagas, and even assuming that in these Moses appears as a thaumaturgist and the like—what conclusions could be drawn from this? On the same page of a book to which the scholar just quoted refers, we first read: "Moses the Faustian magician is an entirely believable figure of the steppes," and thereafter, "the deeds of the ancient heroes were already felt by their contemporary world as wonders and enchantments, and those heroes themselves may likewise easily have regarded them in the same way." [14] That Moses himself experienced and understood many of his own actual deeds, particularly the decisive ones, as "wonders," or more correctly as deeds of his God performed through him, is obvious; which, however, does not transform him into a "Faustian magician," but if anything into the contrary; while the idea that he himself regarded anything he did as "sorcery" seems to me to lie beyond all proof. In legend, to be sure, and to some degree even in the legend that blossomed in the minds and memories of those who were present, something of the kind may have taken place—clearly under the influence of Egyptian conceptions[15]; those people, thirsting for miracle, whose remolding memory allowed them to remember events as they did not occur and could not have occurred, were prepared to transform God Himself into a sorcerer, and with Him His messenger. The same process was doubtless at work, and very early at that, in the legend of Jesus. It was not enough to glorify his healings; the legend set him also walking on the sea, giving his commands to the winds and turning water into wine. Great is the work of the Saga, and as ever it still thrills our heart[16]; that, however, should not prevent us from penetrating wherever possible beyond the veil of legend and, as far as we can, viewing the pure form which it conceals.

In this nothing helps us so much, with Moses as with Jesus and others, as those utterances that, by use of criteria other than a general judgment derived from the saga material about the "religious attitude" of a person, may properly be attributed to that specific man with whom we deal. There is certainly no doubt that Moses took over archaic rites that were charged with magical meaning. Yet, as we have seen in the case of the Passover, the Sabbath, and the Blood Covenant, he brought about a fundamental transformation of meaning in them without in this way depriving them of any of their vitality, but rather while rejuvenating this very vitality by transmuting it from a nature vitality to a historical one. The change in meaning he introduced was drawn by him from the same ground of faith, the same kind and power of faith, that was given imperishable form in the first three of the Ten Commandments. It is not hard to understand, when one has at length touched this ground of faith, that Moses worded these and specifically these basic demands—no less but likewise no more—and fashioned them into a unity.

An attempt must be made, however, to render the situation even more clear in its details.

What the critics have been arguing more recently against the Mosaic origin of the Decalogue refers, as has been said, not to the content of the individual commandments but to their elevation to the level of fundamentals of religion; or, I would prefer to say, to fundamentals of community life under the rule of God. This has been demonstrated with particular impressiveness in connection with the prohibition of statues and images; nor can we choose any better example in order to elucidate the actual facts.

One of the most radical of critics has admitted [17] that the iconoclastic movement in later Israel may with some justification have referred itself to Moses. As among the ancient Arabs and in the early days of the Semitic cultures in general, art does not appear to have been put to use in the cult practices. We know that the pre-Islamic Arabs[18] were beginning to convert stones to images of gods by bringing out a natural resemblance, say to a human head, with the aid of art. Between this primitive cultural situation and the later tendencies directed against images of the god, there lay the essential difference that the primitive Semites regarded their imageless cult as a natural usage, whereas it constituted a program of reform for the later ones. What is natural would not require to be fixed by any separate or special commandment. The cult in which absence of images is a principle

could therefore, it is claimed, not derive from the days of
Moses.

    Edvard Lehmann has justly pointed out[19] that it is often
difficult to decide whether a cult is imageless because it does
not yet require images or because it no longer requires them.
But there are historically important constellations in which
the appearance of a great personality during the pre-image
period anticipates the highest teachings of the post-image period in a simple form that cannot be improved upon.

    We must first realize that matters are by no means sim-
ple as regards the pre-image stage in Mosaic Israel, if we assume that the latter was under Egyptian influence; not as
regards the belief in some gods or other, but in respect of the
custom of making images of the gods believed in. If this was
indeed the case, a conflict must necessarily have come about
between those who could not or did not wish to break down
this influence, and those who wished to eradicate it. If, however, we assume that the unabbreviated wording of the "prohibition of images" is of early date (I mean that, although
only verse 4a belongs to the original text, the rest of the verse
has been added very early), the prospects continue to ex-
pand before us, seeing that in that case we have before us
more than a prohibition of images. For that prohibition is
followed by a prohibition of the worship of any of the figures
that could be perceived in the heavens, on the earth, or in
the water ("And every figure that . . . and that . . . and
that . . . , bow not down before them and serve them not").
In Egypt the great national gods appeared in the forms of
beasts and other natural beings. Hence, once the "other
gods" have been excluded in verse 3, there is an implicit prohibition of worshipping YHVH Himself in an image or in one
of the natural forms.

    We penetrate even deeper when we base our viewpoint
on what we know of the God of Israel.

    Originally He was what has been called a "god of
way," [20] but He differed in character from all the other gods
of way. The function of a god of way, who accompanies and
protects the wandering nomads and the caravans through
the wilderness, was exercised in Mesopotamia by the moon,

the god "who opens the way," and his assistants. In Syria it was the evening star who served this purpose. (Characteristically enough such a god of way of the Nabataeans, whose name meant roughly "He who accompanies the tribe," was apparently considered by Epiphanius to be the deified Moses.[21]) It is assuredly something more than a mere coincidence that the name of the city of Haran, which together with Ur was the chief city of the moon cult and in which Abraham separated from his clan, meant way or caravan, and would appear to have designated the spot "where the caravans met and from which they started out." [22] The God by whom Abraham, after "straying away" from Haran, is led in his wanderings, differs from all solar, lunar, and stellar divinities, apart from the fact that He guides only Abraham and His own group,[23] by the further fact that He is not regularly visible in the heavens, but only occasionally permits Himself to be seen by His chosen—whenever and wherever it is His will to do so. This necessarily implies that various natural things and processes are on occasion regarded as manifestations of the God, and that it is impossible to know for certain where or wherein He will next appear.

It may be supposed and is readily understood that among the Hebrew tribes resident in Egypt the guiding function of the ancient clan God had been forgotten. But this clearly is what revives within the spirit of Moses in Midian when he meditates upon the possibility of bringing forth the tribes. The God who meets him wishes to resume His guiding function, but for "His people" now. With His words, "I shall be present howsoever I shall be present," He describes Himself as the One who is not restricted to any specific manner of manifestation, but permits Himself to be seen from time to time by those He leads and, in order to lead them, to be seen by them after the fashion He prefers at the given moment.[24]

Thus it can be understood that clouds, and smoke, and fire, and all kinds of visual phenomena are interpreted by Moses as manifestations from which he has to decide as to the further course through the wilderness—as to the whither and the how. But always, and that is the fundamental characteristic, YHVH remains the invisible One, who only permits Himself to be seen in the flame, in "the very heavens," in the flash of the lightning. Admittedly anthropomorphic manifestations also alternate with these; but none of them shows an unequivocally clear-cut figure with which YHVH might be identified.

For this reason He should not be imaged, that is, limited to any one definite form; nor should He be equated to one or other of the "figures" in nature, that is, restricted to any one definite manifestation. He is the history God, which He is only when He is not localized in nature—and precisely because He makes use of everything potentially visible in nature, every kind of natural existence, for His manifestation. The prohibition of "images" and "figures" was absolutely necessary for the establishment of His rule, for the investiture of His absoluteness before all current "other gods."

No later hour in history required this with such force; every later period that combated images could do nothing more than renew the ancient demand. What was immediately opposed to the founder-will of Moses makes no difference: whether the memories of the great Egyptian sculptures or the clumsy attempts of the people themselves to create, by means of some slight working of wood or stone, a reliable form in which the Divinity could be taken with them. Moses certainly saw himself as facing a contrary tendency, namely that natural and powerful tendency which can be found in all religions, from the most crude to the most sublime, to reduce the Divinity to a form available for and identifiable by the senses. The fight against this is not a fight against art, which would certainly contrast with the report of Moses' initiative in carving the images of the cherubim; it is a fight to subdue the revolt of fantasy against faith. This conflict is to be found again, in more or less clear-cut fashion, at the decisive early hours, the plastic hours, of every "founded" religion, that is, of every religion born from the meeting of a human person and the mystery. Moses more than anybody who followed him in Israel must have established the principle of the "imageless cult," or more correctly of the imageless presence of the Invisible, who permits Himself to be seen.[25]

Thus in the case of the sentence whose antiquity has been the most strongly disputed, we have shown that the roots of these commandments and prohibitions derive from a specific time and situation. However, this leaves open the decisive question as to whether the whole Decalogue as such, as collection and composition, can be explained in terms of this specific time and situation; whether it can be assumed that Moses separated and unified precisely these phrases as an absolute norm, out of the wealth of existent or nascent sentences regarding the right and the unright, regarding what should be and what should not be, while excluding all cultic elements.

First we once again meet the argument of "primitivity," although in attenuated form. It is claimed [26] that at the Mosaic epoch the religion of Israel could not have possessed tendencies such as would have permitted the manifestation of a "catechism," in which the cult is consciously thrust into the background and the main content of the religion is reduced to purely ethical sentences. An assumption that this could have occurred is said to be based on "a lack of understanding of both the mentality and the civilization of the Mosaic epoch." [27] The "prelogical" thinking of those times is supposed to have included the primacy of the "sacral system"; for "in his religion and the practice of his cult primitive man has the means of producing everything that he needs badly." [28] And in this sense even "the loftiest efflorescence of Egyptian culture" is regarded as primitive.

The use of such a concept of primitivity leads to a questionable simplification of religious history. Religions as complexes of popular practices and traditions are more or less "primitive" at all times and among all peoples. The inner conflict for faith, for the personally experienced reality, is non-primitive in all religions. A religious change, an interior transformation which also alters the structure, never takes place, however, without an internal conflict. Particularly as far as the religion of Israel is concerned, we cannot compre-

hend its ways and changes at all unless we pay attention to
the inner dialectic, to the struggle, ever recurrent at various
stages and in various forms, for the truth of belief, for revelation.

That this conflict began at the time of Moses, and indeed that he waged the primal fight from which everything
subsequent, including the great protests of the prophets
against a cult emptied of intention, can find only its starting-
point is proved, even though generally in legendary form, by
the great and small stories that tell of the "murmuring," the
rebellion, the insurrection; and in most of which we recognize or sense the presence of a religious problem in the background. The people wish for a tangible security, they wish to
"have" the God, they wish to have Him at their disposal
through a sacral system; and it is this security that Moses
cannot and must not grant them.

This, however, should not in any way be taken to mean
that Moses had "founded a clear and conscious anti-cultic
religion" [29]; that is, a religion directed against the cult. Nothing is so likely to interfere with a historical cognition, which
is one not of categories but of facts, as the introduction of
alternatives formulated in so extreme a fashion. There can
be no talk here of simple rejection of the cult. It is quite
enough to bear in mind, to begin with, that a seminomadic
life does not encourage a high degree of cult practices and
institutions; here in particular there is clearly a very ancient
tendency "to place morality above the cult." [30] Further, it
should also be remembered that all those elements that were
liable to militate against the exclusive service of YHVH have
been eliminated. For what remained there was need of a
change not of form, but only of sense and content, in order to
satisfy the purpose of Moses. The sacral principle remained;
but the sacral assurance, the sacral power of utilizing
the God, was uprooted—as was demanded by His character and essence. This sacral power was replaced by the
consecration of men and things, of times and places, to the
One who vouchsafes His presence amid His chosen people,
if only the latter persevere in the Royal Covenant.

And why are there no cultic ordinances in the Deca-

logue? Why is it that in the domain of cult nothing more is
done than the prohibition of the false—not the prescription
of the correct—deeds? Why is the prescription of circumcision not to be found? Why is Sabbath observance required,
but not that of the New Moon festival? Why the Sabbath but
not the Passover? Does not this, for instance, indicate a late
origin, seeing that in exile, far from the Temple, the Sabbath
came to be the center of religious life?

All these and similar questions taken together mean:
Why does the Decalogue contain these precise commandments, these and none other, no more and no less? Why have
these been joined together as the norm, and where in those
early days could the principle be found in accordance with
which the association took place? Naturally this question
also comprehends the analogous questions that arise within
the ethical field, such as: Is it possible to suppose that in the
time of Moses there could have been a prohibition of "covet-
ing," which, in contrast to all the other prohibitions, was
aimed not at action but at a state of mind? Or on the other
hand, why is there no prohibition of lying? [31]

It is desirable to offer a single and comprehensive answer to all these questions; and necessarily that answer will
have to deal with both selection and composition. Hence the
literary category as such must be a subject of interest. Why
should there be a decalogue or anything resembling a decalogue? Why these ten commandments and no others? Why,
which in turn means: to what end? To what end, and that in
turn means: when?

In order to find an answer we must first disabuse ourselves of the widely-held view that the Decalogue is a "catechism" which supplies the essence of the Israelite religion in
summary fashion, in articles of faith that can be counted on
the ten fingers, and are specially "prepared for learning by
heart." [32] If we have to think of ten fingers, then rather those
of the law-giver himself, who was first a law-finder and who,
so to say, sees in his two hands an image of the completeness
requisite ere he raise those two hands toward the multitude.
We miss the essential point if we understand the Decalogue
to be "the catechism of the Hebrews in the Mosaic pe-

riod." [33] A catechism means an instruction for the person
who has to be in a position to demonstrate his full membership of a religious community on the basis of general sentences which he recites either in complete or in abbreviated
form. Such a catechism is correspondingly prepared partly
in the third person as a series of statements, and partly in the
first as a series of articles of personal faith.

The soul of the Decalogue, however, is to be found in
the word "thou." Here nothing is either stated or confessed;
but orders are given to the one addressed, to the listener. In
distinction to all catechisms and compositions resembling
catechisms, everything here has reference to that specific hour
in which the words were spoken and heard. It is possible
that only the man who wrote down the words had once had
the experience of feeling himself addressed; possibly he
transmitted that which he heard to his people not orally, taking the "I" of the god in his own mouth as though it were his
own, but only in written form, preserving the necessary distance. At all times, in any case, only those persons really
grasped the Decalogue who literally felt it as having been
addressed to themselves; only those, that is, who experienced
that original state of being addressed as an address to
themselves. Thanks to its "thou," the Decalogue means the
preservation of the divine voice.

And if we now no longer formulate the question from
the point of view of literary criticism but in accordance with
strictly historical categories, the Decalogue again shows its
difference in kind, its antithesis in fact to all catechisms. It is
both legislation and promulgation, in the precise historical
sense. What this means is that the intention to be recognized
in it refers neither to articles of faith nor to rules of behavior,
but to the constituting of a community by means of common
regulation. This state of affairs has been obscured through
the fact that the contents of the single commandments are
partly "religious" and partly "ethical," and that if the single
commandments are considered on their own they seem, even
in their totality, to be directed toward the religious and ethical
life of the individual, and appear to be capable of realization there. Only when the Ten Commandments are consid-

ered as a whole can it be recognized that, no matter how
repeatedly the individual alone is addressed, it is nevertheless
not the isolated individual who is meant. If the "religious"
commandments are taken by themselves and the "ethical" by
themselves, it is almost possible to gain the impression that
they derived from a culture in which religion and morality
have already become separate spheres, each with a special
system and a special form of speech. If they are regarded in
their connection, it will be observed that there are no such
separate fields at all here, but only one as yet undifferentiated common life, which requires a constitution containing
"religious" and "ethical" elements in order to achieve a uniform growth.

Here the unifying force has to start from the conception
of a divine Lord. The disparate material out of which the
people develop shapes itself into a closed national form as a
result of their common relation to Him. Only as the people
of YHVH can Israel come into being and remain in being. The
constitution appears not as something objective, to be taken
at its own intrinsic value, but as an allocution by Him, a
thing that can be actualized only in and through a living relationship with Him. It therefore begins by His designation
of Himself as the One who brought forth and liberated Israel, including each and every person addressed in Israel.
God does not wish to speak as the Lord of the world that He
is (Exod. 19:5b), but as the One who has led them forth
from Egypt. He wishes to find recognition in the concrete
reality of that historic hour; it is from that starting-point that
the people have to accept His rule.

This calls for and conditions a threefold commandment
through a threefold prohibition. First: a commandment of an
exclusive relationship of worship by means of the prohibition
of other gods "in my face." Secondly: a commandment of
self-dedication to His invisible but nevertheless manifesting
presence, by means of a prohibition of all sensory representations. Thirdly: a commandment of faith to His name as the
truly "Present One" through the prohibition of carrying that
name over to any kind of "illusion," [34] and thus of admitting
that any kind whatsoever of illusive thing can participate in

the presence of the Present One. This, to be sure, prohibits idol-worship, image-worship, and magic-worship. But the essential reason for which they have been prohibited is the exclusive recognition of the exclusive rule of the divine lord, the exclusive leadership of the divine leader; and to this end it is necessary to recognize Him as He is, and not in the shape with which people would like to endow Him.

This first part of the Decalogue, which bases the life of the community on the rule of the Lord, is built up in five phrases, all beginning "Thou shalt not" (the two phrases beginning with "for" appear to be later supplements). If the final verse of the third section is restored to an original shorter version, it can be seen to consist likewise of five phrases beginning "Thou shalt not." (We therefore, to be precise, have a group of twelve commandments before us.) Between these two groups comes a central section containing the commandment of the Sabbath and the commandment to honor parents (in shorter versions), both commencing with a positive injunction. The first, a "religious" one, refers back to what went before; the second as "ethical" refers ahead to those that follow.

Between the two of them, however, there is a connection other than the purely formal one. The two of them, and only these two among all of the Ten Commandments, deal with *time,* articulated time; the first with the closed succession of weeks in the year, the second with the open succession of generations in national duration. Time itself is introduced into the constitutional foundation of national life by being partly articulated in the lesser rhythm of the weeks, and partly realized in its given articulation through the greater rhythm of the generations. The former requirement is provided for through the repeated "remembering" of the Sabbath day as that which has been consecrated to YHVH; and the latter by the "honoring" of the parents. Both of them together ensure the continuity of national time: the never-to-be-interrupted consecution of consecration, the never-to-be-broken consecution of tradition.

There is no room here for the mention of special individual festivals alongside the Sabbath. The Sabbath represents the equal measure, the regular articulation of the year; and further, one that is not simply taken over from nature, that is not strictly lunar, but is based on the concept of the regular consecration of every seventh day. It is not the exceptional, not that which has to be done only at certain times and on certain occasions, but that which is of all time, that which is valid at all times, for which alone place must be found in the basic constitution. The cult is not in any way excluded, but only its general prerequisite postulates, as they are expressed in the first part of the Decalogue, and not its details, have found acceptance here in accordance with the main purpose.

If the first part deals with the *God* of the community and the second with the *time,* the one-after-the-other of the community, the third is devoted to the *space,* the with-one-another of the community insofar as it establishes a norm for the mutual relations between its members. There are four things above all that have to be protected, in order that the community may stand firm in itself. They are life, marriage, property, and social honor. And so the damaging of these four basic goods and basic rights of personal existence is forbidden in the most simple and pregnant of formulas. In the case of the first three the verb does not even possess any object, as a result of which the impression is given of a comprehensive and absolute prescription.

But these four commandments in themselves are not enough to protect the community from disorganization, on account of all the kinds of inner conflicts which might break out. They apply only to actions, to the active outcome of passions or feelings of ill-will directed against the personal sphere of other people; they do not involve attitudes that have not passed into action.

There is one attitude, however, that destroys the inner connection of the community even when it does not transform itself into actual action; and which indeed, precisely on account of its passive or semipassive persistence, may become a consuming disease of a special kind in the body politic. This is the attitude of envy. The prohibition of "covetousness," no matter whether it was without any object in its original form[35] or it read, "do not covet the house—i.e., the content of the personal life in general, household, property, and prestige—of your fellow man," is to be understood as a prohibition of envy. The point here is not merely a feeling of the heart but an attitude of one man to another that leads to a decomposition of the very tissues of society. The third part of the Decalogue can be summarized in its basic tendency as: Do not spoil the communal life of Israel at the point upon which you are placed.

Since, as we have seen, it is the will toward inner stability of the community that determined the selection of commandments and prohibitions, we must, if the Decalogue is ascribed to a later period, necessarily note the absence of some phrase reading more or less as follows: "Do not oppress thy fellow man." In a community that was being broken up from within, as we know was the case during the period of the kings in Israel, by a vast increase of social inequality, by the misuse of the power of property in order to gain possession of smaller properties, by the exploitation of the strength of the economically weaker and dependent; in a community wherein, generation after generation, rang the great protest of the prophets, no central and authoritative collection of the laws indispensable for the inner strengthening of the community could have been thinkable that did not expressly combat social injustice. It is appropriate to a period in which, to be sure, inequality of property is already to be found, but in which, taking the whole situation into account, that inequality does not yet lead to any fateful misuses, so that the immediately obvious danger deriving from it is envy and not oppression.

But we can fix the period in question even more precisely. Within the individual clan and even the individual tribe there had always been, as we are also aware from other Semitic peoples, a solidarity that interdicted and directly punished every transgression of a member against the personal sphere of life of another. What was lacking in wandering Israel, fused together of related and unrelated elements, and joined on its wanderings by other elements, was a sense of solidarity among the tribes. What Israel needed was the extension of its tribal solidarity to the nation. The members of each separate tribe knew "thou shalt not kill," "thou shalt not commit adultery," "thou shalt not steal"; they had them deeply engraved in their consciousness in respect of other members of their own tribe. An analogous "Israelite" consciousness, however, had hardly begun to come into being. The constituting of a people out of clans and tribes, which Moses undertook, made the expansion of the specific tribal prohibitions to the relations between the components of the people as a whole an unconditional necessity. At no later period was the need so urgent as at this plastic and fateful hour, in which it was necessary to build the "House of Israel" out of unequally suited, unequally cut stones. A wandering into the unknown had begun under the most difficult external circumstances. Before that wandering could be given a destination it was necessary to shape, no matter in how raw and clumsy a fashion, a folk-character that would have the capacity, as a homogeneous being, to follow a road to a destination. This, in turn, indispensably required the proclamation of a basic constitution founded on the principles of unlimited rule of the one God, equable duration of Israel throughout the changes of years and generations, and the inner cohesion of those members of Israel living as contemporaries at any one period.

The situation of Moses has been compared, not unjustly,[36] with that of Hammurabi, who made his code in order to establish a strong unity among all the city communities of his kingdom, despite their many and varied customs and laws. But Hammurabi was the victorious ruler of a firmly established kingdom; Moses was the leader of an inchoate, stubborn horde during the transition of that horde from a lack of freedom into a problematic freedom.

Admittedly we must not imagine Moses as a planning, selecting and composing legislator directed by certain motives of "biological social necessity"; for his consciousness as for that of his successors in the work of codification, admittedly, "only the demand of the law was decisive, in order to manifest divine commands that are of absolute authority." [37] But here we are not justified in attempting to discriminate too precisely between conscious and unconscious processes. Moses can only be understood as deriving from the terrain of an elemental unity between religion and society. He undertook the paradoxical task of leading forth the Hebrew tribes only because he had been possessed, in his direct experience, by the certainty that this was the will of the God who called those tribes His People. He aims at nothing else than to prepare the community for this God, who has declared that He is ready to be their covenantal Lord; but, and for that very reason, he must provide Israel with a basic constitution, in order to make Israel united and firm in itself. For him God's dominion over the people and the inner cohesion of the people are only two aspects of the same reality. From out of those words, "I, YHVH, am thy God who brought thee out of the land of Egypt," which flood into his expectant spirit, gush forth all the remaining ones in a stream that is not to be stayed; and as they gush they gain their strict order and form. To be sure, he is not concerned with the soul of man, he is concerned with Israel; but he is concerned with Israel for the sake of YHVH. For this reason all those who came after him in Israel, and were concerned with the soul of man, had to start from his law.

Thus, in so far as any historical conclusions are at all permissible from texts such as those before us, we have to recognize in the Decalogue "the constitution by which the host of Moses became united with their God and likewise among themselves" [38]; save that this host should not, as sometimes happens, be understood to be a "religious" union, a "Yahveh League," [39] a cult association,[40] a "congregation" [41]; for, despite their deliquescent state, reminiscent as it is of a saturated solution before crystallization, they are a complete society, a people that is coming into being. It is a "unique event in human history" [42] that the decisive process of crystallization in the development of a people should have come about on a religious basis. Irrespective of the importance of the typological view of phenomena in the history of the spirit, the latter, just because it is history, also contains the atypical, the unique in the most precise sense. This is true

particularly of the religious document of that crystalloid uni-
fication: of the "Decalogue."

It has been supposed [43] that, in spite of the fact that the
original short form to be laid bare within it "contains nothing which speaks against its composition at the time of
Moses," nevertheless "it is impossible to trace it back to
Moses himself, because in its literary style every decalogue
is impersonal." But do we really know so much of "decalogues" in general that we have to subject this one to a typological view in order to discover what is possible and what is
impossible in respect of it? All other sections of the Pentateuch and other books of the Bible, which it has been the
practice to describe as decalogues, are either loose and, as
it were, accidental or else are of indubitably literary origin;
this one alone is fully self-consistent in its nucleus and aims
at the mark like a perfect instrument, each word charged
with the dynamism of a historical situation. We cannot under any condition regard something of this kind as an "impersonal" piece of writing but, if at all, only as the work of
that particular man upon whom it was incumbent to master
the situation. This may be a hypothesis; it is undoubtedly the
only one that affords us what is requisite: namely, to insert a
combination of words found in literature into a sequence of
events such as would be possible within history.

A demand is voiced, and quite properly, to ascertain
what "position in life" such a text may have had; which
means, more or less, at which celebration it was likely to
have been regularly read aloud. Even more important, however, than the question of that which is regularly recurrent,
namely, of the reality of the calendar, is that of the first time,
that of the reality of innovation. This too can be answered
only by hypothesis and assumption; but it can be answered.

If we attempt to gain the view of a sequence of events
from the texts we have sifted, it is first necessary, despite
everything that may appear to speak in its favor, to reject
the theory that "the Decalogue was the document on the
basis of which the Covenant was made." [44] The concept of
the document in the making of the Covenant appears to me

to be secondary, and to have derived from the fact that the Covenant was misunderstood at a later period as the conclusion of a contract. In any case, however, the Decalogue has the Covenant not as its subject, but as a prerequisite condition.

In a message which must underlie our Eagle Speech, but which cannot be reconstructed from it, Moses brings to his rank and file, as he had already brought to the elders, YHVH's offer to establish the *berith,* which would unite both of them, the God and the human host, into a living community; in which YHVH would be the *melekh* and Israel His *mamlakhah,* His regal retinue, YHVH would be the owner and Israel the special personal property chosen by Him, YHVH would be the hallowing leader and Israel the *goy* hallowed by Him, the national body made holy through Him. These are concepts I take out of the version before us, but which must already have been either contained or latent in an undifferentiated form in the original source, if the latter was to fulfill its function.

The host accepts the offer; and in the blood rite which had already begun earlier, and wherein the two partners share in the identical living substance, the Covenant by which YHVH becomes "*melekh* in Yeshurun" (Deut. 33:5) is concluded. The process is completed in the contemplation of the heavens and the holy meal. This might be the proper place for a report of the representative to those represented, in which the motto "Israel" was given out and taken up—a report that has not come down to us. What now has to follow sooner or later is the proclamation of the *melekh* YHVH. It is this that seems to me to be preserved in the "Decalogue" as restored to its original nucleus. Here YHVH tells the tribes united in "Israel" what has to be done and what left undone by them as Israel, and by each individual person in Israel (an induction into such a new and exclusive relationship will consist, naturally, for the greater part, in a prohibition of that which must henceforward be left undone), in order that a people, the people of YHVH which has to come into being, should come into being. In order that it should really become

His people it must really become a people, and vice versa.
The instruction to this is the Ten Commandments.

Whether this proclamation was made immediately after
the conclusion of the Covenant or only in the course of the
"many days" (Deut. 1:46) of the sojourning at the oasis of
Qadesh is a question that may be left open. It seems to me,
on the other hand, as already said, more likely both from the
introduction to the passage commencing "I," as well as from
the prose-like structure of the sentences, that the manifestation took place in written form. That it was written down on
two tables is a tradition that is worthy of belief. Tables or
stelæ with laws ascribed to the divinity are known to us both
from Babylon and from early Greece; as against which there
is not a single historical analogy,[45] to the best of my knowledge, for the frequently-assumed imaginary transformation
of stone fetishes, thought to have been kept in the Ark, into
tablets of the law. It may well be conceived that the tablets
on which Moses wrote in truly "lapidary" sentences the basic
constitution given by YHVH to His people "in order to instruct them"[46] were erected and again and again inspected
and read out; until the departure from that spot made it necessary to place them in the Ark.

The story of the tables as told in the Book of Exodus
consists of a series of tremendous scenes, which have always
aroused the fervent emotions of believing hearts. Moses summoned to the summit of the mountain in order to receive the
tables that YHVH Himself has written for the instruction of
the children of Israel (Exod. 24:12); Moses ascending into
God's cloud and remaining there for forty days and forty
nights (24:18); Moses receiving from God the "Tablets of
the Testimony" written by His finger (31:18); Moses on the
way down from the mountain becoming aware of the "un-
bridled" people, and in flaming fury flinging the tables away
from his hands, so that they smash below on the mountain-
side (32:19); Moses, at the command of YHVH, hewing two
fresh tables from the stone "like the first," in order that God
may write upon them again and again ascending the mountain with them (34:1, 4); Moses with the tables in his hand

receiving from the mouth of the God who "passes him by" the revelation of God's qualities (34:5 ff.); Moses again standing forty days and forty nights on the mountain without food and drink and writing on the tables "the words of the covenant, the ten words"; he and not YHVH, although YHVH had promised him to do this Himself, and hence, from the viewpoint and for the purpose of the redactor, who considered that the two passages were mutually reconcilable, functioning as the writing finger of YHVH (34:28); and Moses going down with the new tables, the skin of his face radiant from his contact with God, and he himself unaware of it (34:29).

If we wish to keep before us a sequence of events possible in our human world, we must renounce all such tremendous scenes. Nothing remains for us except the image, capable of being seen only in the barest outline and shading, of the man who withdraws to the loneliness of God's mountain, far from the people and overshadowed by God's cloud, in order to write God's law for the people. To this end he has hewn stelæ out of the stone for himself. It must be stone and not papyrus. For the hard stone is called to testify, to serve as a witness. It sees what there is to see, it hears what there is to hear; and it testifies thereto, makes present and contemporary for all coming generations that which it has to see and hear. The stone outlasts the decaying eyes and ears, and goes on speaking. In the same way Moses, before the Covenant was made, had erected twelve memorial stones— such as men making covenants were accustomed to erect (Gen. 31:45 ff.)—for the twelve tribes that were to become Israel at that hour.

Now, however, he goes further. After all, there is one means of placing a more comprehensive, clearer, verbally dependable witness upon the stone. That is the wondrous means of writing, which for early Israel was still surrounded by the mystery of its origin, by the breath of God, who makes a gift of it to men. By means of it one can embody in the stone what has been revealed to one, so that it is no longer simply an event, the making of the Covenant, but also, word by word, it continues to serve as evidence of a revelation, of the law of the King. What Moses says may be clumsy, but not what he writes; that is suitable for his time and for the later times in which the stone will testify.

And so he writes on the tables what has been introduced to his senses, in order that Israel may come about; and he writes it fittingly, as a finger of God. And the tables remain as "tables of the testimony" or "tables of making present" (Exod. 32:15),[47] whose function it is to make present unto the generations of Israel forever what had once become word; that is, to set it before them as something spoken to them in this very hour. It may well be assumed, although there is no tradition extant to this effect, that in the days before Samuel the tables were taken out of the Ark at extraordinary moments and elevated before the people, as had once been done in the wilderness, in order to restore them to the situation in which they had been at Sinai. Reports about this may have been destroyed after the tables were placed in the Holy of Holies of Solomon's Temple together with the Ark, which was now deprived of its mobile character (I Kings 8:9), obviously in order that they might become immovable themselves, and no longer serve as the occasionally reviving original witnesses, but should remain nothing more than relics of dead stone.[48]

And at an unknown hour they pass out of our ken. The Word alone endures.

WHAT ARE WE TO DO
ABOUT THE TEN COMMANDMENTS?

Y OU WANT to know what I think should be done about the Ten Commandments in order to give them a sanction and validity they no longer possess.

In my opinion the historical and present status of the Decalogue derives from a twofold fact.

The Ten Commandments are not part of an impersonal codex governing an association of men. They were uttered by an *I* and addressed to a *Thou*. They begin with the *I* and every one of them addresses the *Thou* in person. An *I* "commands" and a *Thou*—every *Thou* who hears this *Thou*—"is commanded."

In the Decalogue, the word of Him who issues commands is equipped with no executive power effective on the plane of predictable causality. The word does not enforce its own hearing. Whoever does not wish to respond to the Thou addressed to him can apparently go about his business unimpeded. Though He who speaks the word has power (and the Decalogue presupposes that He had sufficient power to create the heavens and the earth), He has renounced this power of His sufficiently to let every individual actually decide for himself whether he wants to open or close his ears to the voice, and that means whether he wants to choose or reject the I of "I am." He who rejects Him is not struck down by lightning; he who elects Him does not find hidden treasures. Everything seems to remain just as it was. Obviously

God does not wish to dispense either medals or prison sentences.

This, then, is the situation in which "faith" finds itself. According to all criteria of predictable causality, the hearing of what there is to hear does not pay. Faith is not a mere business enterprise which involves risk balanced by the possibility of incalculable gain; it is the venture pure and simple, a venture that transcends the law of probability. This holds especially for those hardened believers whose idea about death and what comes after death is that it will all be revealed in due time, but cannot be anticipated by the imagination—not even by "religious" imagination.

Now human society, and by that I mean the living community at any definite period, as far as we can recognize the existence of a common will in its institutions, has at all times had an interest in fostering and keeping the Ten Commandments. It has been, to be sure, less interested in those commandments that refer to the relationship to God, but it certainly wants the rest to be kept, because it would not be conducive to the welfare of society if murder, for example, ceased to be a crime and became a vice. To a certain extent this holds even for the prohibition against adultery, at least as long as society believes that it cannot get along without marriage, and indeed it never has gotten along without it, not even in its "primitive" stages of polyandry and polygamy. And as long as society cares about maintaining the connection between generations and transmitting forms and contents in a well-regulated manner, it must respect the command to honor one's parents. The Soviet Union has proved that even a society built up to achieve communistic goals must care about honoring that commandment.

It is understandable that society does not want to base so vital a matter on so insecure a foundation as faith—on wanting or not wanting to hear. So, society has always endeavored to transfer those commands and prohibitions it considered important from the sphere of *"religion"* to that of *morals,* to translate them from the language that uses the personal imperative to the impersonal formulation of

"musts." Society wishes these commandments to be upheld
by public opinion, which can to a certain extent be con-
trolled, rather than by the will of God whose effectiveness
cannot be predicted or counted on. But since even the security of opinion is not entirely dependable, the commands and
prohibitions are once more transferred, this time to the
sphere of "law," i.e., they are translated into the language of
if-formulations: "If someone should do this or that, then
such-and-such a thing shall be done to him." And the purpose of the threat of "such-and-such a thing" is not to limit
the freedom of action of the law-breaker, but to punish him.
God scorned to regulate the relation between what a man
does and what, as a result of his doing, is done to him, by
exact mathematical rules, but that is exactly what society attempts. To be sure, society certainly *has* the personnel to
carry out its rulings, a personnel which, at least in principle,
has well-defined work to perform: the courts, the police,
jailers, and hangmen. Oddly enough, however, the result is
still far from satisfactory. Statistics, for example, do not
show that the death penalty has had the effect of diminishing
the number of murders.

For the sake of clarity, I have oversimplified the situation. In history, all these processes are far more circumstan-
tial and interconnected. All this is not reprehensible just so
long as the "translation" does not claim to be a translation.
Plagiarism is legitimate here, but citation is not. Provided
society does not insist that the moral and legal forms into
which it has tranformed the Ten Commandments—that that
product which is an I-and-Thou deprived of the I and the
Thou—are still the Ten Commandments, its activities are
unobjectionable; it is as a matter of fact impossible to imagine how society could exist without them. But nothing of
its vast machinery has anything to do with the situation of
the human being who in the midst of a personal experience
hears and feels himself addressed by the word "thou." "Thou
shalt not take the name of the Lord thy God in vain" (Exod.
20:7), or "Thou shalt not bear false witness against thy
neighbor" (20:13). The vast machinery of society has nothing to do with the situation that prevails between the all-

powerful Speaker who avoids exerting His power and him who is spoken to; and it has nothing to do with the daring, catastrophic, redeeming situation of faith. But if society were to have the temerity to pretend that its voiceless morals and its faceless law are really the Word—adapted to the times and extricated from the husk of superstitions and outmoded ideas—something would take place which has not yet happened in the history of mankind. And then it would, perhaps, be too late for society to discover that there is One who rejects jailers and hangmen as executors of His will.

Now, provided you have not given me up as someone who is simply behind the times, but ask me more insistently than before what should be done with the Ten Commandments, I shall reply: Do what I am trying to do myself: to lead up to them. Not to a scroll, not even to the stone tablets on which "the finger of God" (Exod. 31:18) once wrote the commandments, after they had been uttered; but to the Spoken Word.

THE PRAYER OF
THE FIRST FRUITS
(DEUTERONOMY 26)

IN THE Hebrew Bible in which there are so many prayers, gathered together in the Psalms as well as scattered among the narrative and prophetic texts, we find only two that are prescribed to be said at a certain annually recurring period (Deut. 26). The first of them is the prayer to be said at the offering of the first fruits, the "first of all the fruit of the earth" (26:2). The commandment to offer choice fruits from the early produce of the land in the sanctuary recurs on several occasions in the five books of the Instruction. Here now, in the last of these passages, it is stated how and with what accompanying words the action is to be carried out.

Gifts to the gods of the first fruits of the harvest are a universally familiar custom, not least in the countries that influenced the ancient culture of Israel, namely Babylon, Egypt, and Canaan. Prayers, too, from many different stages of development have come down to us, prayers expressing the purposes of the offering. The gods are thanked for the blessings of the earth; they are invited to the meal; they are asked to bestow new fertility. But of all the prayers of the first fruits in the world that I know there is only one in which, in contrast to all the others, God is glorified for His gift of a *land* to the worshipper.

The opening instruction already points to this: "And it shall be when thou art come in unto the land, which the Lord thy God giveth thee for a possession, and inheritest it, and dwellest therein. . . ." Apart from this passage there is only one other in which the formula is to be found: the one in which the question of "setting a king over thee" is mentioned (17:14). But whereas in that instruction the people as a whole is addressed as "thou," here it occurs only at the beginning in the preliminary sentence already quoted: the "thou" of the following sentence—"that thou shalt take of the first of all the fruit of the earth, which thou shalt bring of the land that the Lord thy God giveth thee, and shalt put it in a basket, and shalt go unto the place which the Lord thy God shall choose to place His name there and shalt come to the priest that shall be in those days and say unto him . . ."—the "thou" in this sentence obviously no longer refers to the people as a whole but to the individual, each individual landowner in Israel throughout all generations. The presupposition is a collective one, the duty a personal one. Furthermore, the presupposition is a never-to-be-repeated historical event, the duty one that returns with every year.

This dual reference of the "thou" is not, however, simply incidental. The first words that the landowner is to speak to the priest show that clearly enough: "I report this day to the Lord thy God that I am come unto the country which the Lord sware unto our fathers for to give us." Even in the latest ages the man who offers the first fruits is not to say, for instance, "My fathers have come into the country" but "I have come into the country." Here the people and the individual are merged into one. "I am come into the country" means first of all "I, the people of Israel, am come into the country." The speaker identifies himself with Israel and speaks in its name. The saying "I am come into the country" corresponds to the reference to Israel in the first sentence, "When thou art come in unto the land": even the son of a later generation speaks for the generation that once came into Canaan and therefore for the whole people that came to Canaan in that generation. But that does not exhaust the full meaning of this "I." The man does not simply say: "I am come into the country"; he says that he is "reporting to the Lord" that he has come into the country. That can hardly mean anything else but: "I report as one who has come into

the country." Every year when he brings the first fruits of his
land he reports anew as one who has come into the country.
If he were speaking merely for the people he would not need
to "report." He does so because he is under an obligation to
say: "Not merely Israel, but also this very person here has
come into the land—I as an individual feel and profess myself as one who has come into the land, and every time that I
offer its first fruits I acknowledge that anew and declare it
anew." To understand this rightly one must recall another
passage in the same book (5:2 f.) in which Moses says to
the people, before he repeats the Ten Commandments which
he once heard on the holy mountain: "The Lord our God
made a Covenant with us on Horeb. The Lord made not this
Covenant with our fathers, but with us, even us, who are all
of us here alive this day." This sentence, which expresses the
eternal actuality of the Covenant with such emphatic directness, does not say: "not with our fathers *alone,* with our
fathers who have meanwhile died in the wilderness," but
more uncompromisingly: "not with our fathers"; not with
a single generation, but with each generation of Israel that
lives before His face God has made His Covenant. And just
as the making of the Covenant is the concern of all generations of the people, so too is the coming into the land promised in the Covenant. This acquisition of land is a gift of
land, a gift that God is constantly renewing. Every peasant
in each generation of Israel, when he brings the first fruits,
thanks God for the land into which He has brought *him.*
This "bringing" into the land and that "bringing" the first
fruits are in fact set into a mutual relationship to one another
that is stressed in the prayer itself: "And He hath *brought* us
into this place . . . and now, I have *brought* the first fruits
of the land." Thus is expressed the reciprocity between God
and the individual members of His people. The peasant says:
"I have been brought by Him into this fruitful land and now
I bring Him of its fruits." That is something more than mere
thanksgiving. The whole land has been bestowed by God on
the people; the harvest, which the man whom God has
brought into the land produces from the soil, comes from
God's blessing and work. It is impossible to give Him any-

thing of it, but one can bring Him something, the best of the first fruits, as a symbol and for consecration. Even today a sacrificial formula of the Palestinian Arabs begins with the words: "From Thee and unto Thee."

He, God, is the giver. As so often in the Bible, the heart of the matter is brought out by the sevenfold repetition of the verb "to give" in the passage containing the instruction and the prayer. In the first three and last three cases it is used of God's gift to Israel; between the two groups of three, however, there is a strange "giving," obviously not merely to make up the full seven but chiefly to emphasize the negative background of the divine giving; it is the Egyptians, who "gave us hard bondage" (Deut. 26:6). Of such kind are the historical "gifts" made to Israel by the other peoples of the world. God's gift frees it from the bondage laid upon it by the other peoples. But God's great gift to Israel—it is this that the fivefold repetition impresses on us—is the land. Finally (26:11), in order to prevent any misunderstanding at all, it is summed up in more general terms: "every good thing," not only the land, but also its annual yield comes from God as His gift.

In accordance with tradition the land is described as "a land flowing with milk and honey" (26:9). No peasant describes the land of his desire in that way. When the peasant praises his land, he says: "A land of wheat and barley and vines and fig trees and pomegranates" (8:8). It is not, however, this or a similar description that has become the familiar one but the other. Some think it is a later interpolation only to be found in later texts and that "milk and honey" refers to the sacred food that recurs in the mythologies of various peoples; in this case the term will have arisen not out of the basic feeling of an early and creative hour in the history of the people but from a romantic, almost literary trend of thought. But it is not usual for sayings of such simplicity and pregnancy to arise in this way. It would also be more than strange if a later epoch were, by reason of some romantic proclivity, subsequently to have given to the promised land a name that expresses not the peasant's interests but those of the pasture-seeking, roving shepherd, in whom the

old food-gathering instinct survives, and which expresses his
delight in discovering the honey of the wild bees.[1] The saying
refers to representative products that the land offers to the
newcomer without the need for any effort on his part: milk,
into which the energy of the rich pastures, as it were of one
tremendous oasis, is converted and honey for the refreshment
of passers-by. It is essentially a very old saying, the expression of a promise made to nomads or seminomads. In the
centuries following the entry into the promised land it seems
in literature to have given way to the peasants' new pride,
although it continued to be current in the oral language; later
on, urban circles in Judea, especially the clergy of Jerusalem
and other nearby holy places, gave the saying a more prom-
inent place in the literary language in an attempt really to do
justice to early conditions from a historical point of view,
and in so doing they may have had in mind the people of the
South who had remained more attached to cattle-breeding
than the people of Ephraim. The description of the land is,
however, not the only remnant of the old tradition here. The
prayer begins with the words: *Arammi obed abi,* "An Aramæan gone astray was my father." The alliterative connection of the three words, the thrice-recurring guttural sound
is, as almost always in the Bible, not incidental and no mere
stylistic ornament: the intention is that these words should
be impressed upon the listener or the reader in a particular
way; they form a phrase that is easy to learn by heart. Even
at a first hearing the connection with the words that follow
appears to be questionable: "An Aramæan gone astray was
my father; and he went down into Egypt" does not sound
like a straightforward narrative. If we enquire who this "father" is, it becomes even clearer that different and disparate
material has been combined here. Judging from the text further on, we are to think of Jacob; it is he who goes down into
Egypt, "sojourns" there and "becomes there a nation"—obviously the reference cannot be to Abraham's short stay in
Egypt. On the other hand, how would Jacob come to be
spoken of as an "Aramæan gone astray"? The fact that his
mother is the sister of Laban the "Aramæan" and he is his
son-in-law does not make him his fellow countryman. And

the fact that he spends more than twenty years of his life far away from his tribe is no justification for describing him as having "gone astray." This word "gone astray" is pastoral language. It is used when a sheep has lost the flock to which it belongs (Jer. 50:6; Ezek. 34:4, 16; Psalm 119:176). "My people hath been lost sheep; their shepherds have caused them to go astray, they have turned them away on the mountains: they have gone from mountain to hill, they have forgotten their resting place," we read in Jeremiah. "Their shepherds have caused them to go astray"—in the same words and with the same meaning, though in quite a different tone of voice Abraham tells the king of the Philistines about his life (Gen. 20:13): "And it came to pass, when God caused me to go astray from my father's house . . ." A bad shepherd causes a sheep to go astray from the flock because he is careless; Abraham's God, of whom he speaks in the plural in order to make himself understood to the Philistine, caused him to go astray from his flock because, He, the good shepherd, was caring for him. In Haran, in the land of Aram, where the tribe of the Terahites, Abraham's tribe, had settled, this God had caused him to go away from his kindred and his father's house "unto a land that I will show thee" (12:1), into this land of Canaan. No matter whether the Terahites really sprang from the Aramæans, who had once migrated to Ur, for which there is some evidence, or whether they were called Aramæans because they had settled in "Paddan Aram"; Abraham was in fact a "lost Aramæan." The fact that he is nowhere else described as such, but only as a Hebrew (14:13)—the latter is presumably not a tribal designation but merely signifies membership of the community of the "travelers" or "immigrants"—is naturally bound up with the tradition that Abraham had been fetched by God from his father's house and brought to Canaan to become the ancestor of a new people: in the hour of "going astray" he is still an Aramæan, in Canaan no longer.

   It is impossible to ascertain how the connection of the old saying with the prayer came about. Jacob's Aramæan sojourn obviously made it easier to associate the "Aramæan" with his name.

The instruction to make a feast of the first fruits, which follows the prayer, ends with the order that "the sojourner that is in your midst" shall, like the poor Levite also, participate therein. There is some suggestion of an instruction here, not unlike the one that is given full expression in another place: your fathers, of whom you have just spoken, once sojourned in this land; now that you are its masters, let the strangers that are in your midst participate without stint in all the delights of the land, in all the good things that YHVH, thy God, has given thee and thy house.

In order to appreciate the spiritual background of the passage, however, one must read it in connection with the words of Jeremiah (2:3): "Israel is sacredness unto the Lord, the first fruits of His increase." The world is God's field, the peoples His plantation, Israel His first fruits. Just as the tree offers Him, the giver of the land, the first fruits every year, so Israel must offer itself to Him as the first fruits of His world harvest.

One must not completely spiritualize such a conception and deprive it of the bodily substance without which the spiritual content would have no real stability. No symbol has authentic existence in the spirit if it has no authentic existence in the body. In order that Israel may become the first fruits of the divine harvest, it needs a real land as well as a real people. For this reason the word of the Lord in Jeremiah introduces the saying thus: "I remember thee the kindness of thy youth, the love of thy betrothal-time, when thou wentest after me in the wilderness, in the land that is not sown." That is the historic progress of the people into the land that God has promised and given to it.

Twice seven times the name of God is mentioned in the short passage and nine times with the addition "thy God." [2] As has already been shown, this working with numbers on the part of the author or the editor has a didactic purpose. If, repeatedly, at every stage of the action, in every important section of the statement, YHVH is called "thy God," if stress is laid, in exactly the same way, on the fact that the sanctuary is His sanctuary, the altar His altar, that He is the God addressed in the prayer, then this is a declaration of faith of decisive importance. For the Canaanite the fertility of the soil is the work of natural gods, of many local Baals or, in the more advanced Phœnician culture, of the "heavenly" Baal, the result of the sexual associations of water-giving and water-receiving divinities. This conception was not restricted to the religious sphere: it determined the cultivation of the soil itself with its magical and orgiastic sexual customs, it permeated the whole life of the peasant. In view of the influence of these pagan beliefs it was a matter of life or death for the faith of Israel, and one that became increasingly serious from the time of the entry into the promised land onwards, to make every citizen absolutely and invincibly certain that the God who gives him the fruit of the land, "corn, wine, and oil" (Hosea 2:10) is the same God who gave Israel the land. The God of history and the God of nature cannot be separated and the land is the token of their unity. The God who brought Israel into this land, it is even He whose eyes are always upon it "from the beginning of the year even unto the end of the year" (Deut. 11:12). The uniformly recurring seasons with their blessings are bound to that unique historical act in which God led the people with whom He had made the Covenant into the promised land. The creation itself bears witness to the revelation. The land is its witness.

It is only from early talmudic times that a description of how the offering of the first fruits was celebrated has come down to us. The report of the Mishnah sounds as though the intention was to preserve something lost and past for the memory of future generations.[3] We hear how the people from the surrounding country come to Jerusalem with the first fruits, those living close at hand with fresh fruits, those far away with dried. In the early morning the procession enters the city, headed by pipers, then the sacrificial bull with gilded horns, and behind it the men, bearing baskets filled with fruits and garlanded with grapes, each according to his wealth, golden baskets, silver baskets, and baskets woven from stripped willow-twigs. The artisans of Jerusalem come out to meet them, greeting those from each place in turn: "Brothers, men from the place of such-and-such a name, may you come in peace!" But when they stood by the temple

hill the king himself took his basket on his shoulders and
entered in with them. In the forecourt the Levites sang the
verse from the Psalms: "I will exalt Thee, YHVH, for Thou
hast drawn me up." The verb described the lifting of the
bucket from the well. In the context of the action and the
prayer that follows, which gives thanks for the deliverance
from Egypt, the quotation comes to mean: "Israel gives
thanks to God for raising it from the well of Egypt into the
daylight and freedom of its own land."

What emerges from the report of the Mishnah is the living unity—from the small peasant and the artisan right up
to the king—of a people experiencing and glorifying the
blessings of nature as the blessings of history. Thus we appreciate the full meaning of the passage on the offering of the
first fruits, the unique document of a unique relationship between a people and a land.

SAMUEL AND THE ARK

(I SAMUEL)

T HE narrator of the prophecy regarding the house of Eli
most emphatically connects Samuel with the ark, and this
connection—especially in the story of his Call—rings truer
than the idyll of his childhood. YHVH's revelation, which he
receives in chapter 3 and which overcomes the sterility of
the priestly oracle (3:1b) with a new and fruitful divine
initiative, occurs at the ark. The information that he was
lying in the *hekhal* [temple] of YHVH (3:3)—emphasized by
the sevenfold recurrence of *shakhab* [lie down]—is supplemented with special intent by the apparently unnecessary
observation, "where the ark of God was." Even taken together with verse 21, one may not infer from this "that there
was an incubation oracle which people would seek out in
Shiloh which owed its origin to this experience of Samuel." [1]
Etiology is a powerful element in the history of oral literature, but tradition cannot be dissolved in it. In I Samuel 3:
2 ff. both the reader interested in the history of religion and
the naive reader can tell how the narrator is ruled by the
impression of the colossally unique. The ark is stressed because the ark is at issue. The revelation to Samuel that now
follows—whether in the entire substance of its core or in its
beginning—has the catastrophe of the ark as its object. Only
in this way can the manifestly early verse 11 be understood;
the Master of the ark announces its capture and desecration.
(At this point an original connection with the ark—not a
subsequent one—is evident.) The fact that this announce-

ment is made to Samuel indicates what the narrator wanted
to express emphatically from the beginning: YHVH, who is
preparing Himself for judgment, has selected Samuel to re-
place the condemned priesthood in a period without ark or
sanctuary and to bear the divine voice without *ephod* as an
independent *nabi.*

This basic perception will manifestly also enable us to
understand the initial situation in the narrative of Samuel
and Saul. It has been correctly designated as "one of the
strangest circumstances of a strange age" [2] that the ark was
not brought from the border area, where it is last to be
found, to one of the sanctuaries within the actual territory
of Israel. To whatever cause it may be ascribed—opposition
of the people of Kiriath-jearim, objection of the Philistines,
its desecration either on account of its sojourn among the
enemy as such or on account of the plunder of its contents,
etc.—the narrative makes clear: YHVH has indeed brought
His ark from Philistine dominion, but He does not want—
not yet—to return it to Israel. This is the background of the
report regarding the community's confession of sin. YHVH's
ark signifies His leading presence, but He has cruelly withdrawn it from the people. How shall the people free itself of
the yoke without it? Samuel meets this complaint in that he,
the non-priest who has called together the assembly, "cries
out" "for Israel," and YHVH "answers him," which is confirmed by the repulsion of the Philistine attack upon the assembly.

As in the verses between the narrative concerning the
house of Eli and that concerning the ark (3:20; 4:1) YHVH
had revealed Himself to Samuel at Shiloh beyond His curse,
so now He reveals Himself to him again before all the people; He answers him, the independent *nabi* without ark or
ephod, as He usually answers only the priest. The ark does
not return; but the ark is not needed to receive the presence
of YHVH.

In the story of the curse of the house of Eli, which in
its essence may have originated soon after the story of the
ark, Samuel is made to utter the first non-anonymous proph-

ecy of doom in the Bible. Despite the manifest tendency of
the narrative to put Samuel in the right against the priesthood of the family of Eli and to justify his attitude toward it,
there is no reason to doubt the genuineness of the tradition.
If the text on Samuel did not contain the data that he had
auditory experiences, it would be completely impossible to
picture a historical person of that name. Moreover, it is evident from his conduct after the catastrophe that he opposes
the priesthood, i.e., in a person of auditory experiences, that
he is made aware of his opposition to them. Samuel should
not be regarded as a frondeur priest; there is no indication
that he tried to establish a rival priestly line. In the time in-
terval between the narrative of the defeat and the beginning
of the assembly of lament, Samuel has already gained recognized authority over the people (7:5). The man who
proclaimed the catastrophe of the priestly center must afterwards have seized the priestly prerogatives crucial for influence upon the community, and, apparently without aggressive
force, he makes them in fact dispensable within the sphere
of his influence. He does so as a *nabi,* i.e., as one who
speaks also of his own accord, *unasked,* the message of
revelation. We never hear the like in regard to any of the
priests of Israel. It is the probable intent of the author
of verses 3:20–4:1, and certainly of the editor who inserted
them at this point, to show that through his message of revelation—the catastrophe he foretold—he is conclusively
proven *neeman,* entrusted and authenticated. However, such
conduct as his, which changes the sacred and thus also the
secular power structure, is only possible when it is supported
by an active circle. The attempt to derive a picture of the historical Samuel necessarily leads to his connection with the
nebiim.

Opinion is mounting that the trace of a great "religious
popular movement," [3] stretching over many generations, can
be found in the scant accounts of evanescently appearing
prophetic bands [*nebiim*]. Moreover, especially during the
period of Philistine domination, these bands are responsible
for "one of the most vigorous drives for independence." [4]

Samuel appoints the *moshia* [savior], who is then accepted
into their inspired community. Only when his working together with them is clearly recognized, as intended by the narrator, can one understand the origins and beginnings of the
liberation movement. Simply on the basis of this working together as early as the time of the catastrophe, it becomes clear
that Samuel, as a *nabi* and supported by the *nebiim,* supplants
the ruined priesthood, and that he replaces priestly leadership with prophetic; dependent oracle with independent;
and, apparently, also the communal offering exacted at the
seat of the priesthood with an itinerant one.

I have tried to show[5] that the *nabi* movement of early
Israel—regardless of when and how the name originated—
began in the outer and inner crises of the nascent people
during the period after the decisive acts of the Conquest. It
is the sentiment of this movement—to cite only the undis-
puted—that is expressed plainly and authentically in the
saying of Deborah (Judges 4:14) and in the Song of Deborah, so that, already on this account, the designation of
Deborah as a *nebiah* deserves at least posthumous justification. *Ha-lo* YHVH *yatza lefanekha* (is not YHVH gone out before thee?)—thus Deborah addresses Barak. It is God Himself who leads His people into battle. "Nay; but there shall
be a king over us; that we also may be like all the nations;
and that our king may judge us, and go out before us (*ve-
yatza lefanenu*), and fight our battles"—thus the elders of
Israel address Samuel (I Sam. 8:19 f.). After their will, mod-
ified by the will of YHVH, has been carried out, he answers
(12:12): "For YHVH your God is your king!" YHVH is the
true vanguard, the true champion, the true leader, the true
king.[6] That is the *nabi* attitude—with or without the applica-
tion of the term—and wherever it manifests itself, the essence of the *nabi* manifests itself, namely that primal essence
which prompts Deborah's speech. The Samuel of chapter 12
—apparently a late composition—says basically the same
thing.

The catastrophe of the ark and its consequences should
be regarded anew from this point of view. Already on the
people's journey to Canaan the ark preceded them (Num.

10:33). "Let Thine enemies be scattered; and let them that hate Thee flee before Thee!" (10:35). Thus goes the old formula, reminiscent of the conclusion of the Song of Deborah, which they exclaimed when the ark set forward. Now, in the most dire straits of war, the people bring the ark into the camp (I Sam. 4:3 ff.) and it goes forth before them—into disaster. According to the story, it is returned to a border town under Israelite control (that the tale has a historical kernel can scarcely be denied), but Samuel, the proclaimer of YHVH who is Himself the vanguard, does not retrieve it. Beyond all the motivations that are possible here, one suspects what the narrator cannot say: he does not want to do it. For an ark that could be captured by the Philistines can henceforth only be the sign that for the present YHVH marches in advance the way He Himself wants to, leads the way He Himself wants to, and not as one would like Him to march in advance and to lead. You do not have YHVH when you have the ark; just when you think you have Him, you do not. None less than YHVH Himself has let His ark be taken. Now He has retrieved it from the control of the Philistines, but He does not want—not yet—to return it to Israel. For He does not desire to be used but to be worshipped. YHVH does not want to be conjured or prayed into the position of leader, nor to be given "divine service" in order to be made use of. What He wants is obedience. "Hearkening is better than the best sacrifice" (I Sam. 15:22) could be the genuine word of Samuel.[7] In the hour of the catastrophe that he predicted, the leadership of God without the ark is Samuel's "idea." It is a prophetic idea. The priesthood, which is responsible for the calamity, must be eliminated. The seat of the ark was in a sanctuary supervised by priests; as its *mesharet* [minister, I Sam. 2:18] the young Samuel once slept in its *hekhal,* but in that very place he received the proclamation of disaster. No ark—no more rigid adherence to the cult; the sacrificial service is now loosened, free to move about. No ark—no more pilgrimages to an oracle bound by objects; the man of God himself wanders from place to place, YHVH speaks to him, and he is able to convey His guiding will. YHVH's hand cannot be forced, not even against the Philistines; the continuation of their dominion belongs to His dealings with Israel and His plans for them. They have sinned against Him; they must confess and pray and are allowed to do so. He is not a pseudo-king to whom one can dictate; He is the true *melekh*. Only those who fear Him and hearken unto His voice (I Sam. 12:14) will He lead to redemption.

BIBLICAL LEADERSHIP

I DO NOT imagine that you will expect me to give you any
so-called character sketches of biblical leaders. That
would be an impossible undertaking, for the Bible does not
concern itself with character, nor with individuality, and one
cannot draw from it any description of characters or individ-
ualities. The Bible depicts something else, namely, persons
in situations. The Bible is not concerned with the difference
between these persons; but the difference between the situations in which the person, the creaturely person, the appointed person, stands his test or fails, is all-important to it.

But neither can it be my task to delve beneath the
biblical account to a picture more trustworthy historically,
to historical data out of which I could piece together a historically useful picture. This too is impossible. It is not that
the biblical figures are unhistorical. I believe that we are
standing at the beginning of a new era in biblical studies;
whereas the past era was concerned with proving that the
Bible did not contain history, the coming era will succeed
in demonstrating its historicity. By this I do not mean that
the Bible depicts men and women and events as they were
in actual history; rather do I mean that its descriptions and
narratives are the organic, legitimate ways of giving an
account of what existed and what happened. I have nothing
against calling these narratives myths and sagas, so long as
we remember that myths and sagas are essentially memories
which are actually conveyed from person to person.

What kind of memory is it that manifests itself in these accounts? I say again: memory; not imagination. It is an organic memory molding its material. We know of it today, because occasionally, though indeed in unlikely and indeed in incredible ways, the existence of great poets with such organic memories still extends into our time. If we want to distinguish between narrators, between a great narrator and one who is simply very talented, the best way is to consider how each of them handles the events of his own life. The great narrator allows the events to drop into him as they happen, careless, trusting, with faith. And memory does its part: what has thus been dropped into it, it molds organically, unarbitrarily, unfancifully into a valid account and narrative; a whole on which admittedly a great deal of conscious work has then to be done, but the distinguishing mark was put upon it by the unarbitrarily shaping memory. The other narrator registers, he makes an inventory in what he also calls the memory, but which is really something quite different; he preserves the events while they are happening in order to be able to draw them forth unaltered when he needs them. Well, he will certainly draw them forth from the preservative after a fashion unaltered, and fit for use after a fashion, and then he may do with them what he can.

I said that the great poets show us in their way how the nascence of myths and sagas takes place. Each myth, even the myth we usually call the most fantastic of all, is creation around a memory core, around the kernel of the organically shaping memory. It is not that people to whom something like the exodus from Egypt has happened subsequently improvise events, allowing their fancy to add elements they do not remember and to embroider on what happened; what happened continues to function, the event itself is still active and at work in their souls, but these souls, this community soul, is so made that its memory is formative, myth-creating, and the task before the biblical writers is then to work on the product of this memory. Nowhere is there any point where arbitrariness is observable or interference by alien elements; there is in it no juggling.

This being the case, we cannot disentangle the historical

from the biblical. The power of the biblical writing, which springs from this shaping memory, is so great, the elemental nature of this memory so mighty, that it is quite impossible to extract any so-called historical matter from the Bible. The historical matter thus obtained would be unreal, amorphous, without significance. But it is also impossible to distill "the historical matter" from the Bible for another reason. In contrast to the sacred historiography of the other nations, there exists in the case of Israel no evidence from profane parallels by which one might correct the sacred documents; there is no historiography of another tendency than that which resides in this shaping memory; and this shaping memory stands under a law. It is this law that I shall try to elucidate by the examples with which I deal today.

In order to bring out still more clearly and exactly what I have in mind, I shall ask you to recall one of the nations with whom Israel came into historical contact and dispute; I do so for the purpose of considering the aspect under which this nation must have regarded one of the biblical leaders. Let us try to imagine how Abraham must have been regarded by one of the nations against whose kings he fought, according to Genesis 14, a chapter whose fundamental historical character seems to me beyond doubt. Undoubtedly Abraham was a historical figure to this nation in the same sense in which we usually speak about history today. But he was no longer Abraham. That which is important for us about Abraham, that which makes him a biblical character, a Father, that which is the reason why the Bible tells us about Abraham—that is no longer embraced under this aspect; the significance of the figure has vanished. Or, take for instance the Egyptians and Moses, and imagine how an Egyptian historian would have described Moses and his cause. Nothing essential would have been left; it would be a skeleton taking the place of the living person.

All we can do, therefore, is to refer to the Bible, to that which is characteristic of the biblical leader as the Bible, without arbitrariness, tells of him and thinks of him, under the law of *its* conception of history, *its* living of history, which is unlike everything we are accustomed to call history.

But from this law, from this biblical way of regarding leader and leadership, different from all other ways in which leader and leadership have been regarded, from this have we— from this has Judaism—arisen.

As I now wish to investigate the question of the essence of biblical leadership, I must exclude from the inquiry all those figures who are not *biblical* leaders in the strict sense of the term: and this means, characteristically enough, I must exclude all those figures who appear as continuators, all those who are not called, elected, appointed anew, as the Bible says, directly by God, but who enter upon a task already begun without such personal call—whether it is a disciple to whom the person who is not permitted to finish the task hands over his office, breathing as it were toward his disciple the spirit that breathes upon him; or whether it is a son who succeeds an elected, originally anointed king, without receiving any other anointing than the already customary official one, which is thus no longer the anointing that comes upon a person and turns him into another man.

Thus I do not consider figures like Joshua and Solomon because the Bible has such figures in common with history —they are figures of universal history. Joshua is a great army leader, a great conqueror, but a historical figure like any other, only with special religious affiliations added, which, however, do not characterize his person. Solomon is an oriental king, only a very wise one; he does his task, he builds the Temple, but we are not shown that this task colors and determines him. What has happened here is simply that the completion of a task, the completion of a task already intended and already begun, has been taken over by a disciple or a successor. The task of Moses, which he had already begun but was not allowed to finish, was taken over by Joshua; the task of David, which he was not allowed to finish, was taken over by Solomon. In this connection I recall the words that David and God exchanged on the proposed building of the Temple and the prohibition against David's carrying it out: "It is not for you," says God, reproving David (II Sam. 7:5) as He had reproved Moses when He told Moses that it was not for him to bring into their land the people whom he had led out of Egypt. The work is taken away from him, and taken away from him, moreover, in view of his special inner and outer situations; another man has nothing more to do than to bring the work to its conclusion.

Only the elected, only those who begin, are then comprised under the biblical aspect of leadership. A new beginning may also occur within a sequence of generations, as for instance within those that we call the generations of the patriarchs; this is clearly seen in the case of Jacob, with whom something new begins, as the particular way in which revelation comes to him indicates.

I would like first to attempt a negative characterization of the essential features of biblical leadership. It goes beyond both nature and history. To the men who wrote the Bible, nature, as well as history, is of God; and that in such a way that the biblical cosmogony relates each separately. In the first chapter the creation of the world is described as the coming of nature into being; and then in the second chapter this same creation of the world is described as the rise of history. Both are of God, but then the biblical event goes beyond them, God goes beyond them, not in the sense that they—nature and history—come to be ignored by God, but in the sense that time and again God's hand thrusts through them and interferes with what is happening—it so chooses, so sends, and so commands, as it does not seem to accord with the laws of nature and history to send, to choose, and to command.

I shall here show only by two particularly clear examples what I mean by this. First of all, it is the weak and the humble who are chosen. By nature it is the strong, those who can force their cause through, who are able and therefore chosen to perform the historical deeds. But in the Bible it is often precisely the younger sons who are chosen—from Abel, through Jacob, Joseph and Moses, to David; and this choosing is accompanied by a rejection, often a very emphatic rejection, of the older sons; or else those who are chosen were born out of wedlock, or of humble origin. And if it happens that a strong man like Samson appears, a man who has not all these limitations, then his strength is not his own, it is only loaned, not given, and he trifles it away, squanders it, in the way in which we are told, to get it back only in order to die.

A different but no less telling expression of what is meant by this peculiar election against nature is represented by the battle and victory of Gideon. The Bible makes him do the strangest thing any commander ever did. He has an army of ten thousand men, and he reduces its numbers again and again, till only three hundred men remain with him; and with these three hundred he gives battle and conquers (Judg.7).

It is always the same story. The purpose of God is fulfilled, as the Bible itself says in one place, not by might, nor by power, but "by my spirit" (Zech. 4:6).

It is "against nature" that in one way or another the leaders are mostly the weak and the humble. The way in which they carry out their leadership is "contrary to history." It is the moment of success that determines the selection of events that seem important to history. World history is the history of successes; the heroes who have not succeeded but who cannot be excluded from it on account of their very conspicuous heroism serve only as a foil, as it were. True, the conquered have also their place in world history; but if we scrutinize how it treats the conquerors and the conquered, what is of importance to history becomes abundantly clear. Granted that one takes Croesus together with Cyrus, that Herodotus has a use for him; nevertheless, in the heart of history only the conquerors have value. It murmurs a low dirge over the overpowered heroes, but its paean for those who stand firm, who force their cause through, for those who are crowned with success, rings out loud. This is current history, the history that we are accustomed to identify with what happens, with the real happenings in the world, in spite of the fact that this history is based only on the particular principle of picking and choosing, on the selection made by the historian, on the so-called historical consciousness.

The Bible knows nothing of this intrinsic value of success. On the contrary, when it announces a successful deed, it is duty bound to announce in complete detail the failure involved in the success. When we consider the history of Moses, we see how much failure is mingled in the one great successful action, so much so that when we set the individual events that make up his history side by side, we see that his life consists of one failure after another, through which runs the thread of his success. True, Moses brought the people out of Egypt; but each stage of this leadership is a failure. Whenever he comes to deal with this people, he is defeated by them, let God ever so often interfere and punish them. And the real history of this leadership is not the history of the Exodus, but the history of the wandering in the desert. The personal history of Moses' own life, too, does not point back to his youth and to what grew out of it; it points beyond, to death, to the death of the unsuccessful man, whose work, it is true, survives him, but only in new defeats, new disappointments, and continual new failures—and yet his work survives also in a hope that is beyond all these failures.

Or let us consider the life of David. So far as we are told of it, it consists essentially of two great stories of flight. Before his accession to the throne there are the manifold accounts of his flight from Saul, and then follows an interruption which is not trifling in terms of length and its value for profane history, but which in the account appears paltry enough, and after this there is the flight from Absalom, painted for us in detail. And even where the Bible recounts David's triumph, as for instance with the entry of the Ark into Jerusalem, this triumph is clearly described as a disgrace in a worldly sense; this is very unlike the language of world history. What Michal, his wife, says to David of his triumph, how he ought to have felt ashamed of himself behaving as he did in front of his people (II Sam. 6:20)—that is the language of profane history, i.e., of history *par excellence*. To history such a royal appearance is not permitted, and rightly so, seeing that history is what it is.

And, finally, this glorification of failure culminates in the long line of prophets whose existence is failure through and through. They live in failure; it is for them to fight and not to conquer. It is the fundamental experience of biblical leadership, of the leadership described by one of them, a nameless prophet whose words are preserved in the second part of the Book of Isaiah where he speaks in the first person of himself as "the servant of the Lord," and says of God:

> "He hath made my mouth like a sharp sword,
> In the shadow of His hand hath He hid me;
> And He hath made me a polished shaft,—
> In His quiver hath He concealed me!" (Isa. 49:2)

This existence in the shadow, in the quiver, is the final word of the leaders in the biblical world; this enclosure in failure, in obscurity, even when one stands in the blaze of public life, in the presence of the whole national life. The truth is hidden in obscurity and yet does its work; though indeed in a way far different from that which is known and lauded as effective by world history.

Biblical leadership falls into five basic types, not according to differences in the personality and character of the leader—I have already said that personality and character do not come into consideration—but according to the difference in the successive situations, the great stages in the history of the people which the Bible describes, the stages in the dialogue between God and the people. For what the Bible understands by history is a dialogue in which man, in which the people, is spoken to and fails to answer, yet where the people in the midst of its failure continually rises up and tries to answer. It is the history of God's disappointments, but this history of disappointments constitutes a way, a way that leads from disappointment to disappointment and beyond all disappointments; it is the way of the people, the way of man, yes, the way of God through mankind. I said that there are five basic types in accordance with the successive stages of the situations in the dialogue: first, the Patriarch; second, the Leader in the original sense of one who leads the wandering; third, the so-called Judge; fourth, the King, but of course not the king who is a successor, a member of a dynasty, but the founder of the dynasty, called the first anointed; fifth, the Prophet. All these constitute different forms of leadership in accordance with the different situations.

First the Patriarch. This is a current conception which is not quite correct. No rulership is here exercised, and, when we understand the conception in its accurate sense, we cannot here speak of any leadership, for there is as yet no people to lead. The conception indicates a way along which the people are to be led beginning with these men. They are Fathers. It is for them to beget a people. It is the peculiar point in biblical history where God, as it were, narrows down His original plan for the whole of mankind and causes a people to be begotten that is called to do its appointed work toward the completion of the creation, the coming of the kingdom. The fathers of this people are the men of whom I speak. They are Fathers, nothing else. Patriarch expresses too much. They are the real fathers, they are those from whom this tribe, this people, proceeds; and when God speaks to them, when God blesses them, the same thing is always involved: conception and birth, the beginning of a people. And the great story that stands in the middle of the story of the patriarchs—the birth and offering of Isaac—makes exactly this point, in a paradoxical manner. Kierkegaard has presented this paradox very beautifully in the first part of his *Fear and Trembling.* This paradoxical story of the second in the line of the patriarchs, of his being born and very nearly being killed, shows what is at stake: a begetting, but the begetting of a people standing at the disposal of God; a begetting, but a begetting commanded by God.

We have a people, and the people is in bondage. A man receives the charge to lead it out. That is he whom I have described as the leader in the original meaning of the word. It is he who serves in a human way as a tool for the act God pronounces, "I bore you on eagles' wings, and brought you unto myself" (Exod. 19:4). I have already spoken of his life. But in the middle of his life the event takes place in which Moses, after the passage through the Red Sea, intones the song in which the people joins, and which is the proclamation of a king. The words with which the song ends proclaim it: "King shall the Lord be for ever and ever" (Exod. 15:18). The people has here chosen God Himself for its King, and that means that it has made a vital and experi-

enced truth out of the tradition of a divine kingdom which
was common to all Semitic peoples but which never had been
taken quite seriously. The Hebrew leaders are so much in
earnest about it that after the land has been conquered they
undertake to do what is "contrary to history": they try to
build up a society without a ruling power save only that of
God. It is that experiment in primitive theocracy of which
the Book of Judges tells, and which degenerates into anarchy, as is shown by the examples given in its last part.

The so-called Judge constitutes the third type of leadership. This type is to be understood as the attempt made by
a leading group among the people that is dominated by the
desire to make actual the proclamation of God as king, and
try to induce the people to follow it. This attempt miscarries
time and again. Time and again the people, to use the biblical phrase, falls away from God. But we can also express this
in the language of history: time and again the people fall
apart; it is one and the same thing whichever language we
use. The attempt to establish a society under no other dominion than God's—this too can be expressed in the language of history, or if one likes, in the language of sociology:
the attempt to establish a society on pure voluntarism fails
over and over again. The people falls away. This is always
succeeded by an invasion by one of the neighboring peoples,
and Israel, from a historical point of view fallen apart and
disunited, does not stand firm. But in its conquered state it
again makes itself subject to the will of God, resolves anew
to accept God's dominion, and again a divine mission occurs; there is always a leader whom the spirit lays hold of as
it laid hold of Moses. This leader, whose mission it is to free
the people, is the Judge, or more correctly, "he who makes
right"; he makes this right exist in the actual world for the
people, which after its return to God now again has right
on its side, by defeating the enemy. This is the rhythm of
the Book of Judges; it might almost be called a tragic
rhythm, were it not that the word tragic is so foreign to the
spirit of biblical language.

But in this Book of Judges there is also something being
prepared. The experience of failure, of the inability to bring

about this intended, naive, primitive theocracy, becomes ever deeper; ever stronger grows the demand for a human kingdom. Judges itself is in its greater part written from an anti-monarchical standpoint. The kings of the peoples file before one in a way determined by this point of view, which reaches its height in that ironic fable of Jotham's (Judg. 9). But in its final chapters the Book of Judges has to acknowledge the disappointment of the theocratic hope, because the people is as it is, because men are as they are. And so kingship is demanded under Samuel. And it is granted by God. I said before, the way leads through the disappointments. Thus the demand of the people is as it were laid hold of and consecrated from above; for by the anointing of the King a man is transformed into the bearer of a charge laid upon him. But this is no longer—as was the case with the Judge— a single charge the completion of which brings his leadership to an end; it is a governor's charge which goes beyond individual acts, indeed beyond the life of individual men. Anointing may also imply the beginning of a dynasty, when the king is not rejected by God, as Saul was.

The kingdom is a new stage in the dialogue, a new stage of attempt and failure, only in this stage the account lays the burden of the failure on the king and not any longer, as in the Book of Judges, on the whole people. It is no longer those who are led but the leader himself who fails, who cannot stand the test of the charge, who does not make the anointing come true in his own person—a crucial problem in religious history. The history of the great religions, and in general all great history, is bound up with the problem: How do human beings stand the test of what is here called anointing?

The history of the kings is the history of the failure of him who has been anointed to realize the promise of his anointing. The rise of Messianism, the belief in the anointed king who realizes the promise of his anointing, is to be understood only in this context.

But now in the situation of the failure of kings the new and last type of leader in biblical history arises, the leader who above all other types is "contrary to history," the

Prophet, he who is appointed to oppose the king, and even more, history. When God says to Jeremiah, "I have made thee . . . a brazen wall against the whole land" (Jer. 1:18), it is really so; the prophet stands not only against the ruler but against the people itself. The prophet is the man who has been set up against his own natural instincts that bind him to the community, and who likewise sets himself up against the will of the people to live on as they have always lived, which, naturally, for the people is identical with the will to live. It goes without saying that not only the rulers but also the people treat the prophet as their enemy in the way in which, as a matter of history, it falls to the lot of such men to be treated. These experiences of suffering which thus come upon the prophet join together to form that image of the servant of the Lord, of his suffering and dying for the sake of God's purpose.

When the Bible then tries to look beyond these manifestations of leadership to one that no longer stands amidst disintegration and failure, when the idea of the Messianic leader is conceived, it means nothing else by it than that at last the answer shall be given: from out of mankind itself the word shall come, the word that is spoken with the whole being of man, the word that answers God's word. It is an earthly consummation that is awaited, a consummation in and with mankind. But this precisely is the consummation toward which God's hand pushes through that which He has created, through nature and through history. This is what the Messianic belief means, the belief in the real leader, in the setting right of the dialogue, in God's disappointment being at an end. And when a fragment of an apocryphal gospel has God say to Jesus: "In all the prophets have I awaited thee, that thou wouldst come and I rest in thee, for thou art my rest," [1] this is the late elaboration of a truly Jewish conception.

The biblical question of leadership is concerned with something greater than moral perfection. The biblical leaders are the foreshadowings of the dialogical man, of the man who commits his whole being to God's dialogue with the world, and who stands firm throughout this dialogue. The

life of those people to whom I have referred is absorbed in
this dialogue, whether the dialogue comes about through an
intervention, as in Abraham's talk with God about Sodom,
or Moses' after the sin of the golden calf; or whether it
comes about through a resistance they offer against that
which comes upon them and tries to overpower them, but
their resistance ends in submission, which we find docu-
mented from Moses to Jeremiah; or whether the dialogue
comes about through the struggle for a purpose and a task,
as we know from that dialogue which took place between
David and God. Whatever the way, man enters into the dialogue again and again; imperfect entry, but yet one that is not
refused, an entry that is determined to persevere in the dialogical world. All that happens is here experienced as
dialogue; what befalls man is taken as a sign; what man tries
to do and what miscarries is taken as an attempt and a failure to answer, as a stammering attempt to respond as well as
one can.

Because this is so, biblical leadership always means a
process of being led. These men are leaders insofar as they
allow themselves to be led, that is, insofar as they accept that
which is offered them, insofar as they take upon themselves
the responsibility for that which is entrusted to them, insofar
as they make real that which has been laid upon them from
outside of themselves, make it real with the free will of their
own being, in the autonomy of their person.

So long as we remember this, we can make the lives of
these leaders clear. Almost always what we see is the taking
of a man out of the community. God lifts the man out of the
community, cuts him off from his natural ties; from Abraham
to Jeremiah he must go forth out of the land in which he has
taken root, away to the place where he has to proclaim the
name of God; it is the same story, whether it is a wandering
over the earth like Abraham's, or a becoming utterly alone in
the midst of the people like the prophets'. They are drawn
out of their natural community; they fight with it, they experience in this community the inner contradiction of human
existence. All this is intensified to the utmost precisely in the
prophets. The great suffering of the prophets, preserved for

us by Jeremiah himself in a small number of (in the highest sense of the word) autobiographical sayings is the ultimate expression of this condition.

But this ever widening gulf between leader and community, the ever greater failure of the leader, the leader's ever greater incompatibility with "history"—this means, from the biblical standpoint, the gradual overcoming of history. What we are accustomed to call history is from the biblical standpoint only the façade of reality. It is the great failure, the refusal to enter into the dialogue—not the failure in the dialogue, as exemplified by biblical man. This great refusal is sanctioned with the imposing sanction provided by so-called history.

The biblical point of view repudiates with ever increasing strength this two-dimensional reality, most strongly in the prophets; it proclaims that the way, the real way, from the Creation to the Kingdom is trod not on the surface of success, but in the deep of failure. The real work, from the biblical point of view, is the late-recorded, the unrecorded, the anonymous work. The real work is done in the shadow, in the quiver. Official leadership fails more and more, leadership devolves more and more upon the secret. The way leads through the work that history does not write down, and that history cannot write down, work that is not ascribed to him who did it, but which possibly at some time in a distant generation will emerge as having been done, without the name of the doer—the secret working of the secret leadership. And when the biblical writer turns his eyes toward the final, Messianic overcoming of history, he sees how the outer history becomes engulfed, or rather how both the outer history and the inner history fuse, how the secret which the leadership had become rises up out of the darkness and illumines the surface of history, how the meaning of biblical history is consummated in the whole reality.

PLATO AND ISAIAH

(ISAIAH 6)

P LATO WAS about seventy-five years old when the assassi-
nation of the prince Dion, master of Syracuse, his friend
and disciple, put an end to the enterprise of founding a republic in accordance with the concepts of the philosopher. It
was at this time that Plato wrote his famous letter to his
friends in Sicily, in which he rendered an account of his life-
long ambition to change the structure of the state (which for
him included the structure of society), of his attempts to
translate this purpose into reality, and of how he failed in
these attempts. He wrote them that, having observed that all
states were poorly governed, he had formed the opinion that
man would not be free from this evil until one of two things
happened: either true philosophers were charged with the
function of government, or the potentates who ruled states
lived and acted in harmony with the precepts of philosophy.
Plato had formulated this thesis—though somewhat differently—about twenty years earlier as the central passage of
his *Republic*. This central position which he gave this passage indicates that in the final analysis he believed that individuals, above all, leaders, were of prime importance rather
than any particular institutions—such institutions as the
book deals with. According to Plato, there are two ways of
obtaining the right persons as leaders: either the philosopher
himself must come to power, or he must educate those who
rule to conduct their lives as philosophers.

In his memorable tractate *Perpetual Peace,* Kant opposed this thesis of Plato's without mentioning him by name. The rebuttal is part of a passage that appeared only in the second edition and that Kant designated as a "secret article" of his outline on international law. He wrote: "Because the wielding of power inevitably destroys the free judgment of reason, it is not to be expected that kings should philosophize or philosophers be kings, nor even to be desired. But one thing is indispensable to both philosophers and kings, because the possession of sovereign power inevitably corrupts the free judgment of reason, and that is that kings or kingly nations, i.e., nations which govern themselves on the basis of laws of equality, should not dispense with or silence the class of philosophers, but let them express themselves in public." Previously, Kant emphasized that this was not meant to suggest that the state should prefer its power to be represented by the principles of the philosopher rather than the dicta of the jurist, but merely that the philosopher should be heard. This line of thought is a clear indication not only of resignation, but also of disappointment in the spirit (*Geist*) itself, for Kant had been forced to relinquish faith in the spirit's ability to rise to power and, at the same time, remain pure. We may safely assume that Kant's disillusionment is motivated by his knowledge of the course of Church history, which in the more than two thousand years intervening between Plato and Kant came to be the spirit's actual history of power.

Plato believed both in the spirit and in power, and he also believed in the spirit's call to the assumption of power. The power he saw was decadent, but he thought it could be regenerated and purified by the spirit. The young Plato's own epochal and grave encounter with "history" took place when the city-state of Athens condemned and executed his teacher Socrates because he had disobeyed the authority of power, and obeyed the Voice. And yet, among all those who concerned themselves with the state, Socrates alone knew how to educate the young for a true life dedicated to the community; like the seer Tiresias in Hades, he was the only one spiritually alive amid a swarm of hovering shades. Plato regarded himself as Socrates' heir and deputy. He knew himself to be called to renew the sacred law and to found the just, law-abiding state. And he knew that for this reason he had a right to power. But while the spirit is ready to accept power at the hands of God or man, it is not willing to seize it.

In the *Republic,* Socrates is asked whether the philosophic man would, if he is as Socrates describes him, be at all apt to concern himself with affairs of state. To this question Socrates replies that the philosophic man, in his own state, would certainly concern himself with such matters, but the state that he conceives and that is suitable to him would have to be one other than his native land, "unless there is some divine intervention." But even prior to this passage, he speaks of the man who is blessed with spirit and yet confronts a furious mob, confronts them without confederates who could help maintain justice, and feels like one who suddenly finds himself surrounded by wild beasts. Such a man, he goes on to say, will henceforth keep silence, attend to his own work, become a spectator, and live out his life without doing any wrong to the end of his days. But when Socrates' listeners interpose that such a man will thus have accomplished a great work by the time he dies, he contradicts them, saying: "But not the greatest, since he has not found the state which befits him."

That is the gist of Plato's resignation. He was called to Syracuse and went there time after time, even though there too he suffered one disappointment after another. He went because he was called and because there is always the possibility that the divine voice may be speaking in the voice of man. According to Dion's words, there was a possibility that then, if ever, the hope to link the philosophers and the rulers of great states to each other could be fulfilled. Plato decided to "try." He reports that he was ashamed not to go to Syracuse, lest he should seem to himself to be nothing but "words." "Manifest" is the word he once used to Dion—we must manifest ourselves by truly being what we profess in words. He had used the word "must," not "should." He went and failed, returned home, went once more and still another time, and failed again. When he came home after the

third failure, he was almost seventy. Not until then did the
man Plato had educated come into power. But before he was
able to master the confusion of the people, he was murdered
by one who had been his fellow student at Plato's Academy.

Plato held that mankind could recover from its ills only
if either the philosophers—"whom we termed useless"—became kings, or the kings became philosophers. He himself
hoped first for the one and then for the other of these alternatives to occur as the result of "divine intervention." But he
was not elevated to a basileus in Greece and the prince whom
he had educated to be a philosopher did not master the chaos
in Sicily. One might possibly say that the peace that Timo-
leon of Corinth established in Sicily after the death of this
prince was achieved under the touch of Plato's spirit, and
that Alexander, who later united all of Greece under his rule,
had certainly not studied philosophy with Plato's most re-
nowned disciple without benefit to himself, but neither in the
one case nor the other was Plato's ideal of the state actually
realized. Plato did not regenerate the decadent Athenian de-
mocracy, and he did not found the republic he had projected
in theory.

But does this glorious failure prove that the spirit is
always helpless in the face of history?

Plato is the most sublime instance of that spirit which
proceeds in its intercourse with reality from its own possession of truth. According to Plato, the perfect soul is one that
remembers its vision of perfection. Before its life on earth,
the soul had beheld the idea of the good. In the world of
ideas, it had beheld the shape of pure justice and now, with
the spirit's growth, the soul recollects what it had beheld in
the past. The soul is not content to know this idea and to
teach others to know it. The soul wishes to infuse the idea of
justice with the breath of life and establish it in the human
world in the living form of a just state. The spirit is in possession of truth; it offers truth to reality; truth becomes reality through the spirit. That is the fundamental basis of Plato's
doctrine. But this doctrine was not carried out. The spirit did
not succeed in giving reality the truth it wished to give. Was
reality alone responsible? Was not the spirit itself responsi-

ble as well? Was not its very relationship to the truth responsible? These are questions that necessarily occur to us in
connection with Plato's failure.

But the spirit can fail in another and very different way.
"In the year that King Uzziah died" (Isa. 6:1) Isaiah
had a vision of the heavenly sanctuary in which the Lord
chose him as His prophet. The entire incident points to the
fact that King Uzziah was still alive. The king had been suffering from leprosy for a long time. It is well known that in biblical times leprosy was not regarded merely as one ailment
among others, but as the physical symptom of a disturbance in
man's relationship to God. Rumor had it that the king had
been afflicted because he had presumed to perform sacral
functions in the sanctuary of Jerusalem which exceeded his
rights as a merely political lieutenant of God. Moreover, Isaiah feels that Uzziah's leprosy was more than a personal
affliction, that it symbolized the uncleanliness of the entire
people, and Isaiah's own uncleanliness as well. They all have
"unclean lips" (Isa. 6:5). Like lepers they must all cover
"their upper lip" (Lev. 13:45), lest by breath or word their
uncleanliness go forth and pollute the world. All of them have
been disobedient and faithless to the true King, to the King
whose glory Isaiah's eyes now behold in His heavenly sanctuary. Here God is called *ha-Melekh* and this is the first time
in the Scriptures that He is designated so nakedly, so plainly,
as the King of Israel. *He* is the King. The leper whom the
people call "king" is only His faithless lieutenant. And now
the true King sends Isaiah with a message to the entire people, at the same time telling him that his message will fail;
he will fail, for the message will be misunderstood, misinterpreted and misused, and thus confirm the people—save for
a small "remnant"—in their faithlessness, and harden their
hearts. At the very outset of his way, Isaiah, the carrier of
the spirit, is told that he must fail. He will not suffer disappointment like Plato, for in his case failure is an integral part
of the way he must take.

Isaiah does not share Plato's belief that the spirit is a
possession of man. The man of spirit—such is the tradition
from time immemorial—is one whom the spirit invades and

seizes, whom the spirit uses as its garment, not one who houses the spirit. Spirit is an event, it is something that happens to man. The storm of the spirit sweeps man where it will, and then storms on into the world.

Neither does Isaiah share Plato's belief that power is man's possession. Power is vouchsafed man to enable him to discharge his duties as God's lieutenant. If he abuses this power, it destroys him, and in place of the spirit that came to prepare him for the use of power (I Sam. 16:14), an "evil spirit" comes upon him. The man in power is responsible to One who interrogates him in silence, and to whom he is answerable, or all is over with him.

Isaiah does not believe that spiritual man has the vocation to power. He knows himself to be a man of spirit and without power. Being a prophet means being powerless, and powerless confronting the powerful and reminding them of their responsibility, as Isaiah reminded Ahaz "in the highway of the fullers' field" (Isa. 7:3). To stand powerless before the power he calls to account is part of the prophet's destiny. He himself is not out for power, and the special sociological significance of his office is based on that very fact.

Plato believed that his soul was perfect. Isaiah did not. Isaiah regarded and acknowledged himself as unclean. He felt how the uncleanliness that tainted his breath and his words was burned from his lips so that those lips might speak the message of God.

Isaiah beheld the throne and the majesty of Him who entrusted him with the message. He did not see the just state which Plato beheld in his mind's eye as something recollected. Isaiah knew and said that men are commanded to be just to one another. He knew and said that the unjust are destroyed by their own injustice. And he knew and said that there would come a dominion of justice and that a just man would rule as the faithful lieutenant of God. But he knew nothing and said nothing of the inner structure of that dominion. He had no idea; he had only a message. He had no institution to establish; he had only to proclaim. His proclamation was in the nature of criticism and demands.

His criticism and demands are directed toward making

the people and their prince recognize the reality of the invisible sovereignty. When Isaiah uses the word *ha-Melekh* it is not in the sense of a theological metaphor, but in that of a political, constitutional concept. But this sovereignty of God which he propounded is the opposite of the sovereignty of priests, which is commonly termed theocracy and which has very properly been described as "*the* most unfree form of society," for it is "unfree through the abuse of the Highest knowable to man." [1] None but the powerless can speak the true King's will with regard to the state, and remind both the people and the government of their *common* responsibility toward this will. The powerless man can do so because he breaks through the illusions of current history and recognizes potential crises.

That is why his criticism and demands are directed toward society, toward the life men live together. A people that seriously calls God Himself its King must become a true people, a community all the members of which are governed by honesty without compulsion, kindness without hypocrisy, and the brotherliness of those who are passionately devoted to their divine Leader. When social inequality, when distinction between the free and the unfree splits the community and creates chasms between its members, there can be no true people, there can be no more "God's people." So, the criticism and demands are directed toward every individual on whom other individuals depend, everyone who has a hand in shaping the destinies of others, and that means they are directed toward every one of us. When Isaiah speaks of justice, he is not thinking of institutions but of you and me, because without you and me the most glorious institution becomes a lie.

Finally, the criticism and demands apply to Israel's relationship to other nations. They warn Israel not to consent to the making of treaties, not to rely on this or that so-called world power, but to "keep calm" (Isa. 7:4; 30:15), to make our own people a true people, faithful to its divine King, and then we will have nothing to be afraid of. "The head of Damascus," Isaiah said to Ahaz in the highway of the fullers' field, "is Rezin, and the head of Samaria, Pekah,"

meaning "but you know who is the Head of Jerusalem—if
you want to know." But "If ye will not have faith, surely ye
shall not endure" (Isa. 7:9).

There has been much talk in this connection of "Utopian" politics which would relate Isaiah's failure to that of
Plato, who wrote the Utopian *Republic*. What Isaiah said to
Ahaz is accepted as a sublimely "religious" but politically
valueless utterance, meaning one that lends itself to solemn
quotation but is not applicable to reality. Yet the only political chance for a small people hemmed in between world
powers is the metapolitical chance to which Isaiah pointed.
He proclaimed a truth that could not, indeed, be tested in
history up to that time, but only because no one ever thought
of testing it. Nations can be led to peace only by a people
that has made peace a reality within itself. The realization of
the spirit has a magnetic effect on mankind which despairs
of the spirit. That is the meaning Isaiah's teachings have for
us. When the mountain of the Lord's house is "established"
on the reality of true community life, then, and only then,
the nations will "flow" toward it (Isa. 2:2), there to learn
peace in place of war.

Isaiah too failed, as was predicted when he was called
to give God's message. The people and the king opposed
him, and even the king's successor, who attached himself to
Isaiah, was found wanting in the decisive hour, when he
flirted with the idea of joining the Babylonian rebel against
Assyria. But this failure is quite different from Plato's. Our
very existence as Jews testifies to this difference. We live by
that encounter in the highway of the fullers' field, we live by
virtue of the fact that there were people who were deadly
serious about this *ha-Melekh* in relation to all of their social
and political reality. They are the cause of our survival until
this new opportunity to translate the spirit into the reality we
have a presentiment of. We may yet experience an era of
history that refutes "history." The prophet fails in one hour
in history, but not so far as the future of his people is concerned. For his people preserve his message as something
that will be realized at another hour, under other conditions,
and in other forms.

The prophet's spirit does not, like Plato's, believe that he possesses an abstract and general, a timeless concept of truth. He always receives only one message for one situation. That is exactly why, after thousands of years, his words still address the changing situations in history. He does not confront man with a generally valid image of perfection, with a Pantopia or a Utopia. Neither has he the choice between his native land and some other country which might be "more suitable to him." In his work of realization, he is bound to the *topos,* to this place, to this people, because it is the people who must make the *beginning.* But when the prophet feels like one who finds himself surrounded by wild beasts, he cannot withdraw to the role of the silent spectator, as Plato did. He must speak his message. The message will be misunderstood, misinterpreted, misused, it will even confirm and harden the people in their faithlessness. But its sting will rankle within them for all time.

REDEMPTION
(ISAIAH AND DEUTERO-ISAIAH)

W E FIND in many peoples of antiquity, and also in talmudic and post-talmudic Jewry, the conception of a
holy place as the center of the earth, its "navel." Apart from
a few isolated hints (Ezek. 38:12), no evidence of such an
idea has come down to us from the Bible, and certainly none
that might suggest the site of the Temple in Jerusalem. On
the other hand, however, we observe how, in the prophetic
writings, an image of Zion as the center of the future, redeemed world is gradually established. This image is peculiar to the prophetic literature of Israel and the Psalms that
derive from it; as far as I know there is nothing analogous
anywhere else in the sacred books of the peoples.

It is particularly the Book of Isaiah in which the image
is fully developed. To see this clearly, however, one must
rid oneself of the familiar idea that speeches, songs, and sayings of the prophet Isaiah are combined in this book with
later material which is foreign to him and was associated
with the earlier material for purely technical reasons. With
a few exceptions the contents of the book are indeed connected with Isaiah; in other words, apart from what has been
preserved of his own utterances, it contains the words of disciples of his, in the main not those who had actually sat
at his feet, but those who adopted his teaching a long time
after his death and elaborated some point or other in it.

Toward the end of the Babylonian exile the most prom-
inent among them is that mysterious man whose real name

has no more come down to us than that of the other followers of Isaiah and who is usually called "Deutero-Isaiah."
Independent as he is—far and away the most independent
figure among the prophets of the Exile and after the Exile—
all the same he deliberately and emphatically models himself
on Isaiah as far as the form and language of his prophecies
are concerned, and he wishes to be considered Isaiah's posthumous disciple, the interpreter and perfecter of his teaching,
as is obvious from a number of unmistakable references.[1]
This peculiar relationship between a son of the Crisis and
the master of the high age of prophecy is shown particularly clearly in the way in which he elaborates Isaiah's doctrine of Zion as the eschatological center of the world.

Of all the prophets of Israel, Isaiah is the only one
whose vision and prophecy are focused on the Temple of
Solomon. It was in the Temple that he had been consecrated
a prophet and, in the vision, he had seen the earthly sanctuary become transformed into the heavenly. From that hour
he knew that this place was chosen to become the center of
the world of God, of God's world-embracing Kingdom. But
it has not yet become that which it has been chosen to become, because the people of Israel that is to build this center, by subjecting the whole of its life to the rule of God,
desecrates the sanctuary in which it treads (1:12) by its
iniquity. It must purify itself and learn righteousness; it must
learn to walk in the light of God (2:5) before the holy
mountain, now superior to all the mountains of the world, is
"ready" (2:2) to receive the delegates of all peoples who
will come to share in the Revelation which shall bring all
strife to an end and create a united humanity. This is the
second Revelation, the second "Torah" (2:3): the first was
given to the people of Israel from the mountain in the wilderness, the second is now given to the whole human race
from the mountain of the Temple. (Hence the promise, in a
fragment [4:5] that perhaps does not come from Isaiah but
was certainly written in his spirit, that the cloud of smoke
and a flaming fire will stand over it as once over Sinai.)
Here, when all evil has been rooted out, will be the center
of a peaceful intercourse of the nations (11:6–8, represented

symbolically as animals) in mutual good will and trust. "In that day shall Israel be the third with Egypt and Assyria"— the two world powers that have waged war on each other and on Israel for so long—as a no less important "third power," "a blessing in the midst of the land" (19:24).

This is the context in which Isaiah's teaching on the *security* of Zion is to be understood. Because it is destined to be the center of the Kingdom of God, thus the prophet declares, no earthly power can do it any harm. Therefore the Assyrians and their auxiliary troops, the "throng of all the nations that fight against Mount Zion" (29:8), shall be scattered as chaff: God Himself, "YHVH of hosts," will come down "to fight for Mount Zion" (31:4)—the same verb is deliberately used here, in a sense that is otherwise quite unusual, to describe the action of God and of the enemy. And there as here Zion is called "the hearth of God"; this refers of course to the sacrificial rites, but, for Isaiah, the altar fire of the Temple is fundamentally different from all other sacrificial fires of the peoples, a token of the presence of the "King" (6:5) and of that divine dominion over all the world which will move to its consummation from this place.

The danger of this teaching, the fact that it is apt to produce a false sense of security in the people, which may work against the prophetic call to purification, is realized by the line of prophets from Micah—perhaps a rebellious disciple of Isaiah—to Jeremiah. They do their very utmost to strike the hearts of the careless people who make the existence of the sanctuary an excuse for their evasion of the divine challenge: they prophesy the destruction of the Temple. Fourteen years after the fulfillment of this prophecy, Ezekiel plans the building of the new temple; but there is no sign in his writing of the templocentric view according to which the sanctuary in Jerusalem is the center of the redeemed earth of the future. Nevertheless in the hours of the catastrophe and those that follow it a new elaboration of Isaiah's view is prepared, the essential statements of which have, quite logically, been incorporated into the Book of Isaiah, which we may thus regard as the templocentric book *par excellence* in the corpus of Israelite prophecy.

The first of these statements is contained in the small collection of fragments (chapters 24–27) consisting chiefly of pieces that come, in my opinion, from the last phase of the catastrophe and the early period of the Exile. Here it is proclaimed (24:23) that "YHVH of hosts shall reign in Mount Zion." It is a reign over all people and "in this mountain shall YHVH of hosts make unto all people a feast" (25:6), a homage feast: it is repeated three times that the invitation and the consolations of God "which shall wipe away the tear from off all faces" apply to all peoples. Just as the veil of sorrow that God lifts from the faces of all peoples probably does not signify the sadness of the single person but the sufferings that arise from the conflicts of the peoples, so the mysterious "swallowing up of death forever" (25:8) seems to refer not to the bestowal of immortality on the single person but to the overcoming of the power of death that governs the relationships between the peoples. No less mysterious, however, is the taking away of the "reproach of His people" from "all the earth." In this context Israel, of which one naturally tends to think here, can hardly be meant. If we compare this statement with the cognate Psalm 47, one of those in which the accession of God as king over "the peoples" is glorified, we see that "the noble men of the peoples" who gather around the "throne of His holiness"—probably Mount Zion is meant here too—are conjointly called "the people of the God of Abraham," because he, "the father of the multitude of the peoples" (a phrase that is certainly not meant to be taken genealogically) is the one in whom "all the clans of the earth shall bless themselves." Thus the words of Isaiah may also refer to the human people gathered together from all the peoples of the earth whose "reproach," namely the disintegration into hostile, mutually foreign peoples that originated in the Tower of Babel, is now removed from the whole earth. Here Isaiah's prophecy of the peoples streaming to the mountain (to which the final words "for the Lord hath spoken it" probably refer) seems to have been elaborated into a new and uniform image of the divine King, who on His mountain throne wipes away the tears from all His peoples as a father wipes them from the faces of all his

children and thus redeems them, through the fellowship of
His table and His hand, from the common reproach.

The transformation of Isaiah's Zionist outlook by
"Deutero-Isaiah" and his school, which begins in the late period of the Exile, is far more comprehensive and far-reach-
ing. The hour that is proclaimed here is that in which God
returns to Zion to begin His reign as King (52:7). The reign
of the one great Messianic peace that now begins is described
in pictures that readopt the motifs of Isaiah, partly using the
same words as when (65:25) the prophecy of the mutual
understanding of wild and tame animals—in this context
they are probably intended to be taken as animals and not
as symbols of peoples—ends, like that of Isaiah, with the
words: "they shall not hurt nor destroy in all my holy mountain." But something new is added, namely, the characterization of the hour announced by the prophet as a moment of
world-historical importance. This is only what we should
expect from the prophet who first welcomes Cyrus as the
liberator of both Israel and the enslaved nations and then,
when he is disappointed by him, assigns the task not merely
of bringing Israel back into its own land, but of being a light
of the nations (42:6; 49:6) and of "bringing them that sit
in darkness out of the prison house" (42:7; 49:9), to "the
servant of the Lord" coming from Israel. He, the servant, is
to "make them possess the desolate possessions" (49:8),
just as Israel, returning from Babel, is now restored to the
possession of its land.

Through this work of liberating and restoring humanity
around the liberation and restoration of Israel, the servant
becomes the "covenant of the people": through him the peoples are bound together into one people; in him the people
compounded of the peoples is represented. And through him
redeemed Zion becomes the center of the redeemed world.
The redemption is valid, however, not only for humanity but
for the whole world, and it is precisely this world-redemption
that is centered in Zion. At one and the same time God
"plants" the heaven and says to Zion, "Thou art my people"
(51:16); at one and the same time He creates a new heaven
and a new earth and "creates" Jerusalem (65:17 f.). The

renewal of the world and the renewal of Zion are one and
the same thing, for Zion is the heart of the renewed world.
Isaiah's Zionocentric view has here acquired cosmic propor-
tions.

The people of Israel is called upon to be the herald and
pioneer of the redeemed world, the land of Israel to be its
center and the throne of its King. In this doctrine the biblical
view of the unique significance of the connection between
this people and this land reaches its climax.

FALSE PROPHETS

(JEREMIAH 28)

W HEN HANANIAH took the yoke from the prophet Jeremiah's neck, broke it, and announced to the people
that within two years God would break the yoke of Nebu-
chadnezzar from the necks of all the nations, Jeremiah went
his way in silence. Not until God sent him to Hananiah with
a message did Jeremiah go to him and say what he had to
say.

I am always deeply moved when I come to this passage,
and always learn from it anew. Of all the prophets, Jeremiah
is the only one who knew he was elected to his office at the
very hour of his birth—in accordance with the gravity of the
historical juncture and the decisions it dictated. He felt that
the hand of God had touched his mouth and with that touch
had enabled him to speak the words of God. It was God
Himself who told him that he was "set over the nations and
over the kingdoms" (Jer. 1:10) and that the judgment of
God which would be realized in history would be communicated to him. And even more: it was in response to God's
command that Jeremiah had laid the bar, which Hananiah
broke, on his own neck as a sign that in this historical juncture it was God's will that the nations be subject to Nebu-
chadnezzar, his strange "servant" (Jer. 43:10). Yet, in spite
of all this, he was silent when the bar was broken and went
his way. He went in order to listen for God's word. Why did
he go? Obviously, because in spite of everything there were
still things he did not know. Hananiah had spoken like a

man who "knows it all." Jeremiah had heard him speak like
a man who "knows it all," but there were still things Jeremiah himself did not know. God had, indeed, spoken to him
only an hour before. But this was another hour. History is a
dynamic process, and history means that one hour is never
like the one that has gone before. God operates in history,
and God is not a machine which, once it has been wound up,
keeps on running until it runs down. He is a living God.
Even the word God speaks at a certain hour, the word one
obeys by laying a yoke on one's neck, must not be hung up
like a placard. God has truth, but He does not have a system. He expresses His truth through His will, but His will is
not a program. At this hour, God wills this or that for mankind, but He has endowed mankind with a will of its own,
and even with sufficient power to carry it out. So, mankind
can change its will from one hour to the next, and God, who
is deeply concerned about mankind and its will, and the possible changes it may undergo, can, when that will changes,
change His plan for mankind. That means that historical reality can have been changed. One must not rely on one's
knowledge. One must go one's way and listen all over again.
There were things Jeremiah did not know, and knew that he
did not know. Socrates has told something similar about
himself. But Jeremiah differed from Socrates in that he realized that from time to time he could learn something new.
Socrates too—so he tells us—occasionally heard the voice
of Daimonion, but it always told him only what he was not
to do. The voice that instructed Jeremiah told him what he
was to do and say. If one hears Hananiah's voice, and cannot
hear the voice of God, perhaps because "the still small
voice" (I Kings 19:12) can be drowned out by that of the
Hananiahs, it is best to go one's way and to listen.

Hananiah "knew it all." He did not know the truth,
because he "knew it all." What does this mean? He said that
God had spoken and that he would break the yoke of the
king of Babylon. How did he know it? He did not say that
God had spoken to him. He, the false prophet, did not lie.
Hananiah was no liar. He told what truth he knew. But the
unfortunate thing was that he did not know any truth and

could not know any because he never understood what it
meant to go one's way and listen.

He has very aptly been called a caricature of Isaiah.
What is more, he parrots Isaiah. The prophet Isaiah proclaimed God's will to break the yoke of Asshur from off the
necks of His people (Isa. 10:27). From this Hananiah concluded that God had promised to break the yoke of Babylon,
for the situation seemed the same. But the situation was *not*
the same. When Isaiah transmitted the will of God, Israel was
assigned a historical task, not a religious obligation in the or-
dinary sense of the word, but a task concerned with domestic
and foreign politics and comprehending the entire life of the
people. King Hezekiah's generation had been expected to assume and fulfill this task, and it had looked as though it
would. But it did not. King Josiah's generation, which did assume it, was no longer able to accomplish it because the historical conditions had changed. The failure to accomplish it
had led to a situation because of which and for which Jeremiah required the people to accept *destiny* and to fulfill the
deepest meaning of this destiny by turning wholly to God, i.e.,
by taking on themselves the yoke of Babylon and preparing
the new freedom, the true freedom in the midst of servitude.
Later, after the catastrophe had occurred, after the Exile had
begun, Jeremiah made a promise in accordance with altered
conditions and a changing generation. He promised that the
yoke of Babylon would be broken from their neck; so altered,
Hananiah's prophecy had come true. But Hananiah knew
nothing of all this. As far as he was concerned, God was a
man faithful to His principles, who had tied himself down by
the promise He had given Isaiah. He had promised to protect "this city" (Isa. 37:35), and so the false prophets have
Him say—at a completely different historical juncture—that
He would give Israel true peace "in this place" (Jer. 28:4).
Hananiah did not know that there was such a thing as a different historical juncture. He did not know that there was
such a thing as guilt, guilt which means the neglect of the
task of the hour. And so he did not know that something that
had existed was no longer. Neither did he know that there is
a turning through which we are granted a possibility that

only a moment ago did not exist. He did not know that history is a dynamic process. All he knew was the revolving wheel, not the scales and the pointer on the scales that trembles like a human heart.

Hananiah was a forthright patriot, and he was convinced that being patriotic meant being as he was. He was convinced that Jeremiah had no love whatsoever for his country, for if he had, how could he have expected his people to bend their necks to the yoke? But Jeremiah had a concrete concern for what was taking place. "Wherefore should this city become desolate?" Hananiah had no such concern. Instead, he had his patriotism which does not allow such concerns to come up. What he called his fatherland was a political concept. Jeremiah's fatherland was a land inhabited by human beings, a settlement that was alive and mortal. His God did not wish it to perish. He wished to preserve it by putting those human beings under the yoke.

Hananiah considered himself a great politician, for he thought that in an hour of danger he had succeeded in strengthening the people's resistance. But what he actually strengthened was an illusion, which when it collapsed would cause the collapse of the people's strength. Jeremiah, on the other hand, wanted to protect Israel from just that. The only way to salvation is by the steep and stony path over the recognition of reality. The feet of those who take it bleed, and there is always the threat of dizziness, but it is the one and only way.

The true prophets are the true politicians of reality, for they proclaim their political tidings from the viewpoint of the complete historical reality, which it is given them to see. The false prophets, the politicians who foster illusions, use the power of their wishful thinking to tear a scrap out of historical reality and sew it into their quilt of motley illusions. When they are out to influence through suggestion, they display the gay colors; and when they are asked for the material of truth, they point to the scrap, torn out of reality.

As early as the days of Hezekiah, the false prophets with their illusion-politics prevented the persons concerned from growing fully aware of the great task, from resolving to

take it upon themselves and educating the people to its ac-
complishment. They popularized only the promise contained
in Isaiah's tidings, passing over the conditions under which
it would be valid, for every prophecy of salvation is conditional. The false prophets perverted the conditional promise
to an Israel that would accomplish its task into an unconditional promise of security for all time. When this illusion
became dominant and everything happened as it did, they
blocked the way—which was still open—to the people's acceptance of their destiny and their changing it by that very
acceptance. They blocked the way by adapting old, and
manufacturing new and dazzling illusions, by pretending the
existence of a path where there was none, and clouding over
the one and only open way. That was the stubborn situation
which Jeremiah came up against with his powerless word.
How poor is the one reality in the face of the thousand
dreams!

False prophets are not godless. They adore the god
"success." They themselves are in constant need of success
and achieve it by promising it to the people. But they do
honestly want success for the people. The craving for success governs their hearts and determines what rises from
them. That is what Jeremiah called "the deceit of their own
heart" (Jer. 14:14). They do not deceive; they are deceived,
and can breathe only in the air of deceit.

The true prophets know the little, bloated idol that goes
by the name of "success" through and through. They know
that ten successes that are nothing but successes can lead to
defeat, while on the contrary ten failures can add up to a
victory, provided the spirit stands firm. When true prophets
address the people, they are usually unsuccessful; everything
in the people that craves for success opposes them. But the
moment they are thrown into the pit, whatever spirit is still
alive in Israel bursts into flame, and the turning begins in
secret which, in the midst of the deepest distress, will lead to
renewal.

The false prophet feeds on dreams, and acts as if
dreams were reality. The true prophet lives by the true word
he hears, and must endure having it treated as though it only

held true for some "ideological" sphere, "morals" or "religion," but not for the real life of the people.

We have no Jeremiah at this juncture. Neither have we a Micaiah, the son of Imlah (I Kings 22). But at every street corner you are likely to run into Hananiah, or standing slightly to the right, his colleague Zedekiah, the son of Chenaanah, with horns of iron or cardboard on his temples, and empty air issuing from his mouth. Brilliant or insignificant—he is always the same. Look him straight in the eye, as though to say "I know you!" His glance will not waver. But perhaps the next time he dreams his dream, he will remember how you looked at him, and be startled out of his fantasies. And the next time he tells his dream as if it were the word of God, perhaps he will trip over a phrase and pause. No more than an instant, but these instants of incipient reflection are important.

PROPHECY, APOCALYPTIC,
AND THE HISTORICAL HOUR

THE man who, without particularly reflecting on himself, allows himself to be borne along by the bustle of life, still at times unexpectedly finds himself confronted by an hour that has a special and even an especially questionable connection with his personal future. Among his possible reactions, two stand out as essential. The man I speak of can the next instant renounce the beaten track, draw forth forgotten primal forces from their hiding places, and make the decision that answers the situation; he cherishes the until-now-unsuspected certainty of thus being able to participate on the ground of becoming, in the factual decision that will be made about the make-up of the next hour, and thereby in some measure also about the make-up of future hours. Or, in contrast, he may banish all such impulses and resolve, as one says, not to let himself be fooled—not by the situation, which is just an embroilment, and not by himself, who is just a man come to grief; for everything is linked invincibly with everything else, and there is nowhere a break where he can take hold. He surrenders anew to the turmoil, but now, so he thinks, out of insight.

If, disregarding all differences and complications, we transpose this hour, with its indwelling possibilities of these two basic human attitudes set in polar opposition, from the realm of biography into that of history, we catch sight of a problematic it may be instructive to look into.

But from what standpoint is this problematic adequately to be grasped, as is necessary, so that, gazing with clarified spirit into the depths of reality, we can make the right choice between affirmation of choice and denial of choice? How shall we manage to escape from the dilemma whose discursive expression is the old philosophical quarrel between indeterministic and deterministic views of the world? It is not within the province of philosophical dialectic to offer us help here; the highest that it can attain is, instead of setting the two aspects in opposition to each other, understanding them as two irreconcilable-reconcilable sides of the same event. In this, to be sure, philosophy does justice to the life experience in which the moment of beginning the action is illumined by the awareness of freedom, and the moment of having acted is overshadowed by the knowledge of necessity. But where it is no longer a matter of aspects, either experienced or recalled, and no longer a matter of their connection with each other, but of the soul's innermost question of trust, such philosophizing does not suffice to guide us.

This question is: Do I dare the definitely impossible or do I adapt myself to the unavoidable? Do I dare to become other than I am, trusting that in reality I am indeed other and can so put it to the test, or do I take cognizance of a barrier in my present existence as something that will eternally be a barrier? Transposing the question from biography to history: does a historical hour ever experience its real limits otherwise than through undertaking to overstep those limits it is familiar with? Does the future establish itself ever anew, or is it inescapably destined? For this innermost inwardness of our praxis there is no help besides trust itself or, to call it by its sacral name, faith. But this faith is not our own personal faith alone. The history of human faith also affords us help. Its help is not the kind that simply places the right before our eyes in historical realization as a truth that no contradiction confronts. A glance at man's history of faith may so clarify the antithesis of the two possibilities that the decision between them can take place in full light. In the history of faith, my faith finds irreplaceable support even where it receives only a new manner of choosing.

In the history of Judaism these two basic attitudes rose
into the purity and unconditionality of the religious sphere,
being embodied in two great manifestations of the spirit
which, by virtue of this purity and unconditionality, assumed
a significance for man's way in the world, and particularly for
the present stretch of the way, hardly to be comprehended
deeply enough.

These embodiments are the prophets in the ages of the
kings of Judah and Israel and the apocalyptic writings of
Jewish and Jewish-Christian coinage in the age of late Hel-
lenism and its decline. The question here is not one of the
changing historical events and the judgments concerning
them passed under the divine summons by the prophet or
apocalyptic writer living at that time. It is rather a question
of two essentially different views from the standpoint of
which the prophetic sayings on the one side and the apocalyptic texts on the other are to be understood. Common to
both is faith in the one Lord of the past, present, and future
history of all existing beings; both views are certain of His
will to grant salvation to His creation. But how this will manifest itself in the pregnant moment in which the speaker
speaks, what relation this moment bears to coming events,
what share in this relation falls to men, and first and foremost to the hearers of the speaker—at these points the prophetic and the apocalyptic messages essentially diverge.

This difference, as has been said, is by no means of
merely historical significance: it has something of the utmost
importance to teach each generation, and specifically our
own. In order to throw this significance into bold relief, I
must disregard all that is atypical, elementally significant
though it may be. I must disregard the question of what
apocalyptic motifs are already, here and there, to be found
among the classical prophets and what prophetic motifs are
still, here and there, to be found among the late apocalyptics.
I must show the essential difference of the basic attitudes
through the clearest examples.

In a time when the external and internal crisis of the
kingdom of Judah began to manifest itself in momentous

signs, about twenty years before the destruction of Jerusalem by the Chaldeans, Jeremiah received the divine command to go to the workshop of the potter in the valley below; there God would speak to him (Jer. 18:2). We understand what is meant: the prophet shall contemplate a reality that shall come to him as a revelatory parable in the midst of his contemplation. Jeremiah went down and beheld how the potter fashioned the clay on the double wheels. "And if the vessel that he made was marred while still in the clay in the potter's hand, then he made out of it again another vessel, even as it seemed right to make to the potter's eye" (18:4). Three times, in the great biblical style of repetition, the word "to make" is hammered in; the matter in question here is the sovereignty of the making. In contemplating this sovereignty, Jeremiah received the message of God in which, time after time again, that word recurs: "Cannot I do with you as this potter, O house of Israel? Behold, as the clay in the potter's hand, so are you in my hand, O house of Israel! At one instant I may speak over a nation, over a kingdom, to root out, to tear down, to dismantle—but if that nation turn from its evil for the sake of which I have spoken against it, I am sorry for the evil that I planned to make for it. And again at one instant I speak over a nation, over a kingdom, to build up, to plant, but if it do evil in my eyes so that my voice remains unheard, I am sorry for the good with which I have said I would benefit it" (18:6 ff.).

We must bear in mind that in just these verbal terms, the young Jeremiah had received two decades before his summons as "announcer to the nations" (1:5, 7, 10). "To whomever I shall send thee," it was there said to him, "thou shalt go; whatever I shall command thee, thou shalt speak" (1:6). While he felt on his mouth the touch of a finger, he heard further: "I have put my words in thy mouth; see, I appoint thee this day over the nations, over the kingdoms, to root out, to tear down, to dismantle, to annihilate, to build, to plant" (1:9 f.). The communication to him as the chosen *nabi,* the "announcer"—that is, the one who utters the speech of heaven—comes to him now in exact relation to the language of the summons, expanded in meaning, while the lower potter's wheel revolves before him and the vessels are formed on the upper wheel, the successes to remain in the world, the failures to be rejected and shaped anew.

Thus the divine potter works on the historical shapes and destinies of human nations. But, in accordance with His will, this work of His can itself will, can itself either do or not do; with this doing and not-doing that it wills, it touches on the work of the Worker. From the beginning He has granted this freedom to them, and in all sovereignty of His fashioning and destroying, He still gives to them, just in so doing, the answer—fashioning and destroying. He "is sorry for" the planned good when they turn away from Him; He "is sorry for" the planned evil when they turn back to Him.

But the announcer—this creature God once addressed, "Thou shalt be as my mouth" (15:19)—is a part of the happening. For he is obliged at times to say "what God is working," as is said in the prophecy of Balaam (Num. 23: 23)—to say it to those whom it concerns. He can do that, however, in two different ways. The one way is the open alternative. Thus we hear Jeremiah time after time speak to his people in the most direct manner when he delivers to them the concise saying of God: "Better your ways and your affairs and I shall allow you to dwell in this place" (7:5 ff.). But when those so appealed to persistently resist the call, he no longer proclaims the alternative but announces the approaching catastrophe as an unalterable doom. Yet even in this threat the gate of grace still remains open for man when he turns his whole being back to God. Here, too, no end is set to the real working power of the dialogue between divinity and mankind, within which compassion can answer man's turning of his whole being back to God.

This depth of dialogical reciprocity between heaven and earth is brought to its strongest expression by the prophets of Israel—from the early period till the postexilic epoch—through one of those meaningful word-repetitions and word-correspondences that so richly abound in the Hebrew Bible. The turning of the being of man and the divine response are often designated by the same verb, a verb that can signify to turn back as well as to turn away, but also to return and to turn toward someone, and this fullness of meaning was taken advantage of in the texts. Already, in one of the earliest of the biblical prophets, in Hosea, we hear God speak first of all, "Return, Israel, unto the Lord," and once again, "Return"; then it says (just as later in Jeremiah), "I shall heal your turnings away"; but now follows "I shall love them freely, for my wrath is turned away from them" (Hosea 14: 2, 5). This correspondence, expressed through the repetition of the verb, between the action of man and the action of God, which is not at all a causal but a purely dialogical connection between the two, continues in a clear tradition of style into the postexilic age. The late, yet word-powerful prophet Joel sees in his vision a terrible enemy approaching, yet the description of the threatening invasion is followed by God's statement, "Return to me with all your heart." Then the text says once more, "Return to the Lord your God"; but now it is said, "Who knows whether He will not return and be sorry" (Joel 2:12 ff.).

The same turn of speech, "Who knows," as expression of the timid hope of those turning back, we find again in the late fable of Jonah who, contrary to the prevailing interpretation, seems to me to derive from a time when there was still a living tendency to make clear to the people that the task of the genuine prophet was not to predict but to confront man with the alternatives of decision. It is not mere literature; rather, with all its epigonic character, it is still a real echo of the prophetic language in the shape of a reverent paradigm when the king of the Ninevites first calls to his people, to whom the exact data of their destruction have just been announced, "Every one shall turn back from his evil way," and then adds, "Who knows, God may return, He may be sorry and may turn back from the flaming of His wrath, and we shall not perish" (Jonah 3:8 f.).

What view of the ruling of the Ruler underlies all this? Clearly a view that preserves the mystery of the dialogical intercourse between God and man from all desire for dogmatic encystment. The mystery is that of man's creation as a being with the power of actually choosing between the ways, who ever again and even now has the power to choose between them. Only such a being is suited to be God's partner in the dialogue of history. The future is not fixed, for God wants man to come to Him with full freedom, to return to Him even out of a plight of extreme hopelessness and then to be really with Him. This is the prophetic *theologem,* never expressed as such but firmly embedded in the foundations of Hebrew prophecy.

An apocryphal gospel fragment of Jewish-Christian origin has the Holy Ghost say to Jesus at the baptism in the Jordan that he has awaited him "in all the prophets." This historical waiting of the spirit for man's fulfillment of the intention of creation is prophecy's breath of life. The prophetic faith involves the faith in the *factual* character of human experience, as existence that factually meets transcendence. Prophecy has in its way declared that the unique being, man, is created to be a center of surprise in creation. Because and so long as man exists, factual change of direction can take place toward salvation as well as toward disaster, starting from the world in each hour, no matter how late. This message has been proclaimed by the prophets to all future generations, to each generation in its own language.

Many noteworthy mixed forms lead from the historical sphere into that of apocalyptic, but it does not belong to my present task to discuss them. I must, however, call one manifestation to mind because it illustrates not a transitional form but an exception to that type. I refer to that anonymous prophet of the Babylonian exile who has been named after Isaiah, not only because his prophecies have been included in the Book of Isaiah, but also because he clearly understood himself as a posthumous disciple of Isaiah's. Among the prophets he was the man who had to announce world history and to herald it as divinely predestined. In place of the dialogue between God and people he brings the comfort of the One preparing redemption to those He wants to redeem; God speaks here as not only having foreknown but also having foretold what now takes place in history— the revolutionary changes in the life of the nations and the liberation of Israel consummated in it. There is no longer room here for an alternative: the future is spoken of as being established from the beginning.

This transformation of the prophetic perspective was facilitated for "Deutero-Isaiah" through the fact that he associated himself across the centuries with the great announcer who, as the memoir whose author he was (Isa. 6–8) shows, again and again knew himself bound by the cruel duty to withhold from the people the dimension of the alternative and who often can only utter it in symbols. But essentially the transformation had been made possible by the unheard-of new character of the historical situation. Here for the first time a prophet had to proclaim an atonement fulfilled through the suffering of the people. The guilt is atoned for, a new day begins. During this time in which history holds its breath, the alternative is silent. In this moment what is in question is no longer a choosing as a people between two ways, but apprehending as an individual the new, higher summons which shall be fulfilled through a series of "servants of the Lord," a series at the beginning of which the speaker sees himself. An epoch such as ours, entangled in guilt and far from atonement, can learn something great from this prophet, but it cannot take anything directly from him. Here something not dependent upon our wills shines on us comfortingly.

If we aim to set in contrast the historical categories of prophecy and apocalyptic in the greatest possible purity of their distinctive natures, then, just as we proceeded from the prophecy of Jeremiah as one that embodies in the exact sense the prophetic vision of present and future, so for the presentation of the apocalyptic we shall do well to select one of its two most mature late works—the Revelation of John and the so-called Fourth Book of Ezra. Although the work that closes the Christian canon is the more significant of the two, I still prefer the other for our purpose, since it affords a fuller insight into the relationship of the speaker to contemporary history. The book, whose constituent parts probably originated around the middle of the first Christian century, obviously received its final form only decades after

the destruction of Jerusalem by the Romans. Yet the speaker
pretends to be living as a member of the king's house in exile
just after the destruction of Jerusalem by the Chaldeans.

Such a literary fiction, common to most of the apocalyptic writers, is by no means a secondary phenomenon; the
actual historical-biographical situation of the speaker is deliberately replaced by an alien scene taken over as analogous
to his own. That fiction plunges us already into the depths of
the problematic. The time the prophetic voice calls us to
take part in is the time of the actual decision; to this the
prophet summons his hearers, not seldom at the risk of
martyrdom to himself. In the world of the apocalyptic this
present historical-biographical hour hardly ever exists, precisely because a decision by men constituting a factor in the
historical-suprahistorical decision is not in question here.
The prophet addresses persons who hear him, who should
hear him. He knows himself sent to them in order to place
before them the stern alternatives of the hour. Even when
he writes his message or has it written, whether it is already
spoken or is still to be spoken, it is always intended for
particular men, to induce them, as directly as if they were
hearers, to recognize their situation's demand for decision
and to act accordingly. The apocalyptic writer has no audience turned toward him; he speaks into his notebook. He
does not really speak, he only writes; he does not write down
the speech, he just writes his thoughts—he writes a book.

The prophet speaks the word that it is his task to speak;
he is borne by this task, proceeding from a divine purpose
and pointing to a divine goal. The spirit moves him; not only
his organs of speech but the whole man is taken up into the
service of the spirit. The body and life of the man become
a part of this service and by this a symbol of the message.
The burden of a message is at times laid on individual apocalyptic writers, but this message is not joined to a life task.
The author of the Ezra revelation does not recognize at all
a vital task. At the beginning of his book the speaker—we do
not know whether it is the actual speaker or only the ficti-
tious one that is meant—lies on his bed and, visited by a
great anxiety over the fate of Israel and that of the human

race, laments to heaven and complains of the government of the world while relating to God in some detail biblical history from the Creation on, supplemented by critical questions. Conversations with angels follow who disclose to the so-called "Ezra" the mysteries of heaven and of the coming aeons; visions mingle in the conversations, mostly of a schematic-allegorical nature, and are interpreted piece by piece in an orderly fashion. At the conclusion a task is formulated, but this is merely an ingredient of the literary fiction, and apparently is not even of the original one; for instead of that prince of the sixth century, Ezra the Scribe stands before us. Ezra is commanded to write down the twenty-four books of the Old Testament canon and in addition seventy books of secret teaching; when he has accomplished this he disappears.[1]

Nowhere in the book does there stir the prophetic breath of actually-happening history and its fullness of decision. Everything here is predetermined, all human decisions are only sham struggles. The future does not come to pass; the future is already present in heaven, as it were, present from the beginning. Therefore, it can be "disclosed" to the speaker and he can disclose it to others. His innermost question, accordingly, is not concerned with what poor man shall undertake but why things happen to him as they do. In this search, to be sure, the question of Jeremiah and Job, why good befalls the wicked and evil the righteous, is again taken up under the aspect of world history. The query is raised why Zion was destroyed and the certainly no better Babylon spared, but to it is joined the new and altogether different question of how there can be wickedness in general: the problem of the origin of the "evil heart" through whose working Adam and all those begotten by him have fallen into sin and guilt.

Here, however, we must distinguish two stages. In the one a kind of hereditary sin is recognized that was entirely foreign to the Old Testament. There, despite all consciousness of the growing historical burden, each man stood anew in the freedom of Adam; his capacity for decision was not impaired by any inner inheritance. But now the apocalyptic writer writes out, "Ah, Adam, what have you done! When you sinned, your fall did not come upon you alone but also upon us, we who issue from you. What does it avail us that an immortal aeon is promised us when we have done death's work?" And he has God proclaim with the utmost precision: "When Adam disobeyed my command, the creature was condemned." [2]

But the speaker goes further. Adam's sin arose from his own nature, and this he received from God. God had put into him the evil heart, and He had left it in Adam's descendants. Even when He revealed Himself to Israel, He did not take away the evil heart; therefore, the awareness of the truth could not hold its ground against the "bad seed." And the answering angel confirms with still stronger statement, "A grain of evil seed was sown in Adam's heart in the beginning"; now the whole harvest must come up, and only when it is cut can the field of the good appear.[3] This view of the apocalyptic writer contradicts fundamentally the earlier prophetic teaching. It also contradicts the contemporary early-talmudic teaching, according to which an evil urge was not placed in the heart of man at creation, but only the still neutral passion without which nothing could succeed. It depends on man whether this passion takes the direction toward God or falls into directionless chaos.[4] The intention of creation, accordingly, was that the world should become an independent seat of free decision out of which a genuine answer of the creature to his Creator could issue. The apocalyptic writer, on the contrary, though he knows, of course, of the struggle in the soul of man, accords to this struggle no elemental significance. There exists for him no possibility of a change in the direction of historical destiny that could proceed from man, or be effected or coeffected by man. The prophetic principle of the turning is not simply denied in its individual form, but a turning on the part of the community is no longer even thought of. The turning is nowhere acknowledged to have a power that alters history, or even one that manifests itself eschatologically, again in marked contrast to the early-talmudic tradition which held that the historical continuation of existence depends on the turning.

The mature apocalyptic, moreover, no longer knows a historical future in the real sense. The end of all history is near. "Creation has grown old," [5] it notes as a point unalterably established; this is stated still more penetratingly in the Baruch apocalypse: "The procession of the ages is already almost past." [6] The present aeon, that of the world and of world history, "hurries powerfully to the end." The coming age, the transformation of all things through the incursion of the transcendent is at hand. The antithesis of the coming age to all historical ages is expressed most strongly by a sentence of the Johannine Revelation that surpasses all that can be imagined: "Time will no longer be." [7] The proper and paradoxical subject of the late apocalyptic is a future that is no longer in time, and he anticipates this consummation so that for him all that may yet come in history no longer has a historical character. Man cannot achieve this future, but he also has nothing more to achieve.

Prophecy and apocalyptic, regarded through their writings, are unique manifestations in the history of the human spirit and of its relationship to transcendence. Prophecy originates in the hour of the highest strength and fruitfulness of the Eastern spirit, the apocalyptic out of the decadence of its cultures and religions. But wherever a living historical dialogue of divine and human actions breaks through, there persists, visible or invisible, a bond with the prophecy of Israel. And wherever man shudders before the menace of his own work and longs to flee from the radically demanding historical hour, there he finds himself near to the apocalyptic vision of a process that cannot be arrested.

There is also, of course, an optimistic modern apocalyptic, the chief example of which is Marx's view of the future. This has erroneously been ascribed a prophetic origin. In this announcement of an obligatory leap of the human world out of the aeon of necessity into that of freedom, the apocalyptic principle alone holds sway. Here in place of the power superior to the world that effects the transition, an immanent dialectic has appeared. Yet in a mysterious manner *its* goal, too, is the perfection, even the salvation of the world. In its modern shape, too, apocalyptic knows nothing of an inner transformation of man that precedes the transformation of the world and cooperates in it; it knows nothing of the prophetic "turning." Marx could, indeed, occasionally (1856) write, "The new forces of society"—by which the *pre-revolutionary* society is meant—"need new men in order to accomplish good work," although, according to the materialistic interpretation of history, new men can only arise from the new post-revolutionary conditions of society. But such flashing sparks of the prophetic fire are certainly to be found in every apocalyptic. No living man who in his personal experience has known free decision and its share in the objective change of situation can persist uninterruptedly in the thought of a smoothly predetermined course of events bereft of all junctures. Nothing in Marx's basic view of history, however, was altered thereby, and three years later Lasalle could write of it with justification that, linking brazen necessity to necessity, it passes "over and obliterates just for that reason the efficacy of individual resolutions and actions."

Today, despite all assurances to the contrary, this inverted apocalyptic no longer occupies any considerable room in the real thinking of its adherents. Meanwhile, a directly antithetical apocalyptic attitude has taken shape in Western humanity. This appears to resume some doctrines of the Ezra and Baruch apocalypses after they have been divested of all theology of a coming aeon. The wholly other state of being there promised for existence after the end of our world is now annihilated, but the character of the present as late, all too late, has been preserved. The world, to be sure, is no longer called creation, but its irremediable old age is accepted as self-understood. In contrast to what prevailed a short time ago, no one any longer pushes the analogy with the organism so far that he links to the declaration of old age the expectation of early death; prognoses of this kind have today become rare. The specifically modern apocalyptic is not merely completely secularized, but also, after several more grandiose than reliable starts, it has been thoroughly disenchanted. Prognoses, accordingly, have become unpopular, which is to be welcomed at any rate. Instead of assuming this role, the apocalyptic has now, so to speak, expounded itself in permanence. It no longer says, "One cannot swim against the stream"—the image of the stream, to which an outlet belongs, already appears too full of pathos. It says rather, "An old period must behave like an old period if it does not wish to be laughed at." The only poetry that still becomes such an age is one of self-directed irony; the only art that still fits it is one that atomizes things, to employ a striking characterization of Max Picard's; faith has become altogether unseemly. In an aged world one knows exactly what is legitimate and what is not.

If one comes and rebels against the indirectness that has penetrated all human relationships, against the atmosphere of a false objectivity where each sees the other no longer as a partner of his existence but merely as an object among objects in order to register him in already-existing interconnections of "objective" utility, he is upbraided by his critics as a romantic beset by illusions. If he resists the flagging of the dialogical relationship between men, he is forthwith reproached with failing to recognize the fated solitude of present-day living, as if the fundamental meaning of each new solitude were not that it must be overcome on a more comprehensive level than any earlier one. If one declares that one of the main reasons why the crisis in the life of the peoples appears hopeless is the fact that the existential mistrust of all against all prevents any meaningful negotiation over the *real* differences of interest, he is set right by a smile of the shrewd: an "old" world is necessarily shrewd.

The great apocalyptic writings of that earlier turning point of history were of two kinds. The one held that men could no longer have faith in history's taking a new direction, the other that men could believe in an all-determining God only with a special limitation: God can make everything with the exception of a genuine, free Thou for Himself—that He cannot make. Unbelief and belief were here only the two sides of *one* point of view. Of the two, only the unbelief remains in the broken yet emphatic apocalyptic of our time. It steps forward with a heroic mien, to be sure; it holds itself to be the heroic acknowledgment of the inevitable, the embodiment of *amor fati*. But this convulsive gesture has nothing in common with real love.

As in the life of a single person, so also in the life of the human race: what is possible in a certain hour and what is impossible cannot be adequately ascertained by any foreknowledge. It goes without saying that, in the one sphere as in the other, one must start at any given time from the nature of the situation insofar as it is at all recognizable. But one does not learn the measure and limit of what is attainable in a desired direction otherwise than through going in this direction. The forces of the soul allow themselves to be measured only through one's using them. In the most important moments of our existence neither planning nor surprise rules alone: in the midst of the faithful execution of a plan we are surprised by secret openings and insertions. Room must be left for such surprises, however; planning as though they were impossible renders them impossible. One cannot strive for immediacy, but one can hold oneself free and open for it. One cannot produce genuine dialogue, but one can be at its disposal. Existential mistrust cannot be replaced by trust, but it can be replaced by a reborn candor.

This attitude involves risk, the risk of giving oneself, of inner transformation. Inner transformation simply means surpassing one's present factual constitution; it means that the person one is intended to be penetrates what has appeared up till now, that the customary soul enlarges and transfigures itself into the surprise soul. This is what the prophets of Israel understood by the turning in their language of faith: not a return to an earlier, guiltless stage of life, but a swinging around to where the wasted hither-and-thither becomes walking on a way, and guilt is atoned for in the newly arisen genuineness of existence.

Toward the end of the first third of that same century in which those apocalypses were produced that spoke of the aged world and announced the approaching rupture of history, John the Baptist had again taken up the cry of the prophets, "Return!"; and, in complete accord with their belief in real alternatives, he had joined to the imperative the warning that the axe had already been laid to the roots of the trees.[8] He trusted his hearers to trust themselves as capable of the turning that was demanded, and he trusted the human world of his hour to be capable of just this turning, of risk, of giving oneself, of inner transformation. After Jesus and in like manner his emissaries had sounded the call afresh, the apocalyptics and their associates proceeded to disclose that there is no turning and no new direction in the destiny of the world that can issue from the turning. But the depths of history, which are continually at work to rejuvenate creation, are in league with the prophets.

IN THE actual reality of the catastrophe, "honest and wicked" (Job 9:22) are destroyed together by God, and in the outer reality the wicked left alive knew how to assert themselves successfully in spite of all the difficulties; "they lived, became old, and even thrived mightily" (21:7), whereas for the pious, endowed with weaker elbows and more sensitive hearts, their days "were swifter than a weaver's shuttle, and were spent without hope" (7:6); "the robbers' tents are peaceful, and they that anger God have secure abodes" (12:6), whereas the upright is "become a brother of jackals" (30:29). This is the experience out of which the Book of Job was born, a book opposed to the dogmatics of Ezekiel, a book of the question which then was new and has persisted ever since.

I cannot ascribe this book—which clearly has only slowly grown to its present form—in its basic kernel to a time later (or earlier) than the beginning of the exile. Its formulations of the question bear the stamp of an intractable directness—the stamp of a first expression. The world in which they were spoken had certainly not yet heard the answers of Psalm 73 or Deutero-Isaiah. The author finds before him dogmas in process of formation, he clothes them in grand language, and sets over against them the force of the new question, the question brought into being out of experience; in his time these growing dogmas had not yet found their decisive opponents. The book, in spite of its thorough rhetoric—the product of a long-drawn-out literary process—is one of the special events in world literature, in which we witness the first clothing of a human quest in form of speech.

It has rightly been said [2] that behind the treatment of Job's fate in this discussion lie "very bitter experiences of a supra-individual kind." When the sufferer complains, "He breaks me around, and I am gone" (Job 19:10), this seems no longer the complaint of a single person. When he cries, "God delivers me to the wicked, and hurls me upon the hands of the evil-doers" (16:11), we think less of the sufferings of an individual than of the exile of a people. It is true it is a personal fate that is presented here, but the stimulus to speaking out, the incentive to complaint and accusation, bursting the bands of the presentation, are the fruit of supra-personal sufferings. Job's question comes into being as the question of a whole generation about the sense of its historic fate. Behind this "I," made so personal here, there still stands the "I" of Israel.

The question of the generation, "Why do we suffer what we suffer?" had from the beginning a religious character; "why?" here is not a philosophical interrogative asking after the nature of things, but a religious concern with the acting of God. With Job, however, it becomes still clearer; he does not ask, "Why does God *permit* me to suffer these things?" but "Why does God *make* me suffer these things?" That everything comes from God is beyond doubt and question; the question is, How are these sufferings compatible with His godhead?

In order to grasp the great inner dialectic of the poem, we must realize that here not two, but four answers stand over against each other; in other words, we find here four views of God's relationship to man's sufferings.

The first view is that of the Prologue to the book which, in the form in which it has reached us, cannot have come from an ancient popular book about Job, but bears the stamp of a poetic formation. The popular view of God, however, stands here apparently unchanged.[3] It is a God allowing a creature, who wanders about the earth and is subject to Him in some manner, the "Satan," that is the "Hinderer" or "Adversary," to "entice" Him (2:3)—the verb is the same as is used in the story of David being enticed by God or Satan to sin—to do all manner of evil to a God-fearing man, one who is His "servant" (1:8; 2:3), of whose faithfulness God boasts. This creature entices the deity to do all manner of evil to this man, only in order to find out if he will break faith, as Satan argues, or keep it according to God's word. The poet shows us how he sees the matter, as he repeats in true biblical style the phrase "gratuitously." In order to make it clear whether Job serves him "gratuitously" (1:9), that is to say, not for the sake of receiving a reward, God smites him and brings suffering upon him, as He Himself confesses (2:3), "gratuitously," that is to say, without sufficient cause. Here God's acts are questioned more critically than in any of Job's accusations, because here we are informed of the true motive, which is one not befitting to deity. On the other hand man proves true as man. Again the point is driven home by the frequent repetition of the verb *barekh,* which means both real blessing and also blessing of dismissal, departure (1:5, 11; 2:5, 9)[4]: Job's wife tells him, reality itself tells him to "bless" God, to dismiss Him, but he bows down to God and "blesses" Him, who has allowed Himself to be enticed against him "gratuitously." This is a peculiarly dramatic face-to-face meeting, this God and this man. The dialogue poem that follows contradicts it totally: there the man is another man, and God another God.

The second view of God is that of the friends. This is the dogmatic view of the cause and effect in the divine system of requital: sufferings point to sin. God's punishment is manifest and clear to all. The primitive conception of the zealous God is here robbed of its meaning: it was YHVH, God of Israel, who was zealous for the *covenant* with His *people.* Ezekiel had preserved the covenant faith, and only for the passage of time between covenant and covenant did he announce the unconditional punishment for those who refused to return in penitence; this has changed here, in an atmosphere no longer basically historical,[5] into the view of the friends, the assertion of an all-embracing empirical connection between sin and punishment. In addition to this, for Ezekiel, it is true, punishment followed unrepented sin, but it never occurred to him to see in all men's sufferings the avenging hand of God; and it is just this that the friends now proceed to do: Job's sufferings testify to his guilt. The inner infinity of the suffering soul is here changed into a formula, and a wrong formula. The first view was that of a small mythological idol, the second is that of a great ideological idol. In the first the faithful sufferer was true to an untrue God, who permitted his guiltless children to be slain; whereas here man was not asked to be true to an incalculable power, but to recognize and confess a calculation that his knowledge of reality contradicts. There man's faith is attacked by fate, here by religion. The friends are silent seven days before the sufferer, after which they expound to him the account book of sin and punishment. Instead of his God, for whom he looks in vain, his God, who had not only put sufferings upon him, but also had "hedged him in" until "His way was hid" from his eyes (3:23), there now came and visited him on his ash heap *religion,* which uses every art of speech to take away from him the God of his soul. Instead of the "cruel" (30:21) and living God, to whom he clings, religion offers him a reasonable and rational God, a deity whom he, Job, does not perceive either in his own existence or in the world, and who obviously is not to be found anywhere save only in the very domain of religion. And his complaint becomes a protest against a God who withdraws Himself, and at the same time against His false representation.

The third view of God is that of Job in his complaint and protest. It is the view of a God who contradicts His revelation by "hiding His face" (13:24). He is at one and the same time fearfully noticeable and unperceivable (9:11), and this hiddenness is particularly sensible in face of the excessive presence of the "friends," who are ostensibly God's advocates. All their attempts to cement the rent in Job's world show him that this is the rent in the heart of the world. Clearly the thought of both Job and the friends proceeds from the question about justice. But unlike his friends, Job knows of justice only as a human activity, willed by God, but

opposed by His acts. The truth of being just and the reality
caused by the unjust acts of God are irreconcilable. Job cannot forego either his own truth or God. God torments him
"gratuitously" (9:17; it is not without purpose that here the
word recurs, which in the Prologue Satan uses and God repeats); He "deals crookedly" with him (19:6). All man's
supplications will avail nothing: "there is no justice" (19:7).
Job does not regard himself as free from sin (7:20; 14:16 f.),
in contradistinction to God's words about him in the Prologue (1:8; 2:3). But his sin and his sufferings are incom-
mensurable. And the men, who call themselves his friends,
suppose that on the basis of their dogma of requital they are
able to unmask his life and show it to be a lie. By allowing
religion to occupy the place of the living God, He strips off
Job's honor (19:9). Job had believed God to be just and
man's duty to be to walk in His ways. But it is no longer
possible for one who has been smitten with such sufferings
to think God just. "It is one thing, therefore I spake: honest
and wicked He exterminates" (9:22). And if it is so, it is not
proper to walk in His ways. In spite of this, Job's faith in justice is not broken down. But he is no longer able to have a
single faith in God and in justice. His faith in justice is no
longer covered by God's righteousness. He believes now in
justice in spite of believing in God, and he believes in God in
spite of believing in justice. But he cannot forego his claim
that they will again be united somewhere, sometime, although
he has no idea in his mind how this will be achieved. This is
in fact meant by his claim of his rights, the claim of the solution. This solution must come, for from the time when he
knew God Job *knows* that God is not a Satan grown into
omnipotence. Now, however, Job is handed over to the pre-
tended justice, the account justice of the friends, which affects not only his honor, but also his faith in justice. For
Job, justice is not a scheme of compensation. Its content is
simply this, that one must not cause suffering gratuitously.
Job feels himself isolated by this feeling, far removed from
God and men. It is true, Job does not forget that God seeks
just such justice as this from man. But he cannot understand
how God Himself violates it, how He inspects His creature

every morning (7:18), searching after his iniquity (10:6), and instead of forgiving his sin (7:21) snatches at him stormily (9:17)—how He, being infinitely superior to man, thinks it good to reject the work of His hands (10:3). And in spite of this Job knows that the friends, who side with God (13:8), do not contend for the true God. He has recognized before this the true God as the near and intimate God. Now he only experiences Him through suffering and contradiction, but even in this way he does experience God. What Satan designed for him and his wife in the Prologue, recommended to him more exactly, that he should "bless" God, dismiss Him, and die in the comfort of his soul, was for him quite impossible. When in his last long utterance he swears the purification oath, he says: "As God lives, who has withdrawn my right" (27:2). God lives, and He bends the right. From the burden of this double, yet single, matter Job is able to take away nothing, he cannot lighten his death. He can only ask to be confronted with God. "Oh that one would hear me!" (31:35)—men do not hear his words, only God can be his hearer. As his motive he declares that he wants to reason with the deity (13:3); he knows he will carry his point (13:18). In the last instance, however, he merely means by this that God will again become present to him. "Oh that I knew where I might find Him!" (23:3). Job struggles against the remoteness of God, against the deity who rages and *is silent,* rages and "hides His face," that is to say, against the deity who has changed for him from a nearby person into a sinister power. And even if He draw near to him again only in death, he will again "see" God (19:26) as His "witness" (16:19) against God Himself, he will see Him as the avenger of his blood (19:25), which must not be covered by the earth until it is avenged (16:18) by God on God. The absurd duality of a truth known to man and a reality sent by God must be swallowed up somewhere, sometime, in a unity of God's presence. How will it take place? Job does not know this, nor does he understand it; he only believes in it. We may certainly say that Job "appeals from God to God," [6] but we cannot say[7] that he rouses himself against a God "who contradicts His own innermost nature," and seeks a God who will conduct Himself toward him "as the requital dogma demands." By such an interpretation the sense of the problem is upset. Job cannot renounce justice, but he does not hope to find it, when God will find again "His inner nature" and "His subjection to the norm," but only when God will appear to him again. Job believes now, as later Deutero-Isaiah (Isa. 45:15) did under the influence of Isaiah (8:17), in "a God that hides Himself." This hiding, the eclipse of the divine light, is the source of his abysmal despair. And the abyss is bridged the moment man "sees," is permitted to see again, and this becomes a new foundation. It has been rightly said [8] that Job is more deeply rooted in the primitive Israelite view of life than his dogmatic friends. There is no true life for him but that of a firmly established covenant between God and man; formerly he lived in this covenant and received his righteousness from it, but now God has disturbed it. It is the dread of the faithful "remnant" in the hour of the people's catastrophe that here finds its personal expression. But this dread is suggestive of the terror that struck Isaiah as he stood on the threshold of the cruel mission laid upon him—"the making fat and heavy." His words "How long?" are echoed in Job's complaint. How long will God hide His face? When shall we be allowed to see Him again? Deutero-Isaiah expresses (40:27) the despairing complaint of the faithful remnant which thinks that because God hides Himself, Israel's "way" also "is hid" from Him, and He pays no more attention to it, and the prophet promises that not only Israel but all flesh shall see Him (40:5).

The fourth view of God is that expressed in the speech of God Himself. The extant text is apparently a late revision, as is the case with many other sections of this book, and we cannot restore the original text. But there is no doubt that the speech is intended for more than the mere demonstration of the mysterious character of God's rule in nature to a greater and more comprehensive extent than had already been done by the friends and Job himself; for more than the mere explanation to Job: "Thou canst not understand the secret of any thing or being in the world, how much less the secret of man's fate." It is also intended to do more than teach by examples taken from the world of nature about the "strange and wonderful" character of the acts of God, which contradict the whole of teleological wisdom, and point to the "playful riddle of the eternal creative power" as to an "inexpressible positive value." [9] The poet does not let his God disregard the fact that it is a matter of *justice*. The speech declares in the ears of man, struggling for justice, another justice than his own, a divine justice. Not *the* divine justice, which remains hidden, but *a* divine justice, namely that manifest in creation. The creation of the world is justice, not a recompensing and compensating justice, but a distributing, a giving justice. God the Creator bestows upon each what belongs to him, upon each thing and being, insofar as He allows it to become entirely itself. Not only for the sea (Job 38:10), but for every thing and being God "breaks" in the hour of creation "His boundary," that is to say, He cuts the dimension of this thing or being out of "all," giving it its fixed measure, the limit appropriate to this gift. Israel's ancient belief in creation, which matured slowly only in its formulations, has here reached its completion: it is not about a "making" that we are told here, but about a "founding" (38:4), a "setting" (38:5, 9 f.), a "commanding" and "appointing" (38:12). The creation itself already means communication between Creator and creature. The just Creator gives to all His creatures His boundary, so that each may become fully itself. Designedly man is lacking in this presentation of heaven and earth, in which man is shown the justice that is greater than his, and is shown that he with his justice, which intends to give to everyone what is due to him, is called only to emulate the divine justice, which gives to everyone what he is. In face of such divine teaching as this it would be indeed impossible for the sufferer to do aught else than put "his hand upon his mouth" (40:4), and to confess (42:3) that he had erred in speaking of things inconceivable for him. And nothing else could have come of it except this recognition—if he had heard only a voice "from the tempest" (38:1; 40:6). But the voice is the voice of *Him who answers,* the voice of Him that "heard" (31:35), and appeared so as to

be "found" of him (23:3). In vain Job had tried to penetrate
to God through the divine remoteness; now God draws near
to him. No more does God hide Himself, only the storm
cloud of His sublimity still shrouds Him, and Job's eye
"sees" Him (42:5). The absolute power has for human personality's sake become personality. God offers Himself to
the sufferer who, in the depth of his despair, keeps to God
with his refractory complaint; He offers Himself to him as
an answer. It is true, "the overcoming of the riddle of suffering can only come from the domain of revelation," [10] but it
is not the revelation in general that is here decisive, but the
particular revelation to the individual: the revelation as an
answer to the individual sufferer concerning the question of
his sufferings, the self-limitation of God to a person, answering a person.

The *way* of this poem leads from the first view to the
fourth. The God of the first view, the God of the legend
borrowed by the poet, works on the basis of "enticement";
the second, the God of the friends, works on the basis of
purposes apparent to us, purposes of punishment or, especially in the speeches of Elihu which are certainly a later
addition, of purification and education; the third, the God
of the protesting Job, works against every reason and purpose; and the fourth, the God of revelation, works from His
godhead, in which every reason and purpose held by man
are at once abolished and fulfilled. It is clear that this God,
who answers from the tempest, is different from the God of
the Prologue; the declaration about the secret of divine action would be turned into a mockery if the fact of that
"wager" was put over against it. But even the speeches of
the friends and of Job cannot be harmonized with it. Presumably the poet, who frequently shows himself to be a master of irony, left the Prologue, which seems completely opposed to his intention, unchanged in content in order to
establish the foundation for the multiplicity of views that
follows. But in truth the view of the Prologue is meant to be
ironical and unreal; the view of the friends is only logically
"true" and demonstrates to us that man must not subject

God to the rules of logic; Job's view is real, and therefore, so to speak, the negative of truth; and the view of the voice speaking from the tempest is the supralogical truth of reality. God justifies Job: he has spoken "rightly" (42:7), unlike the friends. And as the poet often uses words of the Prologue as motive words in different senses, so also here he makes God call Job as there by the name of His "servant," and repeat it by way of emphasis four times. Here this epithet appears in its true light. Job, the faithful rebel, like Abraham, Moses, David, and Isaiah, stands in the succession of men so designated by God, a succession that leads to Deutero-Isaiah's "servant of YHVH," whose sufferings especially link him with Job.

"And my servant Job shall pray for you"—with these words God sends the friends home (42:8). It is the same phrase as that in which YHVH in the story of Abraham (Gen. 20:7) certifies the patriarch, that he is His *nabi*. It will be found that in all the pre-exilic passages, in which the verb is used in the sense of intercession (and this apparently was its first meaning), it is only used of men called prophets. The significance of Job's intercession is emphasized by the Epilogue (which, apart from the matter of the prayer, the poet apparently left as it was) in that the turning point in Job's history, the "restoration" (Job 42:10) and first of all his healing, begins the moment he prays "for his friends." This saying is the last of the reminiscences of prophetic life and language found in this book. As if to stress this connection, Job's first complaint begins (3:3 ff.) with the cursing of his birth, reminding us of Jeremiah's words (Jer. 20:14 ff.), and the first utterance of the friends is poured out in figures of speech taken from the prophetic world (4, 12 ff.), the last of which (4:16) modifies the peculiar form of revelation of Elijah's story (I Kings 19:12). Job's recollection of divine intimacy, of "the counsel of God upon his tent" (Job 29:4), is expressed in language derived from Jeremiah (Jer. 23:18, 22), and his quest, which reaches fulfillment, to "see" God, touches the prophetic experience which only on Mount Sinai were non-prophets allowed to share (Exod. 24:10, 17).

Jeremiah's historical figure, that of the suffering prophet, apparently inspired the poet to compose his song of the man of suffering, who by his suffering attained the vision of God, and in all his revolt was God's witness on earth (cf. Isa. 43: 12; 44:8), as God was his witness in heaven.[11]

THE HEART DETERMINES
(PSALM 73)

W HAT IS remarkable about this poem—composed of descriptions, of a story, and of confessions—is that a man
tells how he reached the true meaning of his experience of
life, and that this meaning borders directly on the eternal.

For the most part we understand only gradually the
decisive experiences we have in our relation with the world.
First we accept what they seem to offer us, we express it,
we weave it into a "view," and then think we are aware of
our world. But we come to see that what we look on in this
view is only an appearance. Not that our experiences have
deceived us. But we had turned them to our use, without
penetrating to their heart. What is it that teaches us to penetrate to their heart? Deeper experience.

The man who speaks in this psalm tells us how he
penetrated to the heart of a weighty group of experiences—
those experiences that show that the wicked prosper.

Apparently, then, the question is not what was the real
question for Job—why the good do not prosper—but rather
its obverse, as we find it most precisely, and probably for the
first time, expressed in Jeremiah (12:1): "Why does the
way of the wicked prosper?"

Nevertheless, the psalm begins with a prefatory sentence in which, rightly considered, Job's question may be
found hidden.

This sentence, the foreword to the psalm, is

> Surely, God is good to Israel:
> To the pure in heart.

It is true that the Psalmist is here concerned not with the happiness or unhappiness of the person, but with the happiness or unhappiness of Israel. But the experience behind the speeches of Job, as is evident in many of them, is itself not merely personal, but is the experience of Israel's suffering both in the catastrophe that led to the Babylonian exile and in the beginning of the exile itself. Certainly only one who had plumbed the depths of personal suffering could speak in this way. But the speaker is a man of Israel in Israel's bitter hour of need, and in his personal suffering the suffering of Israel has been concentrated, so that what he now has to suffer he suffers as Israel. In the destiny of an authentic person the destiny of his people is gathered up, and only now becomes truly manifest.

Thus the Psalmist, whose theme is the fate of the person, also begins with the fate of Israel. Behind his opening sentence lies the question "Why do things go badly with Israel?" And first he answers, "Surely, God is good to Israel," and then he adds, by way of explanation, "to the pure in heart."

On first glance this seems to mean that it is only to the impure in Israel that God is not good. He is good to the pure in Israel; they are the "holy remnant," the true Israel, to whom He is good. But that would lead to the assertion that things go well with this remnant, and the questioner had taken as his starting point the experience that things went ill with Israel, not excepting indeed this part of it. The answer, understood in this way, would be no answer.

We must go deeper in this sentence. The questioner had drawn from the fact that things go ill with Israel the conclusion that therefore God is not good to Israel. But only one who is not pure in heart draws such a conclusion. One who is pure in heart, one who becomes pure in heart, cannot draw any such conclusion. For he experiences that God is good to him. But this does not mean that God rewards him with his goodness. It means, rather, that God's goodness is revealed to him who is pure in heart: he experiences this goodness. Insofar as Israel is pure in heart, becomes pure in heart, it experiences God's goodness.

Thus the essential dividing line is not between men who sin and men who do not sin, but between those who are pure in heart and those who are impure in heart. Even the sinner whose heart becomes pure experiences God's goodness as it is revealed to him. As Israel purifies its heart, it experiences that God is good to it.

It is from this standpoint that everything that is said in the psalm about "the wicked" is to be understood. The "wicked" are those who deliberately persist in impurity of heart.

The state of the heart determines whether a man lives in the truth, in which God's goodness is experienced, or in the semblance of truth, where the fact that it "goes ill" with him is confused with the illusion that God is not good to him.

The state of the heart determines. That is why "heart" is the dominant key word in this psalm, and recurs six times.

And now, after this basic theme has been stated, the speaker begins to tell of the false ways in his experience of life.

Seeing the prosperity of "the wicked" daily and hearing their braggart speech has brought him very near to the abyss of despairing unbelief, of the inability to believe any more in a living God active in life. "But I, a little more and my feet had turned aside, a mere nothing and my steps had stumbled." He goes so far as to be jealous of "the wicked" for their privileged position.

It is not envy that he feels, it is jealousy, that it is *they* who are manifestly preferred by God. That it is indeed they is proved to him by their being sheltered from destiny. For them there are not,[1] as for all the others, those constraining and confining "bands" of destiny; "they are never in the trouble of man." And so they deem themselves superior to all, and stalk around with their "sound and fat bellies," and when one looks in their eyes, which protrude from the fat-ness of their faces, one sees "the paintings of the heart," the wish-images of their pride and their cruelty, flitting across. Their relation to the world of their fellow men is arrogance and cunning, craftiness and exploitation. "They speak oppression from above" and "set their mouth to the heavens." From what is uttered by this mouth set to the heavens, the Psalmist quotes two characteristic sayings which were supposed to be familiar. In the one (introduced by "therefore," meaning "therefore they say") they make merry over God's relation to "His people." Those who speak are apparently in Palestine as owners of great farms, and scoff at the prospective return of the landless people from exile, in accordance with the prophecies: the prophet of the Exile has promised them water (Isa. 41:17 f.), and "they may drink their fill of water," they will certainly not find much more here unless they become subject to the speakers. In the second saying they are apparently replying to the reproaches leveled against them: they were warned that God sees and knows the wrongs they have done, but the God of heaven has other things to do than to concern Himself with such earthly matters: "How does God know? Is there knowledge in the Most High?" And God's attitude confirms them, those men living in comfortable security: "they have reached power," theirs is the power.

That was the first section of the psalm, in which the speaker depicted his grievous experience, the prosperity of the wicked. But now he goes on to explain how his understanding of this experience has undergone a fundamental change.

Since he had again and again to endure, side by side, his own suffering and their "grinning" well-being, he is overcome: "It is not fitting that I should make such comparisons, as my own heart is not pure." And he proceeded to purify it. In vain. Even when he succeeded in being able "to wash his hands in innocence" (which does not mean an action or feeling of self-righteousness, but the genuine, second and higher purity that is won by a great struggle of the soul), the torment continued, and now it was like a leprosy to him; and as leprosy is understood in the Bible as a punishment for the disturbed relation between heaven and earth, so each morning, after each pain-torn night, it came over the Psalmist— "It is a chastisement—why am I chastised?" And once again there arose the contrast between the horrible enigma of the happiness of the wicked and his suffering.

At this point he was tempted to accuse God as Job did. He felt himself urged to "tell how it is." But he fought and conquered the temptation. The story of this conquest follows in the most vigorous form that the speaker has at his disposal, as an appeal to God. He interrupts his objectivized account and addresses God. If I had followed my inner impulse, he says to Him, "I should have betrayed the generation of Thy sons." The generation of the sons of God! Then he did not know that the pure in heart are the children of God; now he does know. He would have betrayed them if he had arisen and accused God. For they continue in suffering and do not complain. The words sound to us as though the speaker contrasted these "children of God" with Job, the complaining "servant of God."

He, the Psalmist, was silent even in the hours when the conflict of the human world burned into his purified heart. But now he summoned every energy of thought in order to "know" the meaning of this conflict. He strained the eyes of the spirit in order to penetrate the darkness that hid the meaning from him. But he always perceived only the same conflict ever anew, and this perception itself seemed to him now to be a part of that "trouble" which lies on all save those "wicked" men—even on the pure in heart. He had become one of these, yet he still did not recognize that "God is good to Israel."

"Until I came into the sanctuaries of God." Here the real turning point in this exemplary life is reached.

The man who is pure in heart, I said, experiences that God is good to him. He does not experience it as a consequence of the purification of his heart, but because only as one who is pure in heart is he able to come to the sanctuaries. This does not mean the Temple precincts in Jerusalem, but the sphere of God's holiness, the holy mysteries of God. Only to him who draws near to these is the true meaning of the conflict revealed.

But the true meaning of the conflict, which the Psalmist expresses here only for the other side, the "wicked," as he expressed it in the opening words for the right side, for the "pure in heart," is not—as the reader of the following words is only too easily misled into thinking—that the present state of affairs is replaced by a future state of affairs of a quite different kind, in which "in the end" things go well with the good and badly with the bad; in the language of modern thought the meaning is that the bad do not truly exist, and their "end" brings about only this change, that they now inescapably experience their nonexistence, the suspicion of which they had again and again succeeded in dispelling. Their life was "set in slippery places"; it was so arranged as to slide into the knowledge of their own nothingness; and when this finally happens, "in a moment," the great terror falls upon them and they are consumed with terror. Their life has been a shadow structure in a dream of God's. God awakes, shakes off the dream, and disdainfully watches the dissolving shadow image.

This insight of the Psalmist, which he obtained as he drew near to the holy mysteries of God, where the conflict is resolved, is not expressed in the context of his story, but in an address to "his Lord." And in the same address he confesses, with harsh self-criticism, that at the same time the state of error in which he had lived until then and from which he had suffered so much was revealed to him: "When my heart rose up in me, and I was pricked in my reins, brutish was I and ignorant, I have been as a beast before Thee."

With this "before Thee" the middle section of the psalm significantly concludes, and at the end of the first line of the last section (after the description and the story comes the confession) the words are significantly taken up. The words "And I am" at the beginning of the verse are to be understood emphatically: "Nevertheless I am," "Nevertheless I am continually with Thee." God does not count it against the heart that has become pure that it was earlier accustomed "to rise up." Certainly even the erring and struggling man was "with Him," for the man who struggles for God is near Him even when he imagines that he is driven far from God. That is the reality we learn from the revelation to Job out of the storm, in the hour of Job's utter despair (30:20–22) and utter readiness (31:35–39). But what the Psalmist wishes to teach us, in contrast to the Book of Job, is that the fact of his being with God is revealed to the struggling man in the hour when—not led astray by doubt and despair into treason, and become pure in heart—"he comes to the sanctuaries of God." Here he receives the revelation of the "continually." He who draws near with a pure heart to the divine mystery learns that he is continually with God.

It is a revelation. It would be a misunderstanding of the whole situation to look on this as a pious feeling. From man's side there is no continuity, only from God's side. The Psalmist has learned that God and he are continually with one another. But he cannot express his experience as a word of God. The teller of the primitive stories made God say to the fathers and to the first leaders of the people: "I am with thee," and the word "continually" was unmistakably heard as well. Thereafter, this was no longer reported, and we hear it again only in rare prophecies. A Psalmist (23:5) is still able to say to God: "Thou art with me." But when Job (29:5) speaks of God's having been with him in his youth, the fundamental word, the "continually," has disappeared. The speaker in our psalm is the first and only one to insert it expressly. He no longer says: "Thou art with me," but "I am continually with Thee." It is not, however, from his own consciousness and feeling that he can say this, for no man is able to be continually turned to the presence of God: he can say it only in the strength of the revelation that God is continually with him.

The Psalmist no longer dares to express the central experience as a word of God; but he expresses it by a gesture of God. God has taken his right hand—as a father, so we may add, in harmony with that expression "the generation of Thy children," takes his little son by the hand in order to lead him. More precisely, as in the dark a father takes his little son by the hand, certainly in order to lead him, but primarily in order to make present to him, in the warm touch of coursing blood, the fact that he, the father, is continually with him.

It is true that immediately after this the leading itself is expressed: "Thou dost guide me with Thy counsel." But ought this to be understood as meaning that the speaker expects God to recommend to him in the changing situations of his life what he should do and what he should refrain from doing? That would mean that the Psalmist believes that he now possesses a constant oracle, who would exonerate him from the duty of weighing up and deciding what he must do. Just because I take this man so seriously I cannot understand the matter in this way. The guiding counsel of God seems to me to be simply the divine Presence communicating itself direct to the pure in heart. He who is aware of this Presence acts in the changing situations of his life differently from him who does not perceive this Presence. The Presence acts as counsel: God counsels by making known that He is present. He has led His son out of darkness into the light, and now he can walk in the light. He is not relieved of taking and directing his own steps.

The revealing insight has changed life itself, as well as the meaning of the experience of life. It also changes the perspective of death. For the "oppressed" man death was only the mouth toward which the sluggish stream of suffering and trouble flows. But now it has become the event in which God—the continually Present One, the One who grasps the man's hand, the Good One—"takes" a man.

The tellers of the legends had described the translation of the living Enoch and the living Elijah to heaven as "a being taken," a being taken away by God Himself. The Psalmists transferred the description from the realm of miracle to that of personal piety and its most personal expression. In a psalm that is related to our psalm not only in language and style but also in content and feeling, the forty-ninth, there are these words: "But God will redeem my soul from the power of Sheol, when He takes me." There is nothing left here of the mythical idea of a translation. But not only that

—there is nothing left of heaven either. There is nothing here about being able to go after death into heaven. And, so far as I see, there is nowhere in the "Old Testament" anything about this.

It is true that the sentence in our psalm that follows the words "Thou shalt guide me with Thy counsel" seems to contradict this. It once seemed to me to be indeed so, when I translated it as "And afterwards Thou dost take me up to glory." But I can no longer maintain this interpretation. In the original text there are three words. The first, "afterwards," is unambiguous—"After Thou hast guided me with Thy counsel through the remainder of my life," that is, "at the end of my life." The second word needs more careful examination. For us who have grown up in the conceptual world of a later doctrine of immortality, it is almost self-evident that we should understand "Thou shalt take me" as "Thou shalt take me up." The hearer or reader of that time understood simply, "Thou shalt take me away." But does the third word, *kabod,* not contradict this interpretation? Does it not say *whither* I shall be taken, namely, to "honor" or "glory"? No, it does not say this. We are led astray into this reading by understanding "taking up" instead of "taking."

This is not the only passage in the Scriptures where death and *kabod* meet. In the song of Isaiah on the dead king of Babylon, who once wanted to ascend into heaven like the day star, there are these words (14:18): "All the kings of the nations, all of them, lie in *kabod,* in glory, every one in his own house, but thou wert cast forth away from thy sepulcher." He is refused an honorable grave because he has destroyed his land and slain his people. *Kabod* in death is granted to the others, because they have uprightly fulfilled the task of their life. *Kabod,* whose root meaning is the radiation of the inner "weight" of a person, belongs to the earthly side of death. When I have lived my life, says our Psalmist to God, I shall die in *kabod,* in the fulfillment of my existence. In my death the coils of Sheol will not embrace me, but Thy hand will grasp me. "For," as is said in another psalm related in kind to this one, the sixteenth, "Thou wilt not leave my soul to Sheol."

Sheol, the realm of nothingness, in which, as a later text explains (Eccles. 9:10), there is neither activity nor consciousness, is not contrasted with a kingdom of heavenly bliss. But over against the realm of nothing there is God. The "wicked" have in the end a direct experience of their non-being; the "pure in heart" have in the end a direct experience of the Being of God.

This sense of *being taken* is now expressed by the Psalmist in the unsurpassably clear cry, "Whom have I in heaven!" He does not aspire to enter heaven after death, for God's home is not in heaven, so that heaven is empty. But he knows that in death he will cherish no desire to remain on earth, for now he will soon be wholly "with Thee"—here the word recurs for the third time—with Him who "has taken" him. But he does not mean by this what we are accustomed to call personal immortality, that is, continuation in the dimension of time so familiar to us in this our mortal life. He knows that after death "being with Him" will no longer mean, as it does in this life, "being separated from Him." The Psalmist now says with the strictest clarity what must now be said: it is not merely his flesh that vanishes in death, but also his heart, that inmost personal organ of the soul, which formerly "rose up" in rebellion against the human fate and which he then "purified" till he became pure in heart—this personal soul also vanishes. But He who was the true part and true fate of this person, the "rock" of this heart, God, is eternal. It is into His eternity that he who is pure in heart moves in death, and this eternity is something absolutely different from any kind of time.

Once again the Psalmist looks back at the "wicked," the thought of whom had once so stirred him. Now he does not call them the wicked, but "they that are far from Thee."

In the simplest manner he expresses what he has learned: since they are far from God, from Being, they are lost. And once more the positive follows the negative, once more, for the third and last time, that "and I," "and for me," which here means "nevertheless for me." "Nevertheless for me the good is to draw near to God." Here, in this conception of the good, the circle is closed. To him who may draw

near to God, the good is given. To an Israel that is pure in
heart the good is given, because it may draw near to God.
Surely, God is good to Israel.

The speaker here ends his confession. But he does not
yet break off. He gathers everything together. He has made
his refuge, his "safety," "in his Lord"—he is sheltered in
Him. And now, still turned to God, he speaks his last word
about the task which is joined to all this, and which he has
set himself, which God has set him—"To tell of all Thy
works." Formerly he was provoked to tell of the *appearance,*
and he resisted. Now he knows, he has the *reality* to tell of:
the works of God. The first of his telling, the tale of the work
that God has performed with him, is this psalm.

In this psalm two kinds of men seem to be contrasted
with each other, the "pure in heart" and "the wicked." But
that is not so. The "wicked," it is true, are clearly one kind of
men, but the others are not. A man is as a "beast" and purifies his heart, and behold, God holds him by the hand. That
is not a kind of men. Purity of heart is a state of being. A
man is not pure in kind, but he is able to be or become pure
—rather he is only essentially pure when he has become
pure, and even then he does not thereby belong to a kind of
men. The "wicked," that is, the bad, are not contrasted with
good men. The good, says the Psalmist, is "to draw near to
God." He does not say that those near to God are good.
But he does call the bad "those who are far from God."
In the language of modern thought that means that there are
men who have no share in existence, but there are no men
who possess existence. Existence cannot be possessed, but
only shared in. One does not rest in the lap of existence, but
one draws near to it. "Nearness" is nothing but such a drawing and coming near continually and as long as the human
person lives.

The dynamic of farness and nearness is broken by
death when it breaks the life of the person. With death there
vanishes the heart, that inwardness of man, out of which
arise the "pictures" of the imagination, and which rises up
in defiance, but which can also be purified.

Separate souls vanish, separation vanishes. Time that

has been lived by the soul vanishes with the soul; we know of no duration in time. Only the "rock" in which the heart is concealed, only the rock of human hearts, does not vanish. For it does not stand in time. The time of the world disappears before eternity, but existing man dies into eternity as into the perfect existence.

BIBLICAL HUMANISM

I N 1913, I assembled and headed a small circle of Jews interested in education. As we formulated plans for a Jewish school of advanced studies (which the World War prevented from materializing), I proposed that the course of
studies of the prospective institution be guided by the concept of a Hebrew humanism. By this I meant that, just as the
West has for centuries drawn educative vigor from the language and the writings of antiquity, so does the pivotal place
in our system of education belong to the language and the
writings of classical Israel. It is for these forces that we must
win new focal influence, that they may, out of the raw mate-
rials of contemporary life and its tasks, fashion a human
being with new Jewish dignity.

Sixteen years later I attended the Sixteenth Zionist Congress. When I wished to convey, in brief, what I thought was
missing in the educational system of Jewish Palestine and
what I hoped for, I again found no better designation for it
than "Hebrew humanism, in its truest meaning." This newly
added phrase, "in its truest meaning," encompassed my experience of three decades with the Jewish national movement. This movement had activated the people as a people,
had revived the language as a language; but in neither case,
its history or its literature, had it distinguished with prophetic awareness and prophetic demand true values from
false, nor drawn order and direction for the inherited

material. It had failed to understand that the archetype of
this people sprang from the ordering and direction-giving
deed; that the great document of this language was grounded
in the ordering and directing word; that a *formal* "Renaissance" is inflated nonsense; that, rather, the future of a
community beginning anew on the soil of the old homeland
depends on the *rebirth of its normative primal forces*. Hebrew humanism means fashioning a Hebrew man, and a Hebrew man is not at all the same as a Hebrew-speaking man.

   In an important treatise that attempts to determine the
basic nature of Western humanism,[1] Konrad Burdach has
very rightly pointed to a maxim in Dante's *Convivio*: "The
greatest desire Nature has implanted in every thing from its
beginning is the desire to return to its origins." In conform-
ity with these words, Burdach sees as the goal of the spiritual
movement we are accustomed to call humanism a "return to
the wellsprings of humanity, not by way of speculative
thought, but by way of a concrete *transformation* of the total inner life." It is not antiquity in its totality as historical
matter that the humanist receives; he receives that part of it
which by its nature seems capable of furthering the "return."
Thus Goethe in Rome "in the presence of the sculptural cre-
ations of the ancients" feels himself "led back to man in his
purest condition." [2] Similarly, a Hebrew humanism can rise
only from a sensitive selection that out of the totality of Judaism discerns the Hebrew person in his purest state. Thus
our humanism is directed to the Bible.

   To be sure, a Hebrew man is not a biblical man. The
"return" that is meant here cannot in the nature of things
mean a striving for the recurrence or continuation of something long past, but only a striving for its renewal in a gen-
uinely contemporary manifestation. Yet only a man worthy
of the Bible may be called a Hebrew man. Our Bible, however, consists of instruction, admonition, and dialogue with
the Instructor and Admonitor. Only that man who wills to
do and hear what the mouth of the Unconditioned commands him is a man worthy of the Bible. Only that man is
a Hebrew man who lets himself be addressed by the voice

that speaks to him in the Hebrew Bible and who responds to it with his life.

Manifestly, the two concepts are not identical. Manifestly, too, the converse of the proposition that every Hebrew man must be worthy of the Bible is not valid. The Hebrew man is that individual who lets himself be addressed by the voice that speaks to him in the Hebrew language. That is the meaning of biblical humanism.

Humanism moves from the mystery of language to the mystery of the human person. The reality of language must become operative in a man's spirit. The truth of language must prove itself in the person's existence. That was the intent of humanistic education, so long as it was alive.

Biblical humanism moves from the mystery of the Hebrew language to the mystery of the Hebrew being. Biblical humanistic education means fulfillment of the one in the other. Its intent is to lead the Jew of today back to his origins. But his origins are there where he hears the voice of the Unconditional resounding in Hebrew.

Biblical humanism is concerned with a "concrete transformation" of our total—and not alone our inner—lives. This concrete transformation can only follow upon a rebirth of the normative primal forces that distinguish right from wrong, true from false, and to which life submits itself. The primal forces are transmitted to us in the word, the biblical word. Some, like myself, will not let the biblical word usurp the place of the voice; they will not acknowledge the word as that voice's absolute, sufficing, immutably valid expression. Yet even they must feel certain that we can truly retrieve the normative only as we open ourselves to the biblical word, wherein it appears as a primal force. This primal force enables a community to perceive and comply with what has been proclaimed to it; it enables the leader to proclaim to this community as revealed word what they ought to perceive and comply with—for he may not in any way consider himself to be the source of such proclamation. We are no longer a community capable of this. But if we will open ourselves to the biblical word, if the individual will let it affect his personal life and open himself to the authority of the normative, then we may hope that the persons so affected— in various ways, yet all as one—will once again coalesce into a community in the primal meaning of the concept.

Here, however, when I speak of the biblical word, I mean not its content but the word itself. Essential in only the original word in the mystery of its spokenness (*Gesprochenheit*): if we quote it, it must retain its character as a word spoken here and now. The biblical word is translatable, for it encloses a content with which it issues forth to man. It is not translatable, for it encloses a mystery of language with which it issues forth to Israel. At the center of biblical humanism stands the service due the untranslatable word.

I have chosen to call our province of education a humanism because here too the building blocks for the structure of personality must be produced from the depths of language. The adjective "biblical" changes everything basically. For the biblical language is, at base, not only a different language; it is a different manner of speaking and a different mode of expression.

The word of Greek antiquity is detached and formally perfected. It is removed from the block of actual spokenness, sculpted with the artful chisel of thought, rhetoric, and poetry—removed to the realm of form. It would be considered crude and useless—barbarian—were it to retain any immediacy. It is valid only when it becomes pure form.

The purity of the Hebrew Bible's word resides not in form but in originality (*Ursprünglichkeit*). Whenever it was subjected to a consciously artistic adaptation it was polluted. Its full biblical force is present in the biblical word only when it has retained the immediacy of spokenness. It is essential to the biblicality of the biblical word that a psalm is outcry and not poem, that a prophetic speech is appeal and not properly formal elocution. In the Bible the voice of the speaker is not transformed; it remains as is. Yet it seems removed from anything incidental; it is purely original (*ursprünglich*). That is why it also became possible in the domain of this word for the humanized voice of God, resounding in human idiom and captured in human letters, to speak not *before* us, as does a character in the role of a god in the epiphanies of Greek tragedy, but *to* us.

Because the word of Greek antiquity is worked over and hammered into shape—because it is a product—it tends to be monological. The atmosphere of the solitary, sculpting spirit still encompasses it on the platform. That an Athenian orator plans and practices his speeches does not reduce his stature; a prophet who did likewise would be effaced. Socratic irony conceals an elemental immutability in communication; in the Bible, when an idea is expressed, the speaker regards the listener with concern. Whoever is addressed by the tragic chorus—men or gods—is, ultimately, not addressed at all; its foreboding song attains fulfillment by itself. But the psalmodic chorus, which has prayed: "Save us for Thy mercy's sake!" (Ps. 6:5), then listens in the stillness to hear whether its prayer has been granted. Untransfigured and unsubdued, the biblical word preserves the dialogical character of living reality.

Just as the nature of the word differs essentially in these two instances, so too is its apprehension essentially different: it is taught or reported (*berichtet*) in a basically different manner. The Greek logos *is;* it possesses eternal being (Heraclitus). Although the prologue of the hellenizing Gospel of John begins, like the Hebrew Bible, with "In the beginning," it immediately continues with the totally un-Hebraic "*was* the Word." In the beginning of the Bible's account of creation there *is* no word; it comes to be, it is spoken. In this account there is no "word" that is not spoken; the only being of a word resides in its being spoken. But then all being of things that are comes from having been spoken, from the being spoken of the primary word: "He Himself spoke and it was." The Greeks teach the word, the Jews report it.

This essential difference carries over into the educational area. Western humanism conceives language as a formation (*Gebild*), and so it proceeds to "a liberation of the truly formative powers of man" (Burdach); the "spiritual empire" that he wants to establish "might be called the Apollonian." The power of giving shape is set above the world.

The highest faculty of the spirit is the formative one: it wants to *form* the person as perfectly as possible; it wants to *form* the polis as perfectly as possible.

The law of a biblical humanism must be different. It conceives language as an event (*Geschehen*), an event in mutuality. Therefore it must aim at an event, more concretely, at an event in mutuality. Its intent is not the person who is shut up within himself, but the open one; not the form, but the relation; not mastery of the secret, but immediacy in facing it; not the thinker and master of the word, but its listener and executor, its worshipper and proclaimer. Nor is its intent the perfected structure of the polis, nor the free and disciplined interplay of the limbs of a political body; its intent is the *edah,* the present inter-community of this entire people, true immediacy of "justice" and "love," of "esteem" and "faithfulness" between men. But this *edah* is the "*edah* of God," for in fulfilling itself as a community this people provides the proper response to the address of its Master: it fulfills the word. The word is fulfilled, by way of individual man and the people, not in a perfected form (*Gebild*), but in a proof of self (*Bewährung*).

But this proof does not possess the permanence of the formed work; it exists only in the factual moment. Biblical humanism cannot, as does its Western counterpart, raise the individual above the problems of the moment; it seeks instead to train him to stand fast in them, to prove himself in them. This stormy night, these shafts of lightning flashing down, this threat of destruction—do not escape from them into a world of logos, of perfected form! Stand fast, hear the word in the thunder, obey, respond! This terrifying world is the world of God. It lays claim upon you. Prove yourself in it as a man of God!

Thus would biblical humanism declare a rebirth of the normative primal forces of Israel.

NOTES

THE MAN OF TODAY AND THE JEWISH BIBLE

1. Franz Rosenzweig, in his *Stern der Erlösung,* has the great merit of having shown this to our era in a new light. [An English edition, *The Star of Redemption,* translated by William Hallo, will be published shortly.—Ed.]
2. Hebrew Prayerbook.
3. *Ecce Homo,* the chapter on Zarathustra, section 3.
4. Berakhot 31b.

THE TREE OF KNOWLEDGE

1. Thus Otto Procksch in his commentary on Genesis, the only one, as far as I see, to give the correct interpretation here.

ABRAHAM THE SEER

1. Palestinian Talmud, Bikkurim I, 3.

THE BURNING BUSH

1. Cf. W. J. Phythian-Adams, *The Call of Israel* (1934), pp. 144 f., who points out that in the country of the Masai on the Congo a volcano is called "The God Mountain." The author, however, does not notice the fact that the Masai have obviously

been influenced by biblical traditions in the shaping of their mythology.

2. H. Gressmann, *Mose und seine Zeit* (1913), p. 30.

3. *Ibid.*, p. 21. From this statement, which cannot be supported from the text, the author draws the conclusion on pp. 442 f. that "An inner experience such as that enjoyed by the prophets who left writings, or by Jesus, is excluded *ab initio*." That is, it is "not testified to anywhere." Gressmann's addition, namely that an experience of the kind runs counter to "the spirit of antiquity," is quite incomprehensible to me. It is impossible to understand Zarathustra, for example, without positing some actual religious experience; and Moses even less. Cf. also J. Kaufmann, *History of the Religion of Israel* (Hebrew) II, i (1942), 48 f.

4. Gressmann, p. 22.

5. Cf. Isidore Lévy, *La légende de Pythagore de Grèce en Palestine* (1927), pp. 137 ff.

6. B. Jacob, "Mose am Dornbusch," *Monatsschrift für die Geschichte und Wissenschaft des Judentums,* Neue Folge, XXX (1922), 17. Special reference should be made at this point to Jacob's as yet unpublished commentary on Exodus.

7. Cf. Schmoekel, *Das angewandte Recht im Alten Testament* (1930), p. 8.

8. I have given a detailed criticism of this thesis in my work, *Königtum Gottes,* 2d ed., pp. xxxi ff.

9. J. A. Montgomery, *Arabia and the Bible* (1934), p. 10.

10. Gressmann, p. 434.

11. Cf. Buber, *The Prophetic Faith* (1949), pp. 38 ff.

12. Cf. Kaufmann, II, i, 279 ff.

13. That early tribal gods are also creators is known to us from countless myths, of which the Polynesian and North American are particularly characteristic. For the myth-makers the land of the tribe means the entire earth, since it alone affects them directly.

14. God, using the same choice of words, says to Moses (Exod. 33:19) that He will call out the name YHVH before him; and it is told with the identical wording (34:5) that He does so.

15. Cf. Buber, *Königtum Gottes,* pp. 84, 235 ff., and the literature referred to there; Buber–Rosenzweig, *Die Schrift und ihre Verdeutschung* (1936), pp. 201 f., 207 f.; Buber, *The Prophetic Faith,* pp. 27 f., 36 f., and the literature referred to there; more recently A. Vincent, *La religion des Judéo-Araméens d'Eléphantine* (1937), p. 46. Among the literature that reached

me after the completion of this essay the article of J. A. Montgomery, "The Hebrew Divine Name and the Personal Pronoun HŪ," *Journal of Biblical Literature*, LXIII, No. 2 (1944), 161 ff., is noteworthy. It refers to II Kings 2:14 and Jer. 5:12.
16. R. A. Nicholson, *Selected Poems from the Divāni Shamsi Tabriz* (1899), pp. 216 f., 282.
17. S. Mowinckel in a letter to Rudolf Otto, printed in R. Otto, *Das Gefühl des Überweltlichen* (1932), pp. 326 f.
18. L. Koehler, *Theologie des Alten Testaments* (1936), p. 234.

HOLY EVENT

1. E. Sachsse, *Die Bedeutung des Namens Israel* (1922), p. 91; cf. M. Noth, *Das System der zwölf Stämme Israels* (1930), pp. 90 ff.
2. M. Noth, *Die israelitischen Personennamen* (1929), pp. 207 f.; Buber, *Königtum Gottes*, pp. 193, 252 f.; *Moses*, pp. 113 f.
3. P. Volz, *Mose*, p. 88.
4. Cf. *Königtum Gottes*, pp. 119 ff. (against S. Mowinckel, *Psalmenstudien*, II).
5. Cf. Buber, *Moses*, pp. 74 ff.
6. The view connecting these words with the Shechem assembly is without foundation; nothing in the Joshua story fits this hymn of a great theophany.
7. E. Sellin, *Einleitung in das Alte Testament* (1935), p. 22. The view that this is a late psalm (so e.g., H. Schmidt, "Das Meerlied," *Zeitschrift für alttestamentliche Wissenschaft*, Neue Folge, VIII [1931], 59 ff.) cannot be supported from the fact that there is hardly any more mention in it of the dividing of the Red Sea than in other psalms; no other psalm is so built upon the one event and its effects.
8. Cf. *Moses*, pp. 101 ff.
9. The saying is later elaborated many times homiletically (cf. Deut. 4:20; 7:6; 14:2; 26:19; I Kings 8:53); but it differs completely from these in its concentrated style. Its presentation of the deity, to whom the whole earth belongs and who can choose to Himself one people out of all, is *earlier* in the history of faith than the universal liberator deity of Amos.
10. Cf. B. D. Eerdmanns, *De godsdienst van Israel* (1930), I, 56 ff.; P. Volz, *Mose*, pp. 100 ff.; E. Klamroth, *Lade und*

Tempel (1933), pp. 30 ff.; E. Sellin, *Alttestamentliche Theologie* (1933), I, 30 ff.; Buber, *Königtum Gottes,* pp. 228 ff.; *Moses,* pp. 147 ff.

   11. Cf. M. Dibelius, *Die Lade Jahves* (1906).
   12. Cf. especially Johannes Pedersen, "Passahfest und Passahlegende," *Zeitschrift für alttestamentliche Wissenschaft,* Neue Folge, XI (1934), 161 ff.; and my book *Moses,* pp. 69 ff.
   13. Pedersen, p. 168.
   14. J. Hempel, *Das Ethos des Alten Testaments* (1938), p. 43.
   15. P. Volz, *Das Dämonische in Jahwe* (1924), and my *Moses,* pp. 56 ff.
   16. Cf. *Moses,* pp. 80 ff.
   17. Oesterley and Robinson, *A History of Israel,* I (1932), 96; and my *Moses,* pp. 119 ff.
   18. A. Alt, *Die Ursprünge des israelitischen Rechts* (1934), p. 52.
   19. R. Kittel, *Geschichte des Volkes Israel,* I, Supplement I.
   20. Alt, p. 69. For an examination of the types of ordinance style, cf. A. Jirku, *Das weltliche Recht im Alten Testament* (1927).
   21. Alt, p. 47.
   22. *Ibid.,* p. 70.
   23. A. Jirku, "Das israelitische Jobeljahr" (*Seeberg-Festschrift,* 1929), p. 178. Cf. Alt, pp. 65 f.; but he ascribes only the statutes about the Sabbatical year to an early age, and conjectures that in this year there was a complete new allotment of field plots to families, somewhat like that which is to be found among seminomads in our time; cf. also R. H. Kennett, *Ancient Hebrew Social Life and Custom* (1933), p. 77.
   24. Cf. *Königtum Gottes,* pp. 56 ff.
   25. Cf. B. D. Eerdmanns, *Alttestamentliche Studien,* IV (1912), 121 ff.; F. X. Kugler, *Von Moses bis Paulus* (1922), pp. 49 ff.; W. M. Ramsay, *Asianic Elements in Greek Civilization* (1927), pp. 49 f.
   26. Alt, p. 47.
   27. Such an addition is to be seen in the mention of the two kinds of sacrifice in verse 24.
   28. Cf. *Königtum Gottes,* pp. 143 ff.
   29. Cf. L. Rost, *Die Vorstufen von Kirche und Synagoge im Alten Testament* (1938), pp. 7 f.
   30. Cf. *Königtum Gottes,* pp. 157 f., 287 f.
   31. *Ibid.,* pp. 3 ff.

THE ELECTION OF ISRAEL: A BIBLICAL INQUIRY

1. The unquestionably genuine, in fact necessary verse 9:8 must be considered together with 2:10, and both with Gen. 15:16, a specifically "prophetic" verse. (The whole chapter has an early prophetic stamp.)
2. Cf. Jer. 1:5.
3. At first (verse 1) the mountain is called only Horeb; its present-day name will be mentioned only later, but is clearly brought to mind by the fivefold designation of the thornbush as *seneh* (otherwise only Deut. 33:16 has the same intention).
4. In reference to the concept of the key word, cf. the explanation in Buber and Rosenzweig, *Die Schrift und ihre Verdeutschung.*
5. Cf. Franz Rosenzweig's essay "Der Gottesname" in the above volume and my presentation in *Königtum Gottes,* chapter V.
6. Cf. *Die Schrift und ihre Verdeutschung,* pp. 262 ff.
7. For support cf. *Königtum Gottes,* 2d ed., pp. 124 ff., 268 ff.
8. In our passage the concept of *kohanim* as those who are allowed to "come near" (Exod. 19:22) manifestly includes the seventy elders, as follows from chapter 24 (verses 1 f., 9). At this stage of the narrative there are as yet no priests.
9. *Am nahalah* (4:20). The *nahalah* passages express a different, more exclusive and particularistic tendency of interpretation than do the *segulah* passages, which preserve the language of the original spoken word.
10. The verbal form *merahef,* significantly, occurs only in these two passages (the verb as such only once more).
11. The verses 44–53, which are of concern here, are manifestly later than those preceding; however, questions of literary criticism are of no consequence in this presentation.

THE WORDS ON THE TABLETS

1. Karl Buresch, *Klaros* (1889), pp. 89 ff.; the passage on the Decalogue is found on p. 116.
2. J. Wellhausen, *Skizzen und Vorarbeiten I, Die Composition des Hexateuchs,* p. 96.

3. Alt, *op. cit.*, p. 52; cf. W. Rudolph, *Der "Elohist" von Exodus bis Josua,* p. 59: "a conglomerate of little value from the Book of the Covenant, which is in no way source material."

4. B. Duhm, *Israels Propheten* (1916), p. 38.

5. Beer, *Exodus*, p. 162.

6. G. Hoelscher, *Geschichte der israelitischen und jüdischen Religion* (1922), p. 129.

7. C. Steuernagel, *Einleitung in das Alte Testament* (1912), p. 260.

8. Beer, p. 103.

9. K. Budde, *Religion of Israel to the Exile* (1899), p. 33: "both superfluous and impossible."

10. S. Mowinckel, *Le décalogue* (1927), p. 102, is of the opinion that unlike the Decalogue the moral elements "seem to be lost within a long series of ritual and cultic commandments"; but a glance at the texts shows that the ritual and cultic commandments constitute less than half in the Egyptian, and only a small fraction in the Babylonian records.

11. Bruno Gutmann, *Die Stammeslehren der Dschagga* (3 vols., 1932 ff.).

12. Mowinckel, p. 101.

13. Wilhelm Nowack, "Der erste Dekalog" (*Baudissin-Festschrift,* 1918), p. 395.

14. Beer, *Moses und sein Werk* (1912), p. 26.

15. Cf. J. Kaufmann, *History of the Religion of Israel,* II, 1, 77. He connects Aaron with these influences.

16. With regard to the powerful influence exerted particularly by the "Faustian" element in the Moses saga on Goethe, cf. the fine essay by K. Burdach, "Faust und Mose" (*Sitzungsberichte der Königlich Preussischen Akademie der Wissenschaften,* philosophisch-historische Klasse, 1912).

17. Mowinckel, p. 75.

18. J. Wellhausen, *Reste arabischen Heidentums* (1897), p. 102.

19. Chantepie de la Saussaye, *Lehrbuch der Religionsgeschichte,* 4th ed. (1925), I, 89.

20. J. Hempel, *Politische Absicht und politische Wirkung im biblischen Schrifttum* (1938), p. 14; also H. Gressmann, *Mose,* pp. 203, 207, 211. In my book *The Prophetic Faith,* I have dealt with the matter in detail in the chapter "The God of the Fathers"; cf. also *Königtum Gottes,* pp. 73 ff.

21. J. Lagrange, *Études sur les religions sémitiques,* 2d ed.

(1905), p. 507; cf. J. G. Février, *La religion des Palmyréens* (1931), p. 37; cf. also M. I. Rostovtzeff, "The Caravan-gods of Palmyra," *Journal of Roman Studies,* XXII (1932), 111 f.

22. E. Schrader, *Die Keilinschriften und das Alte Testament,* 3d ed. (1903), p. 29.

23. M. Haller, *Religion, Recht und Sitte in den Genesissagen,* p. 23, is of the opinion, to be sure, that YHVH "detached Himself from stone, tree and spring and linked Himself with the person of the shepherd," but also remarks: "Or is the process to be regarded as reversed, so that Yahve was originally a protective spirit that wandered with the shepherds and gradually, as the nomads began to settle, became established at a fixed habitation?" Gunkel noted in his copy of Haller's book that stationary god and settled worshippers as Canaanite are faced by "wandering god and wandering nomads as Israelite." It must, however, be added that this god does not sleep in the tents of the nomads like the *theraphim* fetishes, but from time to time withdraws to the spacious heavens, which are inaccessible to men; Jacob's vision of the gate of heaven is a primordial constituent of the tradition. (That it is therefore impossible to "have" this god may hence have been one of the chief reasons for the women of the tribe to take the *theraphim* about with them.)

24. According to A. Lods, *Israel* (1932), p. 531, the people imagined YHVH with an aerial and therefore invisible body, "susceptible d'apparaître sous des formes diverses."

25. For the relation between imagelessness and invisibility cf. Max Weber, *Gesammelte Aufsätze zur Religionssoziologie,* III (1921), 170, who sees the relation otherwise but as no less close: "A god whose cult has been imageless since immemorial time had to be normally invisible as well, and also had to nourish his specific dignity and uncanny quality by means of that invisibility."

26. Mowinckel, *Le décalogue,* p. 103.

27. *Ibid.,* p. 60.

28. Mowinckel, *Psalmenstudien,* II (1922), 224.

29. Mowinckel, *Le décalogue,* p. 100.

30. O. Eissfeldt, *Hexateuch-Synopse* (1922), p. 275.

31. Cf. L. Koehler, *Theologie des Alten Testaments,* p. 238: "The fact that in the biblical Decalogue any such commandment as 'Thou shalt not lie' is absent, awakens all kinds of thoughts."

32. H. Gunkel, *Die israelitische Literatur* (*Die Kultur der Gegenwart,* I, No. 7 [1906], 73).

33. H. Gressmann, *Mose und seine Zeit* (1913), p. 477.

34. Cf. Buber–Rosenzweig, *Die Schrift und ihre Verdeutschung,* pp. 176 ff.; W. E. Staples, "The Third Commandment," *Journal of Biblical Literature,* LVIII (1939), 325 ff.

35. Cf. O. Procksch, *Der Staatsgedanke in der Prophetie* (1933), p. 5.

36. J. M. Powis Smith, *The Origin and History of Hebrew Law* (1931), pp. 8 f.

37. J. Hempel, *Das Ethos des Alten Testaments* (1938), p. 183.

38. P. Volz, *Mose,* 2d ed., p. 25.

39. Volz, *Mose,* 1st ed. (1907), pp. 93 f.

40. W. Caspari, *Die Gottesgemeinde vom Sinaj* (1922), p. 159.

41. E. Sellin, *Geschichte des israelitisch-jüdischen Volkes,* I, 72.

42. Volz, *Mose,* 2d ed., p. 78.

43. L. Koehler, "Der Dekalog," *Theologische Rundschau,* I (1929), 184.

44. W. Rudolph, *Der "Elohist" von Exodus bis Josua* (1938), p. 47.

45. Cf. Ganszyniec, *Der Ursprung der Zehngebotetafeln* (1920), p. 18. (The little study contains interesting material, from which, however, unwarrantable conclusions are drawn.)

46. B. D. Eerdmanns, *Alttestamentliche Studien,* III (1912), 69 f.

47. J. Morgenstern, *The Book of the Covenant,* I (1928), 34, argues against the originality of the tradition of the Tables that the description "Tables of Witness" is late, and is only found in the Priestly Code. But Exodus 32:15, in general, is not attributed to P.

48. Morgenstern, *loc. cit.,* adduces the absence of any such tradition as his chief argument against the witness character of the Tables. But it seems reasonable to assume that Solomon, with his cult policy that aimed at immobilizing the Ark and its contents in order to withdraw the political coloration from the *melekh* character of yhvh, would have no objection to ordering the removal of all traces of such a tradition (cf. E. Klamroth, *Lade und Tempel* [1933], p. 60; Buber, *The Prophetic Faith,* pp. 82 ff.).

THE PRAYER OF THE FIRST FRUITS

1. Many people imagine that the honey is fruit honey, but the honey referred to in the saying, as also in the case of Jacob's gift to Joseph of "the choice products of the land" (Gen. 43:11), can only be a natural product; no saying would make a land "overflow" with a cultivated product. From Egyptian sources, we know how rich Canaan was in bees' honey as early as about 2000 B.C.

2. Hence, to complete the symbolic number, in all probability the strange addition of "to thy God" in the address to the priest (Deut. 26:3).

3. Bikkurim III.

SAMUEL AND THE ARK

1. K. Budde, "Ephod und Lade," *Zeitschrift für die Alttestamentliche Wissenschaft*, XXXIX (1921), 35; thus already B. Stade, *Biblische Theologie des Alten Testaments*, I (1905), 130 f.

2. J. Kennedy, *I and II Samuel*, p. 325.

3. P. Volz, "Der eschatologische Glaube," *Festschrift Georg Beer* (1935), p. 78.

4. T. H. Robinson, in Oesterley and Robinson, *A History of Israel* (1934), I, 179 f.

5. *Königtum Gottes*, 2d ed., pp. 163 ff.

6. Cf. *ibid.*, pp. xxiii ff., 78 f.

7. Cf. A. Weiser, "I Samuel 15," *Zeitschrift für die Alttestamentliche Wissenschaft*, Neue Folge, XIII (1936), 24.

BIBLICAL LEADERSHIP

1. Quoted in Jerome, Comm. in Isa. 11:2.

PLATO AND ISAIAH

1. Lorenz v. Stein, *System der Staatswissenschaft* (1856), II, 384.

REDEMPTION

1. For more details see the last chapter of my book *The Prophetic Faith* (1949).

PROPHECY, APOCALYPTIC, AND THE HISTORICAL HOUR

1. IV Ezra 14:45–50.
2. *Ibid.*, 7:11, 118 ff.
3. *Ibid.*, 4:30 ff.
4. Genesis Rabba IX, 9; Yoma 69b.
5. IV Ezra 5:55.
6. II Baruch 20:1.
7. Apocalypse 10:6.
8. Matt. 3:10.

JOB

1. [Buber discusses the Book of Job against the background of the prophecy of Ezekiel, who was sent to the "house of Israel" as "watchman" and warner of *persons* (Ezek. 3:17–21) and who spoke his message of personal responsibility. He established the concept of a God in whose justice it is possible to believe, a God whose recompense of the individual is *objectively comprehensible*. Those deserving salvation are saved. Over against this dogmatic principle stood man's experience.—Ed.]

2. Johannes Hempel, *Die althebräische Literatur* (1930), p. 179.

3. I cannot agree with H. Torczyner's view, expressed in his later (Hebrew) commentary on the book (I, 27), that "the story of the framework is later than the poem."

4. The explanation that this expression is a euphemism (according to the view of Abraham Geiger, *Urschrift und Übersetzungen der Bibel* [1857], pp. 267 ff., the language of later emendations, cf. Torczyner, I, 10) does not fit the facts.

5. The atmosphere of the poem is not basically historical, even if the chief characters of the story were historical persons, according to Torczyner's view.

6. A. S. Peake, *The Problem of Suffering* (1904), pp. 94 f.; cf. also P. Volz, *Weisheit* (*Die Schriften des Alten Testaments*, III [1911]), p. 62.

7. F. Baumgaertel, *Der Hiobdialog* (1933), p. 172.

8. Johannes Pedersen, *Israel*, I–II (English ed. 1926), 371.

9. Rudolf Otto, *Das Heilige*, 23–25 ed. (1936), pp. 99 f.; cf. also W. Vischer, *Hiob ein Zeuge Jesu Christi* (1934), pp. 29 ff.; W. Eichrodt, *Theologie des Alten Testaments*, III (1939), 145 f.

10. Eichrodt, p. 146.

11. [The analysis continues with the comparison between the Book of Job and Psalm 73.—Ed.]

THE HEART DETERMINES

1. In what follows I read, as is almost universally accepted, *lamo tam* instead of *lemotam*.

BIBLICAL HUMANISM

1. "Über den Ursprung des Humanismus," reprinted in *Reformation, Renaissance, Humanismus* (1918).

2. *Ibid.*, p. 201.

BIBLIOGRAPHICAL GUIDE

THE MAN OF TODAY AND THE JEWISH BIBLE

From a series of lectures delivered in 1926. *Die Schrift und ihre Verdeutschung*, Berlin, 1936, pp. 13–31. *Israel and the World*, New York, 1948, pp. 89–102. Copyright © 1948 by Schocken Books Inc. Translated by Olga Marx.

THE TREE OF KNOWLEDGE

Good and Evil, New York, 1953, pp. 67–80. Copyright © 1952 and 1953 by Martin Buber. Reprinted by permission of Charles Scribner's Sons and Routledge & Kegan Paul Ltd. Translated by Ronald Gregory Smith.

ABRAHAM THE SEER

Shelihut Avraham, Haaretz, Tel Aviv, 1939. *Sehertum*, Cologne, 1955. *Judaism*, V, 1956. Translated by Sophie Meyer.

THE BURNING BUSH

Moshe, Jerusalem, 1945. *Moses*, Oxford, 1946, pp. 39–55. Copyright © 1946 by East and West Library; reprinted with the publisher's permission. Published in U.S.A. by Harper & Row, New York, 1958. Translated by I. M. Lask.

HOLY EVENT

The Prophetic Faith, New York, 1949, pp. 43–59. Copyright © 1949 by The Macmillan Company; reprinted with the publisher's permission. Translated by Carlyle Witton-Davies.

THE ELECTION OF ISRAEL: A BIBLICAL INQUIRY

Almanach des Schocken Verlags, 5699, Berlin, 1938, pp. 12–31. Translated by Michael A. Meyer.

THE WORDS ON THE TABLETS

Moshe, Jerusalem, 1945. *Moses,* Oxford, 1946, pp. 119–140. Copyright © 1946 by East and West Library; reprinted with the publisher's permission. Published in U.S.A. by Harper & Row, New York, 1958. Translated by I. M. Lask.

WHAT ARE WE TO DO ABOUT THE TEN COMMANDMENTS?

Reply to a circular question. *Literarische Welt,* 1929. *Israel and the World,* New York, 1948, pp. 85–88. Copyright © 1948 by Schocken Books Inc. Translated by Olga Marx.

THE PRAYER OF THE FIRST FRUITS

Ben Am le-Artzo, Jerusalem, 1945. *Israel and Palestine: The History of an Idea,* London, 1952, pp. 3–10. Copyright © 1952 by East and West Library; reprinted with the publisher's permission. Published in U.S.A. by Farrar, Straus and Giroux, New York, 1952. Translated by Stanley Godman.

SAMUEL AND THE ARK

Essays Presented to Leo Baeck on the Occasion of his Eightieth Birthday, London, 1954, pp. 20–25. Copyright © 1954 by East and West Library; reprinted with the publisher's permission. Translated by Michael A. Meyer. The essay was to be a chapter in the projected volume *Der Gesalbte* (Part II of *Das Kommende*); an expanded version appeared in Hebrew, in *Zion,* 1938.

BIBLICAL LEADERSHIP

A lecture delivered in 1928. *Kampf um Israel,* 1933, pp. 84–106. *Israel and the World,* New York, 1948, pp. 119–133. Copyright © 1948 by Schocken Books Inc. Translated by G. Hort.

PLATO AND ISAIAH

From an introductory lecture delivered at the Hebrew University in Jerusalem in 1938. *Ha-Ruah veha-Metziut,* Tel

Aviv, 1942, pp. 10–21. *Israel and the World*, New York, 1948, pp. 103–112. Copyright © 1948 by Schocken Books Inc. Translated by Olga Marx.

REDEMPTION

Ben Am le-Artzo, Jerusalem, 1945. *Israel and Palestine: The History of an Idea*, London, 1952, pp. 30–35. Copyright © 1952 by East and West Library; reprinted with the publisher's permission. Published in U.S.A. by Farrar, Straus and Giroux, New York, 1952. Translated by Stanley Godman.

FALSE PROPHETS

Ha-Ruah veha-Metziut, Tel Aviv, 1942, pp. 64–69. *Israel and the World*, New York, 1948, pp. 113–118. Copyright © 1948 by Schocken Books Inc. Translated by Olga Marx.

PROPHECY, APOCALYPTIC, AND THE HISTORICAL HOUR

Merkur, 1954. *Sehertum*, Cologne, 1955. *Pointing the Way: Collected Essays*, London, 1957, pp. 192–207. Copyright © 1957 by Martin Buber. Used by permission of the publisher, Harper & Row. Translated by Maurice Friedman.

JOB

The Prophetic Faith, New York, 1949, pp. 187–197. Copyright © 1949 by The Macmillan Company; reprinted with the publisher's permission. Translated by Carlyle Witton-Davies.

THE HEART DETERMINES

Ha-Zedek veha-Avel, Jerusalem, 1950. *Right and Wrong: an Interpretation of Some Psalms*, London, 1952, pp. 34–52, and *Good and Evil*, pp. 31–50. Copyright © 1952, 1953 by Martin Buber. Reprinted with the permission of SCM, Ltd., London, and Charles Scribner's Sons, New York. Translated by Ronald Gregory Smith.

BIBLICAL HUMANISM

Morgen, IX (1933), 241–245. *Humanismus Mikrai*, in *Moznayim*, 1933. Translated by Michael A. Meyer. A later version, *Humaniut Ivrit*, appeared in *Hapoel Hatzair*, May 30, 1941; *Israel and the World*, pp. 240–252.

EDITOR'S POSTSCRIPT

1.

EARLY in his career as an interpreter of Judaism Martin Buber became aware of the significance of the Hebrew Bible for the growth and development of Judaism. During those early years hasidic lore and literature fascinated the religious thinker, an interest that persisted into his later years. But the Bible was to him more than literature. In his childhood he had acquired a sound knowledge of the original Hebrew text and was impressed by its earthiness, directness, and clarity. Later, when he came to know Bible translations, he was repelled by the changes in substance, structure, and tone, by the loss of both power and simplicity, boldness and precision, by the amount of "theologization" the translations —both Christian and Jewish—effected. Shortly before World War I he, together with a group of friends, formulated a project for a new, text-faithful translation; this project did not materialize.

In his address "On Youth and Religion" ("Cheruth," 1918) Buber counseled the student "to attempt to understand the spirit of the Bible's original language, Hebrew— with an understanding that has service as its aim; to approach the Bible as the basic documentation of the unconditional's effect on the spirit of the Jewish people; whatever his knowledge of ancient, as well as modern, exegesis, he should search beyond it for the original meaning of each passage; should penetrate beyond modern biblical criticism's distinction between sources to more profound distinctions and connections . . . ; should read the Bible with an appreciation of its poetic form, but also with an intuitive grasp of the suprapoetic element that transcends all form."

This statement conveys both the scholarly and, in the more profound sense of the term, educative tendencies of Buber's study of the Bible. He realized that neither a purely aesthetic and literary nor a linguistic and critical approach would do justice to the texts in question. His ideal was attainment of a synthesis of the two.

A more concentrated effort in this direction commenced when, in 1925, Buber and Franz Rosenzweig were approached by the then young publisher Lambert Schneider to undertake a new translation of the Hebrew Bible into German. Originally conceived as a revision of Luther's rendition, the work soon proved to require a new set of guiding principles. Where Luther tried to follow the text very closely only if and insofar as the text was important to him as a Christian, the new translators could not permit themselves to discriminate between important and unimportant parts. They felt duty-bound to treat the biblical canon as a single great unit of interrelated parts and to apply the greatest possible measure of faithfulness to the entire text. Therefore, rather than being a rendition that would allow the translators a degree of poetic freedom, the new translation endeavored to reproduce the rhythm, stylistic peculiarities, and linguistic structure of the Hebrew original. By means of this translation, the reader could sense the character and feel the flavor of the ancient documents. Even the reader well acquainted with the Hebrew language was made aware of key words, word repetitions, nuances, allusions, word correspondences intended by the text, and often overlooked by the "expert."

Franz Rosenzweig had previously, in his translations of the poetry of Judah ha-Levi, applied the method of following a text closely, both in content and literary form; the Bible presented a challenge in the same direction. Buber, who had become a master of the free, selective rendition of hasidic legends, anecdotes, and words of wisdom, returned to his early concept of a faithful Bible translation where discipline, accuracy, and unstinting attention to detail were required.

Some critics pointed to the fact that the translation was more Hebraic than German and that, indeed, the rules of style and grammar were not followed. They missed the main point of the translators' endeavor. The translators strove, by means of certain linguistic and stylistic devices, to lead the reader from the written record back to the spoken word that lies in the record's core. "Do we mean a book? No, we mean the voice," said Buber in 1926, at the beginning of his work with Rosenzweig. Twenty years later, pointing to the personal address in the Ten Commandments, he stated: "Thanks to its 'thou,' the Decalogue means the preservation of the Divine Voice." And, in the same connection: "At an unknown hour they [the tablets of stone] pass out of our ken. The Word alone endures." In a popular essay, reacting to a question, "What Are We to Do About the Ten Commandments?" he answered, "To lead up to them," qualifying this statement by adding: "Not to a scroll, not even to the stone tablets . . . but to the Spoken Word." In an address on "Hebrew Humanism" Buber pleaded for a "reception of the Bible, not because of its literary, historical, and national values, important though these may be, but because of the normative value of the human patterns demonstrated in the Bible" and for setting these human patterns "before the eyes of our time with its special conditions." "The Book still lies before us, and the voice speaks forth from it as on the first day."

The biblical scholar deals with the text, its parallels, its historical and cultural background, its transmission. Buber, while making understanding of the text the precondition of his work, attempted to penetrate into the realm behind it— a step a scholar denies himself. The intuitive religious thinker does not feel bound by the severe restrictions imposed by scholarship—even if he uses its methods.

Work on the translation, whose publication was transferred to Schocken Verlag shortly after its inception, continued to be a joint labor of Buber and Rosenzweig until the latter's death in 1929; by that time, the Book of Isaiah was completed. Buber continued alone; the work was interrupted by the Nazi era and the war years. It was completed in Jerusalem, in 1961. A four-volume revised edition of the entire work was published by Jacob Hegner Verlag in 1954, 1955, 1958, and 1962. The present editor had the privilege of participating in the editorial meetings, especially during the first years, and of serving as a critical reader of the manuscript; this permitted him a first-hand impression of the proceedings.

2.

Buber's intensive study of biblical issues—occasioned by his work on the translation—led to the publication of numerous monographs and articles, such as "Abraham the Seer," "Biblical Leadership," "False Prophets," "Plato and Isaiah," "Good and Evil," to mention those included in the present volume. Essays of direct relevance to the translation and its problems were included in the volume *Die Schrift und ihre Verdeutschung* ("The Bible and Its Translation into German," 1936, which also contains essays by Franz Rosenzweig) and in supplements (*Beilagen*) to the translation of the third part of the Hebrew Bible (*Ketuvim,* Hagiographa, 1962). In the early 'thirties Buber planned a three-volume work on the subject of Messianism, *Das Kommende* ("That Which Is to Come"). The first volume, *Königtum Gottes* ("The Kingdom of God"), appeared in 1932; an expanded, second, edition was published in 1936; a third, newly revised, edition came out in 1956. The second volume, for which the title *Der Gesalbte* ("The Anointed One") was chosen, never appeared; but four sections from it were published in various learned journals and in the *Festschrift* for Ernst Lohmeyer. The main thesis of the projected third volume is contained in the second part of *The Prophetic Faith,* 1949 (a Hebrew edition, *Torat ha-Neviim,* appeared in 1942). A work on Moses appeared in Hebrew in 1945; an English translation was published in 1946, and reprinted in 1958. Discussion of a given motif appears in diverse contexts in Buber's essays; such duplications, necessary for the development of a theme, are retained in the present volume.

3.

The central theme in Buber's biblical research concerns the concept of the kingdom of God, the origin of the institution of kingship in ancient Israel, and the inception of the idea of the Messianic kingdom.

His introspective reading of the relevant biblical records leads him (in *Königtum Gottes*) to assert a very early realization in Israel of the kingship of God. In contradistinction to the ancient Near Eastern myths of the divine king and rituals based on such myths, the Israelite experience is a historical one. Its theocracy was not a rule by priests, however divinely ordained, but an immediate, unmetaphorical, unlimited, real leadership by the invisible *melekh*, the King, whose kingly domain, *mamlakhah*, is Israel.

Buber admits the influence of Near Eastern thought on Israel, but insists on the historical reality of the biblical concept of theocracy. The wandering tribes took upon themselves the charge that "the Lord shall reign for ever and ever" (Exodus 15:18). This Lord desired Israel to be "a *kingdom* of priests" (19:6); the theophany on Sinai effected the covenant between the people and its kingly leader. "When the heads of the people were gathered, all the tribes of Israel together—there was a king in Jeshurun" (Deuteronomy 33: 5). The two parties, the divine and the earthly, intent upon establishing a kingdom, consecrated their covenant in a unique ceremony (Exodus 24:3–8).

This pure, Sinaitic, theopolitical organization lasted up to the death of Joshua, when it became restricted to a merely "religious" structure. However, the original concept was sustained by the early prophetic, enthusiastic bands, and by the men chosen to be "judges" in Israel. One of the latter, Gideon, to whom the Elders offered the office of hereditary kingship, took a definitive antimonarchal position: "I will not be king over you, neither shall my son be king over you; the Lord shall be king over you" (Judges 8:23). To Buber, this antimonarchal view is represented—at times by implication only—in the entire first part of the Book of Judges.

It was political pressure and the need for a tangible

leader in war that instituted earthly kingship. Whereupon the king became the *mashiah,* the anointed one, of the Lord: a sacred person, God's visible representative on earth. As such he was charged with a responsibility (to execute justice, divine justice) that he was too weak to fulfill.

The prophets criticized the erring king, reminded him of his duties, and, while the monarchy declined, envisioned the coming of a king who would not fail his true calling: the Messiah, the anointed one. The Messianic hope was the expectation of a concrete realization of the kingdom of God on this earth, as a historical, political fact.

In the recent period the themes of God as king and of sacral kingship have occupied many scholars and schools, such as the English myth and ritual group, I. Engnell and the other Scandinavian divine-kingdom school, the American followers of W. F. Albright, Sigmund Mowinckel, author of *He That Cometh* and of studies on the Psalms, and G. Ernest Wright, who investigated the royal terminology in the texts that refer to the covenant concept. Divine kingship in ancient Israel and the eschatological kingdom of God have been further explored by Yehezkel Kaufmann in his *Religion of Israel.* Within these and other similar endeavors Buber's initial insights are rarely, or, to say the least, insufficiently, recognized. "Yet it is true that Buber's many studies on the origins and the history of Messianism are his most important contribution for the understanding of the Old and the New Testaments" (James Muilenberg).

Buber insisted on the philological and historical soundness of his position and polemized against his critics who pointed to the insufficiency of proofs for his assumptions and findings (see the elaborate Introduction to the third edition of *Königtum Gottes*). But his real concern was with those who followed him in his attempts to interpret the text "from within." From the viewpoint of academic expertise Buber stands at the periphery of biblical scholarship, just as his thought is placed at the periphery of professional philosophy. Though cognizant of the methods and findings of both, he refused to curb his intuitive grasp of issues.

4

In his understanding of prophecy Buber transcends the scope of nineteenth-century biblical research. He welds together the various forms of inspired leadership into a coherent phenomenon, an internal history, underlying official biblical history. He postulates Abraham as the first seer, recipient of divine revelation. Moses is presented as belonging to an old family of seers (*nebiim*); he bestows upon the seventy Elders a portion of his spirit (*ruah*); he desires the whole people to be *nebiim*. Classical prophecy in the period of the kings culminates, in Buber's views, in the Deutero-Isaiahnic concept of the Suffering Servant: a prophetic figure that presages the acting, royal, Messiah (*Moses, The Prophetic Faith,* passim).

It is one of the prophet's chief tasks to call upon man to preserve the freedom of choice and action required from the partner in the covenant with God. Man has the power to influence the created world, to further its cause or to hinder it; the prophet formulates this dialogic relationship between the acts of man and the acts of God. (See "Biblical Leadership" in this volume).

The prophet, in Buber's interpretation, is counteracted by the apocalyptic visionary who rises in a late period of Judaic history. The trust in a realization of the kingdom of God within the framework of history is lost; lost too is the confidence in man's meaningful action and in his freedom of choice. The apocalyptic, e.g., the author of Fourth Ezra, proclaims that the world is old and doomed to perish; Adam's sin predestined the fate of future man. Creation has failed. A "new aeon" is the only hope, but this extrahistorical realm is no longer the kingdom of God in which the promise of Creation was to be fulfilled. (See "Prophecy, Apocalyptic, and the Historical Hour" in this volume.)

5

In a measure reminiscent of Franz Rosenzweig's thought, Buber speaks of the triad creation-revelation-redemption as stages of God's communication with world and man. Beginning (creation) and end (redemption) are what the terms imply. However, the center, revelation, is not a stationary point between the origin of the conscious world and its Messianic aim, but an ever-renewed, ever-present manifestation of the divine in a particular human situation: a manifestation that defies generalization, formulation, and recording. Thus, Buber considers the revelation on Sinai an event to which no written account can do justice, and one that cannot be translated into a set of laws and commandments. God is not a law giver; revelation is not legislation.

Such ever-renewed revelation is possible because the world is thought of as "created." It was Marcion, the second-century Christian heretic, who considered creation evil and its God inferior to the God of redemption. The Marcionite threat within Christianity—officially overcome by the fusion of the Old and the New Testaments—is counterposed by Buber with a defense of the "Old Testament" view of the goodness and the grace of creation and the correspondence of creation and redemption, revealed to man whenever such revelation is needed. In this biblical view, as interpreted by Buber, the neutral, indifferent universe is turned into a sphere in which divine address and human response are possible. It is the reference to the mystery and grandeur of creation that forms the divine reply to Job's rebellious quest (see "Job" in the present volume). The world's redemption, the kingdom of God, is but the fulfillment of what was intended in creation.

The reader will not fail to observe the intimate bond between Buber's biblical exegesis and the philosophy of the I-Thou relationship that he represented. Indeed, the two influenced each other, fructified each other. Buber read the Bible (a term he used freely, though not exclusively, for what the Christian calls the Old Testament) as the great document of the "dialogical reciprocity between heaven and earth" ("Prophecy, Apocalyptic, and the Historical Hour"). On the other hand, his religious thought received its deepest confirmation—and clarification—from Scriptures.

N.N.G.

INDEX

Aaron, 45, 54
Abimelech, 29, 36, 79
abodah, 88
Abraham, 22–43, 56, 77, 82, 86, 87, 101, 126, 127, 139, 149, 163, 197, 239
Absalom, 73, 143
Adam, Eve, 14–17, 19–21, 26, 27, 181, 182, 239
Address, being addressed, 11, 106, 107, 120, 144, 159, 176, 203, 204, 212, 213, 215, 240
Adoption 78, 84
Adultery, 119
Ahaz, 156, 158
Albright, W. F., 238
Alexander the Great, 7, 154
Alt, A., 73, 74, 76, 95
Altar, 35, 42, 82, 93, 128
am, umma, ammi, ammim, lo-ammi, 51, 61, 75, 82, 83, 86, 88, 90
am elohim, am qadosh, "people of YHVH," 75, 86, 88
Amaziah, 29
Amenhotep IV, 51
Amos, 29, 65–67, 69, 76, 80, 81, 84
Amphictyony, 78
Amram, 51
Ancient East, Oriental Moral Code, 49, 96
Angels, celestial beings, 14, 17, 20, 45, 182
Anointing, 34, 140, 147, 238

Anthropomorphism, 74, 102
Apocalyptic, 172–87, 239
Apodictical *versus* casuistical style, 73–76
Arabs, 22, 56, 76, 99, 125
Aram, Aramæans, 66, 80, 126, 127
Ark, Ark of the Covenant, 35, 68, 69, 71, 79, 91, 117, 131, 132, 134, 135, 143
Assyria, 158, 162, 168
Athens, 152, 154, 215
Aton, 64
Atonement, 69, 179
Authority, 111
Avesta, 17

Baal, 129
Babylonia, 115, 122, 164, 168, 181, 207
Babylonian exile, 61, 96, 105, 160, 168, 178, 200
Babylonian religion, 51, 96; conjuration tablets, 96
Balaam, 176
Baptism (of Jesus), 178
Barak, 134
Baruch apocalypse, 183, 184
Baumgaertl, F., 193
Beersheba, 31, 35, 41
berakhah, 89
berith, 71, 81, 82, 90, 114
Bethel, 35
"Binding of Isaac," 41, 145
Blessing, 3, 21, 26, 28, 36, 37,